FREE DVD

From Stress . . . to Success!

STRESSED OUT about your upcoming test?

Stress and anxiety on test day can reduce your score by up to 12 percent! Just imagine the difference 12 percent can make . . . that's the difference between passing and failing! Stress and anxiety can be the difference starting your new career and not living the life you've been dreaming of.

You're probably thinking stress won't affect you, but is it worth the risk? Luckily there are scientifically proven methods to avoid **stress and anxiety** on test day.

Calm your nerves and put your trust in the test taking experts! Go into your exam prepared with our From Stress to Success DVD. Guess what! It's FREE with the purchase of this book. Simply email us at:

5star@triviumtestprep.com

Include "Free 5 Star" in the subject line and the following information in your email:

1. The title of the product you purchased.
2. Your rating from 1 – 5 (with 5 being the best).
3. Your feedback about the product, good or bad.
4. Your full name and shipping address so we can send your **FREE DVD**.

Test Confidently!

- Trivium Test Prep Team

** Please note that the free DVD is not included with this book. To receive the free DVD, please follow the instructions above within one week of receiving the book. **

HESI A² Study Guide 2018–2019

HESI Admission Assessment Review Book and Practice Test Questions for the HESI A² Exam

TABLE OF CONTENTS

INTRODUCTION

Congratulations on your decision to join the field of nursing—few other professions are so rewarding! By purchasing this book, you've already taken the first step toward succeeding in your career. The next step is to do well on the HESI Admission Assessment (HESI A^2) exam, which will require you to demonstrate knowledge of high-school level reading, writing, math, and science.

This book will walk you through the important concepts in each of these subjects and also provide you with insider information on test strategies and tactics. Even if it's been years since you graduated from high school or cracked open a textbook, don't worry—this book contains everything you'll need for the HESI A^2.

WHAT IS THE HESI A^2?

The HESI A^2 is an entrance examination used by schools to determine a candidate's suitability for nursing programs. *HESI* stands for Health Education Systems, Inc., and *A^2* stands for *Admission Assessment*. The exam is owned and administered by Elsevier, Inc. The HESI A^2 allows nursing programs to assess candidates' academic strengths in mathematics, science, and English language. It also provides information on candidates' personalities and learning styles.

WHAT'S ON THE HESI A^2?

The HESI A^2 is a computer-based exam with a total of eleven sections. There are eight academic and two personal sections. There is also a section that tests critical thinking ability. Different schools will require different sections as part of their applications, so you'll want to make sure you know what sections you need to take on test day. Most candidates do NOT take all sections of the test.

You can work through the sections on the HESI A^2 in any order, so you should plan in advance how you'd like to tackle the test. Some students like to start with the section they find the hardest, while others like to focus their efforts on sections they know they'll do well on. The time limits listed below are recommendations by the administrators of the HESI A^2 exam. You do not need to strictly adhere to these suggestions, but these limits may be helpful as you practice pacing yourself for other board certification exams. You are allotted four and one-half hours to take the entire exam, so you must manage your time wisely.

Each scored section on the HESI A^2 includes **FIVE PILOT QUESTIONS** that are not scored. These questions are used by the writers of the exam to test new material and will not count toward your final score. However, you won't know which questions these are as you're taking the test, so treat every question like it counts.

Mathematics: 55 questions, 50 minutes

The Mathematics section of the HESI A² is fifty-five questions long. It focuses on skills required for health care professionals. You will see questions on basic addition, subtraction, multiplication, and division. You will also need to have knowledge of roman numerals, calculating dosages, measurements, fractions, and proportions. Finally, be comfortable with unit conversions. You are not allowed to bring a calculator with you to the exam, but one will be provided for you.

Reading: 55 questions, 60 minutes

The Reading section assesses your ability to read, analyze, and comprehend short passages related to health and medicine. This section contains fifty-five questions. You will need to be able to identify the main idea of a passage, make inferences about that passage, and interpret information in the passage from context clues.

Vocabulary and General Knowledge: 55 questions, 50 minutes

In the Vocabulary section, you will be tested on your knowledge of words, specifically those relating to the health field (although not all questions will be health related). There are fifty-five questions in total in this section.

Grammar: 55 questions, 50 minutes

The Grammar section contains fifty-five questions. It will test your knowledge of basic grammar, parts of speech, common grammatical errors, and sentence structure.

Biology: 30 questions, 25 minutes

The Biology section covers topics such as cellular respiration, photosynthesis, genetics, biological molecules, and cells. This, and the other science sections, can be tricky because there are only thirty questions that cover a wide range of material.

Chemistry: 30 questions, 25 minutes

The thirty-question Chemistry section covers topics such as the periodic table, chemical equations, atomic structure, chemical bonding, nuclear chemistry, and chemical reactions.

Anatomy and Physiology: 30 questions, 25 minutes

The Anatomy and Physiology section covers a wide spectrum of body systems, including the muscular, skeletal, nervous, renal/urinary, reproductive, endocrine, circulatory, and respiratory systems. There are thirty questions in this section.

Physics: 30 questions, 25 minutes

Very few test takers will actually have the physics section on their exam, as this is excluded by many colleges. If you do encounter it, you will be tested on mechanics, energy, forces, waves, and light. Even if you do have this section on your test, do not focus your efforts here, as mathematics and the other sciences are typically much more important. Like the other science sections, the physics section has thirty questions.

Critical Thinking: 25 questions, 20 minutes

The Critical Thinking section portion of the exam is scored, but it does not contain academic questions. Instead, the questions are practical, asking you to think about real-life situations that might occur in nursing. Unlike the academic sections of the exam, the scores range from 0 – 1000. You will also receive scores in critical thinking subcategories: **PROBLEM SOLVING, BIASES AND ETHICAL DILEMMAS, ARGUMENT ANALYSIS,** and **DATA ANALYSIS.** There may also be questions on prioritization of care. This section tests your critical thinking as it applies to nursing. A candidate's score indicates his or her ability to think critically within the discipline of nursing. Questions may address situations a nurse might encounter in the professional setting in patient care, relating with patients and the health care team, conflict resolution, and interpreting patient data.

Unscored Learner Profile

You may also encounter other unscored sections on the HESI A². These include the Personality Profile and Learning Style assessments. These sections will not be used as part of your score. Instead, they are designed to help students better understand their strengths and weaknesses, learning styles and habits, and other personality traits.

The Learning Style section includes fourteen test items; it is recommended to spend about fifteen minutes on it. This section will reveal your preferred learning style—visual, auditory, analytical, kinesthetic, and so on.

The Personality Profile contains fifteen questions and should take approximately fifteen minutes. This section will assess your personality as it relates to your preferred learning style. Your dominant personality type—calm, creative, leadership-oriented, or extroverted—will be revealed, with discussion of supporting characteristics.

HOW IS THE HESI A² SCORED?

You cannot "pass" or "fail" the HESI A². Your score is simply indicative of your current level of comprehension. However, each school has its own entrance requirements, so check the requirements of the institutions that you want to attend. Also, each institution has different requirements regarding the sections of the test you will take; make sure to check that you're taking the proper exam before you spend your time studying for a subject that you won't necessarily need.

Each section is scored separately, and your score report will show individual scores for each section you take. The academic sections (Mathematics, Reading, Vocabulary, Grammar, Biology, Chemistry, Anatomy and Physiology, and Physics) are scored out on a scale of 0 – 100. Critical Thinking is scored on a scale of 0 – 1000. The Learning Style and Personality Profile sections are not scored. Check with your program to determine the minimum scores you are required to attain.

MATHEMATICS

TYPES OF NUMBERS

Numbers can be categorized based on their properties. While the HESI A² won't directly test you on the types of numbers, it can be helpful to understand these categories while you review mathematical terms and operations.

- A **NATURAL NUMBER** is greater than 0 and has no decimal or fraction attached. These are also sometimes called counting numbers. {1, 2, 3, 4, ...}
- **WHOLE NUMBERS** are natural numbers and the number 0. {0, 1, 2, 3, 4, ...}
- **INTEGERS** include positive and negative natural numbers and 0. {..., –4, –3, –2, –1, 0, 1, 2, 3, 4, ...}
- A **RATIONAL NUMBER** can be represented as a fraction. Any decimal part must terminate or resolve into a repeating pattern. (Examples: 0.7, $\frac{1}{2}$, –12.36)
- An **IRRATIONAL NUMBER** cannot be represented as a fraction. An irrational decimal number never ends and never resolves into a repeating pattern. (Examples: π, $\frac{3}{7}$, $-\sqrt{2}$)
- A **REAL NUMBER** is a number that can be represented by a point on a number line. Real numbers include all the rational and irrational numbers.

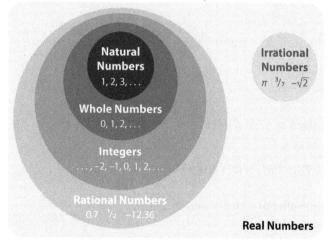

Figure 1.1. Types of Numbers

POSITIVE AND NEGATIVE NUMBERS

You can use a number line to easily find the result when adding and subtracting positive and negative numbers. When adding two numbers, whether they are positive or negative, count to the right; when subtracting, count to the left. Note that adding a negative value is the same as subtracting. Subtracting a negative value is the same as adding.

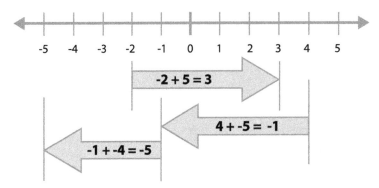

Figure 1.2. Adding and Subtracting Positive and Negative Numbers

Multiplying and dividing with negative and positive numbers is somewhat easier. Multiplying two numbers with the same sign gives a positive result, and multiplying two numbers with different signs gives a negative result. The same rules apply to division. These rules are summarized below:

(+) + (−) = the sign of the larger number

(−) + (−) = negative number

(−) × (−) or (−) ÷ (−) = positive number

(−) × (+) or (−) ÷ (+) = negative number

(+) + (+) or (+) × (+) or (+) ÷ (+) = positive number

Examples

1. Find the product of −10 and 47.

(−) × (+) = (−)

$-10 \times 47 = \textbf{−470}$

2. What is the sum of −65 and −32?

(−) + (−) = (−)

$-65 + -32 = \textbf{−97}$

3. Is the product of −7 and 4 less than −7, between −7 and 4, or greater than 4?

(−) × (+) = (−)

$-7 \times 4 = -28$, which is **less than −7**

4. What is the value of −16 divided by 2.5?

(−) ÷ (+) = (−)

$-16 \div 2.5 = \textbf{−6.4}$

ORDER OF OPERATIONS

Operations in a mathematical expression are always performed in a specific order, which is described by the acronym PEMDAS:

1. Parentheses
2. Exponents
3. Multiplication
4. Division
5. Addition
6. Subtraction

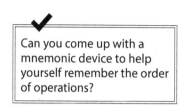

Can you come up with a mnemonic device to help yourself remember the order of operations?

Perform the operations within parentheses first, and then address any exponents. After those steps, perform all multiplication and division. These are carried out from left to right as they appear in the problem.

Finally, do all required addition and subtraction, also from left to right as each operation appears in the problem.

Examples

1. Solve: $-(2)^2 - (4 + 7)$

   First, complete operations within parentheses:

   $-(2)^2 - (11)$

   Second, calculate the value of exponential expressions:

   $-(4) - (11)$

   Finally, do addition and subtraction:

   $-4 - 11 = \mathbf{-15}$

2. Solve: $(5)^2 \div 5 + 4 \times 2$

   First, calculate the value of exponential expressions:

   $(25) \div 5 + 4 \times 2$

   Second, calculate division and multiplication from left to right:

   $5 + 8$

   Finally, do addition and subtraction:

   $5 + 8 = \mathbf{13}$

3. Solve the expression: $15 \times (4 + 8) - 3^3$

   First, complete operations within parentheses:

   $15 \times (12) - 3^3$

   Second, calculate the value of exponential expressions:

   $15 \times (12) - 27$

   Third, calculate division and multiplication from left to right:

   $180 - 27$

   Finally, do addition and subtraction from left to right:

   $180 - 27 = \mathbf{153}$

4. Solve the expression: $\left(\frac{5}{2} \times 4\right) + 23 - 4^2$

First, complete operations within parentheses:

$(10) + 23 - 4^2$

Second, calculate the value of exponential expressions:

$(10) + 23 - 16$

Finally, do addition and subtraction from left to right:

$10 + 23 - 16$

$33 - 16 = \textbf{17}$

DECIMALS AND FRACTIONS

Numbers are written using the base-10 system where each digit (the numeric symbols $0 - 9$) in a number is worth ten times as much as the number to the right of it. For example, in the number 37 each digit has a place value based on its location. The 3 is in the tens place, and so has a value of 30, and the 7 is in the ones place, so it has a value of 7.

Figure 1.3. Place Value

Adding and Subtracting Decimals

When adding and subtracting decimals, write the numbers so that the decimal points are aligned. You want to subtract the ones place from the ones place, the tenths place from the tenths place, etc.

Examples

1. Find the sum of 17.07 and 2.52.

$$\begin{array}{r} 17.07 \\ + \quad 2.52 \\ \hline = \textbf{19.59} \end{array}$$

2. Jeannette has 7.4 gallons of gas in her tank. After driving, she has 6.8 gallons. How many gallons of gas did she use?

$$\begin{array}{r} 7.4 \\ - \, 6.8 \\ \hline = \textbf{0.6 gal.} \end{array}$$

Multiplying and Dividing Decimals

When multiplying decimals, start by multiplying the numbers normally. You can then determine the placement of the decimal point in the result by adding the number of digits after the decimal in each of the numbers you multiplied together.

When dividing decimals, you should move the decimal point in the divisor (the number you're dividing by) until it is a whole number. You can then move the decimal in the dividend (the number you're dividing into) the same number of places in the same direction. Finally, divide the new numbers normally to get the correct answer.

Examples

1. What is the product of 0.25 and 1.3?

    $25 \times 13 = 325$

    There are 2 digits after the decimal in 0.25 and one digit after the decimal in 1.3. Therefore the product should have 3 digits after the decimal: 0.325.

2. Find $0.8 \div 0.2$.

    Change 0.2 to 2 by moving the decimal one space to the right.

    Next, move the decimal one space to the right on the dividend. 0.8 becomes 8.

    Now, divide 8 by 2. $8 \div 2 = \mathbf{4}$

3. Find the quotient when 40 is divided by 0.25.

    First, change the divisor to a whole number: 0.25 becomes 25.

    Next, change the dividend to match the divisor by moving the decimal two spaces to the right, so 40 becomes 4000.

    Now divide: $4000 \div 25 = \mathbf{160}$

Working with Fractions

FRACTIONS are made up of two parts: the NUMERATOR, which appears above the bar, and the DENOMINATOR, which is below it. If a fraction is in its SIMPLEST FORM, the numerator and the denominator share no common factors. A fraction with a numerator larger than or equal to its denominator is an IMPROPER FRACTION; when the denominator is larger, it's a PROPER FRACTION.

Improper fractions can be converted into mixed numbers by dividing the numerator by the denominator. The resulting whole number is placed to the left of the fraction, and the remainder becomes the new numerator; the denominator does not change. The new number is called a MIXED NUMBER because it contains a whole number and a fraction. Mixed numbers can be turned into improper fractions through the reverse process: multiply the whole number by the denominator and add the numerator to get the new numerator.

Examples

1. Simplify the fraction $\frac{121}{77}$.

    121 and 77 share a common factor of 11. So, if we divide each by 11 we can simplify the fraction:

    $$\frac{121}{77} = \frac{11}{11} \times \frac{11}{7} = \mathbf{\frac{11}{7}}$$

2. Convert $\frac{37}{5}$ into a mixed number.

Start by dividing the numerator by the denominator:

$37 \div 5 = 7$ with a remainder of 2

Now build a mixed number with the whole number and the new numerator:

$\frac{37}{5} = 7\frac{2}{5}$

Multiplying and Dividing Fractions

To multiply fractions, convert any mixed numbers into improper fractions and multiply the numerators together and the denominators together. Reduce to lowest terms if needed.

> ⚠️
> Inverting a fraction changes division to multiplication:
> $\frac{a}{b} \div \frac{c}{d} = \frac{a}{b} \times \frac{d}{c} = \frac{ad}{bc}$

To divide fractions, first convert any mixed numbers into improper fractions. Then, invert the second fraction so that the denominator and numerator are switched. Finally, multiply the numerators together and the denominators together.

Examples

1. What is the product of $\frac{1}{12}$ and $\frac{6}{8}$?

Simply multiply the numerators together and the denominators together, then reduce:

$\frac{1}{12} \times \frac{6}{8} = \frac{6}{96} = \frac{1}{16}$

Sometimes it's easier to reduce fractions before multiplying if you can:

$\frac{1}{12} \times \frac{6}{8} = \frac{1}{12} \times \frac{3}{4} = \frac{3}{48} = \frac{1}{16}$

2. Find $\frac{7}{8} \div \frac{1}{4}$.

For a fraction division problem, invert the second fraction and then multiply and reduce:

$\frac{7}{8} \div \frac{1}{4} = \frac{7}{8} \times \frac{4}{1} = \frac{28}{8} = \frac{7}{2}$

3. $\frac{2}{5} \div 1\frac{1}{5} =$

This is a fraction division problem, so the first step is to convert the mixed number to an improper fraction:

$1\frac{1}{5} = \frac{5 \times 1}{5} + \frac{1}{5} = \frac{6}{5}$

Now, divide the fractions. Remember to invert the second fraction, and then multiply normally:

$\frac{2}{5} \div \frac{6}{5} = \frac{2}{5} \times \frac{5}{6} = \frac{10}{30} = \frac{1}{3}$

4. A recipe calls for $\frac{1}{4}$ cup of sugar. If $8\frac{1}{2}$ batches of the recipe are needed, how many cups of sugar will be used?

This is a fraction multiplication problem: $\frac{1}{4} \times 8\frac{1}{2}$.

First, we need to convert the mixed number into a proper fraction:

$8\frac{1}{2} = \frac{8 \times 2}{2} + \frac{1}{2} = \frac{17}{2}$

Now, multiply the fractions across the numerators and denominators, and then reduce:

$\frac{1}{4} \times 8\frac{1}{2} = \frac{1}{4} \times \frac{17}{2} = \frac{17}{8}$ **cups of sugar, or** $2\frac{1}{8}$

Adding and Subtracting Fractions

Adding and subtracting fractions requires a **COMMON DENOMINATOR**. To get a common denominator, you can multiply each fraction by the number 1. With fractions, any number over itself (e.g., $\frac{5}{5}$, $\frac{12}{12}$, etc.) is equivalent to 1, so multiplying by such a fraction can change the denominator without changing the value of the fraction. Once the denominators are the same, the numerators can be added or subtracted.

To add mixed numbers, you can first add the whole numbers and then the fractions. To subtract mixed numbers, convert each mixed number to an improper fraction, get a common denominator, and then subtract the numerators.

Examples

1. Simplify the expression $\frac{2}{3} - \frac{1}{5}$.

   First, multiply each fraction by a factor of 1 to get a common denominator. How do you know which factor of 1 to use? Look at the other fraction and use the number found in that denominator:

   $$\frac{2}{3} - \frac{1}{5} = \frac{2}{3}\left(\frac{5}{5}\right) - \frac{1}{5}\left(\frac{3}{3}\right) = \frac{10}{15} - \frac{3}{15}$$

   Once the fractions have a common denominator, simply subtract the numerators:

   $$\frac{10}{15} - \frac{3}{15} = \frac{7}{15}$$

   > The phrase *simplify the expression* just means you need to perform all the operations in the expression.

2. Find $2\frac{1}{3} - \frac{3}{2}$.

   This is a fraction subtraction problem with a mixed number, so the first step is to convert the mixed number to an improper fraction:

   $$2\frac{1}{3} = \frac{2 \times 3}{3} + \frac{1}{3} = \frac{7}{3}$$

   Next, convert each fraction so they share a common denominator:

   $$\frac{7}{3} \times \frac{2}{2} = \frac{14}{6}$$
   $$\frac{3}{2} \times \frac{3}{3} = \frac{9}{6}$$

   Now, subtract the fractions by subtracting the numerators:

   $$\frac{14}{6} - \frac{9}{6} = \frac{5}{6}$$

3. Find the sum of $\frac{9}{16}$, $\frac{1}{2}$, and $\frac{7}{4}$.

   For this fraction addition problem, we need to find a common denominator. Notice that 2 and 4 are both factors of 16, so 16 can be the common denominator:

   $$\frac{1}{2} \times \frac{8}{8} = \frac{8}{16}$$
   $$\frac{7}{4} \times \frac{4}{4} = \frac{28}{16}$$
   $$\frac{9}{16} + \frac{8}{16} + \frac{28}{16} = \frac{45}{16}$$

4. Sabrina has $\frac{2}{3}$ of a can of red paint. Her friend Amos has $\frac{1}{6}$ of a can. How much red paint do they have combined?

   To add fractions, make sure that they have a common denominator. Since 3 is a factor of 6, 6 can be the common denominator:

$$\frac{2}{3} \times \frac{2}{2} = \frac{4}{6}$$

Now, add the numerators:

$$\frac{4}{6} + \frac{1}{6} = \frac{5}{6} \text{ of a can}$$

Converting Decimals to Fractions

To convert a decimal, simply use the numbers that come after the decimal as the numerator

To convert a fraction to a decimal, just divide the numerator by the denominator on your calculator.

in the fraction. The denominator will be a power of 10 that matches the place value for the original decimal. For example, the denominator for 0.46 would be 100 because the last number is in the hundredths place; likewise, the denominator for 0.657 would be 1000 because the last number is in the thousandths place. Once this fraction has been set up, all that's left is to simplify it.

Example

Convert 0.45 into a fraction.

The last number in the decimal is in the hundredths place, so we can easily set up a fraction:

$$0.45 = \frac{45}{100}$$

The next step is to simply reduce the fraction down to the lowest common denominator. Here, both 45 and 100 are divisible by 5:

$$\frac{45}{100} = \frac{(45 \div 5)}{(100 \div 5)} = \frac{9}{20}$$

COMPARISON OF RATIONAL NUMBERS

Number comparison problems present numbers in different formats and ask which is larger or smaller, or whether the numbers are equivalent. The important step in solving these problems is to convert the numbers to the same format so that it is easier to see how they compare. If numbers are given in the same format, or after they have been converted, determine which number is smaller or if the numbers are equal. Remember that for negative numbers, higher numbers are actually smaller.

To order numbers from least to greatest (or greatest to least), convert them to the same format and place them on a number line.

Examples

1. Which of the following values is the largest? 0.49, $\frac{3}{5}$, $\frac{1}{2}$, 0.55

    Convert the fractions to decimals:

    $$\frac{3}{5} = 0.6$$
    $$\frac{1}{2} = 0.5$$

    Place the values in order from smallest to largest:

    $$0.49 < 0.5 < 0.55 < 0.6$$

    $\frac{3}{5}$ **is the largest number.**

2. Place the following numbers in order from least to greatest:

$\frac{2}{5}$, −0.7, 0.35, −$\frac{3}{2}$, 0.46

Convert the fractions to decimals:

$\frac{2}{5} = 0.4$

$-\frac{3}{2} = -1.5$

Place the values in order from smallest to largest:

−1.5 < −0.7 < 0.35 < 0.4 < 0.46

Put the numbers back in their original form:

$-\frac{3}{2} < -0.7 < 0.35 < \frac{2}{5} < 0.46$

RATIOS

A **RATIO** tells you how many of one thing exist in relation to the number of another thing. Unlike fractions, ratios do not give a part relative to a whole; instead, they compare two values. For example, if you have 3 apples and 4 oranges, the ratio of apples to oranges is 3 to 4. Ratios can be written using words (3 to 4), fractions $\left(\frac{3}{4}\right)$, or colons (3:4).

In order to work with ratios, it's helpful to rewrite them as a fraction expressing a part to a whole. For example, in the example above you have 7 total pieces of fruit, so the fraction of your fruit that are apples is $\frac{3}{7}$, and oranges make up $\frac{4}{7}$ of your fruit collection.

One last important thing to consider when working with ratios is the units of the values being compared. On the HESI A[2], you may be asked to rewrite a ratio using the same units on both sides. For example, you might have to rewrite the ratio 3 minutes to 7 seconds as 180 seconds to 7 seconds.

Examples

1. There are 90 voters in a room, and each is either a Democrat or a Republican. The ratio of Democrats to Republicans is 5:4. How many Republicans are there?

We know that there are 5 Democrats for every 4 Republicans in the room, which means for every 9 people, 4 are Republicans.

5 + 4 = 9

Fraction of Republicans: $\frac{4}{9}$

If $\frac{4}{9}$ of the 90 voters are Republicans, then:

$\frac{4}{9}$ × 90 = **40 voters are Republicans**

2. The ratio of students to teachers in a school is 15:1. If there are 38 teachers, how many students attend the school?

To solve this ratio problem, we can simply multiply both sides of the ratio by the desired value to find the number of students that correspond to having 38 teachers:

$\frac{15 \text{ students}}{1 \text{ teacher}} \times 38 \text{ teachers} = 570 \text{ students}$

The school has **570 students**.

PROPORTIONS

A **PROPORTION** is an equation which states that 2 ratios are equal. Proportions are usually written as 2 fractions joined by an equal sign $\left(\frac{a}{b} = \frac{c}{d}\right)$, but they can also be written using colons ($a : b :: c : d$). Note that in a proportion, the units must be the same in both numerators and in both denominators.

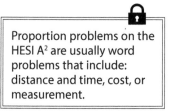

Proportion problems on the HESI A² are usually word problems that include: distance and time, cost, or measurement.

Often you will be given 3 of the values in a proportion and asked to find the 4th. In these types of problems, you can solve for the missing variable by cross-multiplying—multiply the numerator of each fraction by the denominator of the other to get an equation with no fractions as shown below. You can then solve the equation using basic algebra. (For more on solving basic equations, see "Expressions and Equations.")

$$\frac{a}{b} = \frac{c}{d} \rightarrow ad = bc$$

Examples

1. A train traveling 120 miles takes 3 hours to get to its destination. How long will it take for the train to travel 180 miles?

   Start by setting up the proportion:

   $$\frac{120 \text{ miles}}{3 \text{ hours}} = \frac{180 \text{ miles}}{x \text{ hours}}$$

   Note that it doesn't matter which value is placed in the numerator or denominator, as long as it is the same on both sides. Now, solve for the missing quantity through cross–multiplication:

   120 miles × x hours = 3 hours × 180 miles

   Now solve the equation:

   $$x \text{ hours} = \frac{(3 \text{ hours}) \times (180 \text{ miles})}{120 \text{ miles}}$$

   x = 4.5 hours

2. One acre of wheat requires 500 gallons of water. How many acres can be watered with 2600 gallons?

   Set up the equation:

   $$\frac{1 \text{ acre}}{500 \text{ gal.}} = \frac{x \text{ acres}}{2600 \text{ gal.}}$$

   Then solve for x:

   $$x \text{ acres} = \frac{1 \text{ acre} \times 2600 \text{ gal.}}{500 \text{ gal.}}$$

   $x = \frac{26}{5}$ or **5.2 acres**

PERCENTAGES

A **PERCENT** is the ratio of a part to the whole multiplied by 100. The equation for percentages can be rearranged to solve for either the part, the whole, or the percent:

$$percent = \frac{part}{whole}$$
$$part = whole \times percent$$

$$whole = \frac{part}{percent}$$

In the equations above, the percent should always be expressed as a decimal. In order to convert a decimal into a percentage value, simply multiply it by 100. So, if you've read 5 pages (the part) of a 10-page article (the whole), you've read $\frac{5}{10}$ = 0.5 = 50%. (The percent sign (%) is used once the decimal has been multiplied by 100.)

> ⚠️ The word *of* usually indicates what the whole is in a problem. For example, the problem might say *Ella ate two slices of the pizza*, which means the pizza is the whole.

Note that when solving these problems, the units for the part and the whole should be the same. If you're reading a book, saying you've read 5 pages out of 15 chapters doesn't make any sense.

Examples

1. 45 is 15% of what number?

   Set up the appropriate equation and solve. Don't forget to change 15% to a decimal value:

   $$whole = \frac{part}{percent} = \frac{45}{0.15} = \textbf{300}$$

2. Jim spent 30% of his paycheck at the fair. He spent $15 for a hat, $30 for a shirt, and $20 playing games. How much was his check? (Round to nearest dollar.)

   Set up the appropriate equation and solve:

   $$whole = \frac{part}{percent} = \frac{15 + 30 + 20}{.30} = \textbf{\$217.00}$$

3. What percent of 65 is 39?

   Set up the equation and solve:

   $$percent = \frac{part}{whole} = \frac{39}{65} = \textbf{0.6 or 60\%}$$

4. Greta and Max sell cable subscriptions. In a given month, Greta sells 45 subscriptions and Max sells 51. If 240 total subscriptions were sold in that month, what percent were not sold by Greta or Max?

   You can use the information in the question to figure out what percentage of subscriptions were sold by Max and Greta:

   $$percent = \frac{part}{whole} = \frac{(51 + 45)}{240} = \frac{96}{240} = 0.4 \text{ or } 40\%$$

   However, the question asks how many subscriptions weren't sold by Max or Greta. If they sold 40%, then the other salespeople sold 100% − 40% = **60%**.

5. Grant needs to score 75% on an exam. If the exam has 45 questions, how many questions does he need to answer correctly?

   Set up the equation and solve. Remember to convert 75% to a decimal value:

   $$part = whole \times percent = 45 \times 0.75 = 33.75$$, so he needs to answer at least **34 questions correctly**.

EXPRESSIONS AND EQUATIONS

Algebraic expressions and equations include a VARIABLE, which is a letter standing in for a number. These expressions and equations are made up of TERMS, which are groups of numbers and variables (e.g., $2xy$). An EXPRESSION is simply a set of terms (e.g., $3x$ +

$2xy$), while an EQUATION includes an equal sign (e.g., $3x + 2xy = 17$). When simplifying expressions or solving algebraic equations, you'll need to use many different mathematical properties and operations, including addition, subtraction, multiplication, division, exponents, roots, distribution, and the order of operations.

Evaluating Algebraic Expressions

To evaluate an algebraic expression, simply plug the given value(s) in for the appropriate variable(s) in the expression.

Examples

1. Evaluate $2x + 6y - 3z$ if $x = 2$, $y = 4$, and $z = -3$.

   Plug in each number for the correct variable and simplify:

   $2x + 6y - 3z = 2(2) + 6(4) - 3(-3) = 4 + 24 + 9 = \textbf{37}$

2. A hat company's profits are described by the expression below, where x is the number of hats sold, and p is the average price of a hat.

   $xp - 5x - 5000$

   If the company sold 10,000 hats for $13 each, what was its profit?

   Identify the variables:

   $x = 10,000$

   $p = \$13$

   Plug these values into the given expression:

   $xp - 5x - 5000$

   $= (10,000)(13) - 5(10,000) - 5000 = \textbf{\$75,000}$

Adding and Subtracting Terms

Only LIKE TERMS, which have the exact same variable(s), can be added or subtracted. CONSTANTS are numbers without variables attached, and those can be added and subtracted together as well. When simplifying an expression, like terms should be added or subtracted so that no individual group of variables occurs in more than one term. For example, the expression $5x + 6xy$ is in its simplest form, while $5x + 6xy - 11xy$ is not because xy appears in more than one term.

Example

1. Simplify the expression $5xy + 7y + 2yz + 11xy - 5yz$.

   Start by grouping together like terms:

   $(5xy + 11xy) + (2yz - 5yz) + 7y$

   Now you can add together each set of like terms:

   $\textbf{16xy} - \textbf{3yz} + \textbf{7y}$

2. Simplify the expression: $3ac + 4ab^2 - bc + 2ac - 7bc + 3a^3bc$

   Start by grouping like terms together, then add together each set of like terms:

   $(3ac + 2ac) + (-bc - 7bc) + 4ab^2 + 3a^3bc$

   $= \textbf{5ac} - \textbf{8bc} + \textbf{4ab}^2 + \textbf{3a}^3\textbf{bc}$

Multiplying and Dividing Terms

To multiply a single term by another, simply multiply the coefficients and then multiply the variables. Remember that when multiplying variables with exponents, those exponents are added together. For example, $(x^5y)(x^3y^4) = x^8y^5$.

When multiplying a term by a set of terms inside parentheses, you need to **DISTRIBUTE** to each term inside the parentheses as shown in Figure 1.4.

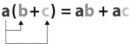

$$a(b+c) = ab + ac$$

Figure 1.4. Distribution

When variables occur in both the numerator and denominator of a fraction, they cancel each other out. So, a fraction with variables in its simplest form will not have the same variable on the top and bottom.

Examples

1. Simplify the expression $(3x^4y^2z)(2y^4z^5)$.

   Multiply the coefficients and variables together:

   $3 \times 2 = 6$

   $y^2 \times y^4 = y^6$

   $z \times z^5 = z^6$

   Now put all the terms back together:

   $\mathbf{6x^4y^6z^6}$

2. Simplify the expression: $(2y^2)(y^3 + 2xy^2z + 4z)$

   Multiply each term inside the parentheses by the term $2y^2$:

   $(2y^2)(y^3 + 2xy^2z + 4z)$

   $(2y^2 \times y^3) + (2y^2 \times 2xy^2z) + (2y^2 \times 4z)$

   $\mathbf{2y^5 + 4xy^4z + 8y^2z}$

3. Simplify the expression: $\frac{2x^4y^3z}{8x^2z^2}$

   Simplify by looking at each variable and crossing out those that appear in the numerator and denominator:

   $\frac{2}{8} = \frac{1}{4}$

   $\frac{x^4}{x^2} = \frac{x^2}{1}$

   $\frac{z}{z^2} = \frac{1}{z}$

   $\frac{2x^4y^3z}{8x^2z^2} = \frac{x^2y^3}{4z}$

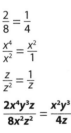

> ⚠️ When multiplying terms with the same base, add the exponents. When dividing terms with the same base, subtract the exponents.

Solving Equations

To solve an equation, you need to manipulate the terms on each side to isolate the variable, meaning if you want to find x, you have to get the x alone on one side of the equal sign. To do this, you'll need to use many of the tools discussed above: you might need to distribute, divide, add, or subtract like terms, or find common denominators.

Think of each side of the equation as the two sides of a see-saw. As long as the two people on each end weigh the same amount the see-saw will be balanced: if you have a 120 lb. person on each end, the see-saw is balanced. Giving each of them a 10 lb. rock to hold changes the weight on each end, but the see-saw itself stays balanced. Equations work the same way: you can add, subtract, multiply, or divide whatever you want as long as you do the same thing to both sides.

Most equations you'll see on the HESI A^2 can be solved using the same basic steps:

1. Distribute to get rid of parentheses.
2. Use the least common denominator to get rid of fractions.
3. Add/subtract like terms on either side.
4. Add/subtract so that constants appear on only one side of the equation.
5. Multiply/divide to isolate the variable.

Examples

1. Solve for x: $25x + 12 = 62$

   This equation has no parentheses, fractions, or like terms on the same side, so you can start by subtracting 12 from both sides of the equation:

   $25x + 12 = 62$

   $(25x + 12) - 12 = 62 - 12$

   $25x = 50$

   Now, divide by 25 to isolate the variable:

   $\frac{25x}{25} = \frac{50}{25}$

   $x = 2$

2. Solve the following equation for x: $2x - 4(2x + 3) = 24$

   Start by distributing to get rid of the parentheses (don't forget to distribute the negative):

   $2x - 4(2x + 3) = 24$

   $2x - 8x - 12 = 24$

   There are no fractions, so now you can join like terms:

   $2x - 8x - 12 = 24$

   $-6x - 12 = 24$

   Now add 12 to both sides and divide by −6.

   $-6x - 12 = 24$

   $(-6x - 12) + 12 = 24 + 12$

   $-6x = 36$

   $\frac{-6x}{-6} = \frac{36}{-6}$

   $x = -6$

3. Solve the following equation for x: $\frac{x}{3} + \frac{1}{2} = \frac{x}{6} - \frac{5}{12}$

   Start by multiplying by the least common denominator to get rid of the fractions:

   $\frac{x}{3} + \frac{1}{2} = \frac{x}{6} - \frac{5}{12}$

   $12\left(\frac{x}{3} + \frac{1}{2}\right) = 12\left(\frac{x}{6} - \frac{5}{12}\right)$

   $4x + 6 = 2x - 5$

Now you can isolate x:

$(4x + 6) - 6 = (2x - 5) - 6$

$4x = 2x - 11$

$(4x) - 2x = (2x - 11) - 2x$

$2x = -11$

$x = -\dfrac{11}{2}$

4. Solve for x: $2(x + y) - 7x = 14x + 3$

This equation looks more difficult because it has 2 variables, but you can use the same steps to solve for x. First, distribute to get rid of the parentheses and combine like terms:

$2(x + y) - 7x = 14x + 3$

$2x + 2y - 7x = 14x + 3$

$-5x + 2y = 14x + 3$

Now you can move the x terms to one side and everything else to the other, and then divide to isolate x:

$-5x + 2y = 14x + 3$

$-19x = -2y + 3$

$x = \dfrac{2y - 3}{19}$

UNITS OF MEASUREMENT

The HESI A[2] will test your knowledge of two types of units: the US customary (or American) system and the metric system. The US system includes many of the units you likely use in day-to-day activities, such as the foot, pound, and cup. The metric system is used throughout the rest of the world and is the main system used in science and medicine. Common units for the US and metric systems are shown in the table below.

Table 1.1. Units

DIMENSION	US CUSTOMARY	METRIC
length	inch/foot/yard/mile	meter
mass	ounce/pound/ton	gram
volume	cup/pint/quart/gallon	liter
temperature	Fahrenheit	kelvin

The metric system uses prefixes to simplify large and small numbers. These prefixes are added to the base units shown in the table above. For example, the measurement 1000 meters can be written using the prefix kilo– as 1 kilometer. The most commonly used metric prefixes are given in the table below.

Table 1.2. Metric Prefixes

PREFIX	SYMBOL	MULTIPLICATION FACTOR
kilo	k	1,000
hecto	h	100
deca	da	10
base unit	--	--

Table 1.2. Metric Prefixes (continued)

PREFIX	SYMBOL	MULTIPLICATION FACTOR
deci	d	0.1
centi	c	0.01
milli	m	0.001

Conversion factors can be used to convert between units both within a single system and between the US and metric systems. Some questions on the HESI A² will require you to know common conversion factors, some of which are shown in the table below.

Table 1.3. Conversion Factors

1 in = 2.54 cm	1 lb = 0.454 kg
1 yd = 0.914 m	1 cal = 4.19 J
1 mi = 1.61 km	$C = \frac{5}{9}(^{\circ}F - 32)$
1 gal = 3.785 L	1 cm³ = 1 mL
1 oz = 28.35 g	1 hr = 3600 s

To perform unit conversion, start with the initial value and multiply by a conversion factor to reach the final unit. This process is shown in Figure 1.5.

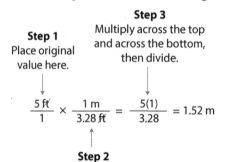

Step 1
Place original value here.

Step 3
Multiply across the top and across the bottom, then divide.

$$\frac{5 \text{ ft}}{1} \times \frac{1 \text{ m}}{3.28 \text{ ft}} = \frac{5(1)}{3.28} = 1.52 \text{ m}$$

Step 2
Add a convesion factor so that the original unit cancels, leaving only the new unit.

Figure 1.5. Unit Conversion

Examples

1. Convert 4.25 km to meters.

$$\frac{4.25 \text{ km}}{1} \times \frac{1000 \text{ m}}{1 \text{ km}} = \textbf{4250 m}$$

2. What is the mass in kilograms of a 150 lb man?

$$\frac{150 \text{ lb.}}{1} \times \frac{0.454 \text{ kg}}{1 \text{ lb.}} = (150)(0.454) = \textbf{68.1 kg}$$

3. A ball rolling across a table travels 6 inches per second. How many feet will it travel in 1 minute?

This problem requires two unit conversions. Start by converting inches to feet:

$$\frac{6 \text{ in.}}{1 \text{ s.}} \times \frac{1 \text{ ft.}}{12 \text{ in.}} = \frac{0.5 \text{ ft.}}{1 \text{ s.}}$$

Now convert seconds to minutes:

$$\frac{0.5 \text{ ft.}}{1 \text{ s.}} \times \frac{60 \text{ s.}}{1 \text{ min.}} = \frac{30 \text{ ft.}}{1 \text{ min.}}$$

The ball will travel **30 feet** in 1 minute.

2

READING COMPREHENSION

THE MAIN IDEA

The **MAIN IDEA** of a text is the argument that the author is trying to make about a particular **TOPIC**. Every sentence in a passage should support or address the main idea in some way.

Identifying the Main Idea

Consider a political election. A candidate is running for office and plans to deliver a speech asserting her position on tax reform, which is that taxes should be lowered. The topic of the speech is tax reform, and the main idea is that taxes should be lowered. The candidate is going to assert this in her speech, and support it with examples proving why lowering taxes would benefit the public and how it could be accomplished.

Topic: The subject of the passage. **Main idea**: The argument the writer is making about the topic.

Other candidates may have different perspectives on the same topic; they may believe that higher taxes are necessary, or that current taxes are adequate. It is likely that their speeches, while on the same topic of tax reform, would have different main ideas supported by different examples and evidence.

Let's look at an example passage to see how to identify the topic and main idea.

> Babe Didrikson Zaharias, one of the most decorated female athletes of the twentieth century, is an inspiration for everyone. Born in 1911 in Beaumont, Texas, Zaharias lived in a time when women were considered second class to men, but she never let that stop her from becoming a champion. Zaharias was one of seven children in a poor immigrant family and was competitive from an early age. As a child she excelled at most things she tried, especially sports, which continued into high school and beyond. After high school, Zaharias played amateur basketball for two years, and soon after began training in track and field. Despite the fact that women were only allowed to enter in three events, Zaharias represented the United States in the 1932 Los Angeles Olympics, and won two gold medals and one silver in track and field events.

The topic of this paragraph is obviously Babe Zaharias—the whole passage describes events from her life. Determining the main idea, however, requires a little more analysis. To figure out the main idea, consider what the writer is saying about Zaharias. The passage describes her life, but the main idea of the paragraph is what it says about her accomplishments. The writer is saying that she is someone to admire. That is the main idea and what unites all the information in the paragraph.

Example

From so far away it's easy to imagine the surface of our solar system's planets as enigmas—how could we ever know what those far-flung planets really look like? It turns out, however, that scientists have a number of tools at their disposal that allow them to paint detailed pictures of many planets' surfaces. The topography of Venus, for example, has been explored by several space probes, including the Russian Venera landers and NASA's *Magellan* orbiter. In addition to these long-range probes, NASA has also used its series of "Great Observatories" to study distant planets. These four massively powerful orbiting telescopes are the famous Hubble Space Telescope, the Compton Gamma Ray Observatory, the Chandra X-Ray Observatory, and the Spitzer Space Telescope. Such powerful telescopes aren't just found in space: NASA makes use of Earth-based telescopes as well. Scientists at the National Radio Astronomy Observatory in Charlottesville, Virginia, have spent decades using radio imaging to build an incredibly detailed portrait of Venus's surface.

Which of the following sentences best describes the main idea of the passage?

A) It's impossible to know what the surfaces of other planets are really like.

B) Telescopes are an important tool for scientists studying planets in our solar system.

C) Venus's surface has many of the same features as Earth's, including volcanoes, craters, and channels.

D) Scientists use a variety of advanced technologies to study the surfaces of the planets in our solar system.

Answer:

D) is correct. Choice A can be eliminated because it directly contradicts the rest of the passage. Choices B and C can also be eliminated because they offer only specific details from the passage. While both choices contain details from the passage, neither is general enough to encompass the passage as a whole. Only choice D provides an assertion that is both backed up by the passage's content and general enough to cover the entire passage.

Topic and Summary Sentences

The topic, and sometimes the main idea of a paragraph, is introduced in the TOPIC SENTENCE. The topic sentence usually appears early in a passage. The first sentence in the example paragraph about Babe Zaharias states the topic and main idea: *Babe Didrikson Zaharias, one of the most decorated female athletes of the twentieth century, is an inspiration for everyone.*

Even though paragraphs generally begin with topic sentences, on occasion writers build up to the topic sentence by using supporting details in order to generate interest or construct an argument. Be alert for paragraphs in which writers do not include a clear topic sentence.

There may also be a SUMMARY SENTENCE at the end of a passage. As its name suggests, this sentence sums up the passage, often by restating the main idea and the author's key evidence supporting it.

Example

The Constitution of the United States establishes a series of limits to rein in centralized power. "Separation of powers" distributes federal authority among three branches: the executive, the legislative, and the judicial. "Checks and balances" allow the branches to prevent any one branch from usurping power. "States' rights" are protected under the Constitution from too much encroachment by the federal government. "Enumeration of powers" names the specific and few powers the federal government has. These four restrictions have helped sustain the American republic for over two centuries.

Which of the following is the passage's topic sentence?

A) These four restrictions have helped sustain the American republic for over two centuries.

B) The Constitution of the United States establishes a series of limits to rein in centralized power.

C) "Enumeration of powers" names the specific and few powers the federal government has.

D) "Checks and balances" allow the branches to prevent any one branch from usurping power.

Answer:

B) is correct. Choice B is the first sentence of the passage and introduces the topic. Choice A is the final sentence of the passage and summarizes the passage's content. Choices C and D are supporting sentences found within the body of the passage. They include important details that support the main idea of the passage.

SUPPORTING DETAILS

SUPPORTING DETAILS reinforce the author's main idea. Let's look again at the passage about athlete Babe Zaharias.

Babe Didrikson Zaharias, one of the most decorated female athletes of the twentieth century, is an inspiration for everyone. Born in 1911 in Beaumont, Texas, Zaharias lived in a time when women were considered second class to men, but she never let that stop her from becoming a champion. Babe was one of seven children in a poor immigrant family and was competitive from an early age. As a child she excelled at most things she tried, especially sports, which continued into high school and beyond. After high school, Babe played amateur basketball for two years, and soon after began training in track and field. Despite the fact that women were only allowed to enter in three events, Zaharias represented the United States in the 1932 Los Angeles Olympics, and won two gold medals and one silver for track and field events.

Remember that the main idea of the passage is that Zaharias is someone to admire—an idea introduced in the opening sentence. The remainder of the paragraph provides details that support this assertion. These details include the circumstances of her childhood, her childhood success at sports, and the medals she won at the Olympics.

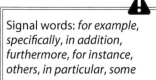

Signal words: *for example, specifically, in addition, furthermore, for instance, others, in particular, some*

When looking for supporting details, be alert for SIGNAL WORDS. These signal words tell you that a supporting fact or idea will follow, and so can be helpful in identifying supporting details. Signal words can also help you rule out certain sentences as the main idea or topic sentence. If a sentence begins with one of these phrases, it will likely be too specific to be a main idea.

Examples

From so far away it's easy to imagine the surface of our solar system's planets as enigmas—how could we ever know what those far-flung planets really look like? It turns out, however, that scientists have a number of tools at their disposal that allow them to paint detailed pictures of many planets' surfaces. The topography of Venus, for example, has been explored by several space probes, including the Russian Venera landers and NASA's *Magellan* orbiter. In addition to these long-range probes, NASA has also used its series of orbiting telescopes to study distant planets. These four massively powerful telescopes include the famous Hubble Space Telescope as well as the Compton Gamma Ray Observatory, the Chandra X-Ray Observatory, and the Spitzer Space Telescope. Such powerful telescopes aren't just found in space: NASA makes use of Earth-based telescopes as well. Scientists at the National Radio Astronomy Observatory in Charlottesville, Virginia, have spent decades using radio imaging to build an incredibly detailed portrait of Venus's surface.

1. According to the passage, which of the following is a space probe used to explore the surface of Venus?

   A) *Magellan* orbiter

   B) Hubble Space Telescope

   C) Spitzer Space Telescope

   D) National Radio Astronomy Observatory

   Answer:

   A) is correct. The passage states, "The topography of Venus, for example, has been explored by several space probes, including the Russian Venera landers and NASA's *Magellan* orbiter." The other choices are mentioned in the passage, but are not space probes.

2. If true, which detail could be added to the passage above to support the author's argument that scientists use many different technologies to study the surface of planets?

   A) Because Earth's atmosphere blocks X-rays, gamma rays, and infrared radiation, NASA needed to put telescopes in orbit above the atmosphere.

   B) In 2015, NASA released a map of Venus that was created by compiling images from orbiting telescopes and long-range space probes.

   C) NASA is currently using the *Curiosity* and *Opportunity* rovers to look for signs of ancient life on Mars.

   D) NASA has spent over $2.5 billion to build, launch, and repair the Hubble Space Telescope.

Answer:

B) is correct. Choice B is the best option because it addresses the use of multiple technologies to study the surface of planets. Choices C and D can be eliminated because they do not address the topic of studying the surface of planets. Choice A can also be eliminated because it only addresses a single technology.

FACTS VS. OPINIONS

In HESI reading passages you might be asked to identify a statement as either a fact or an opinion. A FACT is a statement or thought that can be proven to be true. The statement *Wednesday comes after Tuesday* is a fact—you can point to a calendar to prove it. In contrast, an OPINION is an assumption, not based in fact, that cannot be proven to be true. The assertion that *television is more entertaining than feature films* is an opinion—people will disagree on this, and there is no reference you can use to prove or disprove it.

Which of the following phrases would be associated with opinions? *for example, studies have shown, I believe, in fact, it's possible that*

Example

Exercise is critical for healthy development in children. Today in the United States, there is an epidemic of poor childhood health; many of these children will face further illnesses in adulthood that are due to poor diet and lack of exercise now. This is a problem for all Americans, especially with the rising cost of health care.

It is vital that school systems and parents encourage children to engage in a minimum of thirty minutes of cardiovascular exercise each day, mildly increasing their heart rate for a sustained period. This is proven to decrease the likelihood of developmental diabetes, obesity, and a multitude of other health problems. Also, children need a proper diet, rich in fruits and vegetables, so they can develop physically and learn healthy eating habits early on.

Which of the following in the passage is a fact, not an opinion?

A) Fruits and vegetables are the best way to help children be healthy.

B) Children today are lazier than they were in previous generations.

C) The risk of diabetes in children is reduced by physical activity.

D) Children should engage in thirty minutes of exercise a day.

Answer:

C) is correct. Choice C is a simple fact stated by the author. It is introduced by the word *proven* to indicate that it is supported by evidence. Choice B can be discarded immediately because it is not discussed anywhere in the passage, and also because it is negative, usually a hint in multiple-choice questions that an answer choice is wrong. Choices A and D are both opinions—the author is promoting exercise, fruits, and vegetables as a way to make children healthy. (Notice that these incorrect answers contain words that hint at being an opinion such as *best* or *should*.)

MAKING INFERENCES

In addition to understanding the main idea and factual content of a passage, you will also be asked to take your analysis one step further and anticipate what other information could logically be added to the passage. In a nonfiction passage, for example, you might be asked which statement the author of the passage would agree with. In an excerpt from a fictional work, you might be asked to anticipate what the character would do next.

To answer such questions, you need to have a solid understanding of the topic and main idea of the passage. Armed with this information, you can figure out which of the answer choices best fits the criteria (or, alternatively, which do not). For example, if the author of the passage is advocating for safer working conditions in factories, any details that could be added to the passage should support that idea. You might add sentences that contain information about the number of accidents that occur in factories or that outline a new plan for fire safety.

Example

Exercise is critical for healthy development in children. Today in the United States, there is an epidemic of poor childhood health; many of these children will face further illnesses in adulthood that are due to poor diet and lack of exercise now. This is a problem for all Americans, especially with the rising cost of health care.

It is vital that school systems and parents encourage children to engage in a minimum of thirty minutes of cardiovascular exercise each day, mildly increasing their heart rate for a sustained period. This is proven to decrease the likelihood of developmental diabetes, obesity, and a multitude of other health problems. Also, children need a proper diet, rich in fruits and vegetables, so they can develop physically and learn healthy eating habits early on.

Which of the following statements might the author of this passage agree with?

A) Adults who do not have healthy eating habits should be forced to pay more for health care.

B) Schools should be required by federal law to provide vegetables with every meal.

C) Healthy eating habits can only be learned at home.

D) Schools should encourage students to bring lunches from home.

Answer:

B) is correct. Since the author argues that children need a proper diet rich in fruits and vegetables, we can infer that the author would agree with choice B. The author describes the cost of health care as a problem for all Americans, implying that he would not want to punish adults who never learned healthy eating habits (choice A). Choices C and D are contradicted by the author's focus on creating healthy habits in schools.

TYPES OF PASSAGES

Authors typically write with a purpose. Sometimes referred to as "authorial intention," an author's purpose lets us know why the author is writing and what he or she would like to accomplish. There are many reasons an author might write, but most write for one of four reasons:

- to ENTERTAIN the reader or tell a story
- to PERSUADE the reader of his or her opinion
- to DESCRIBE something, such as a person, place, thing, or event
- to EXPLAIN a process or procedure

Identifying an author's purpose can be tricky, but the writing itself often gives clues. For example, if an author's purpose is to entertain, the writing may include vivid characters, exciting plot twists, or beautiful, figurative language. On the other hand, if an author wishes to persuade the reader, the passage may present an argument or contain convincing examples that support the author's point of view. An author who wishes to describe a person, place, or event may include lots of details as well as plenty of adjectives and adverbs. Finally, the author whose purpose is to explain a process or procedure may include step-by-step instructions or might present information in a sequence.

Related to authorial intention, described above, are the different MODES of written materials. A short story, for example, is meant to entertain, while an online news article is designed to inform the public about a current event.

Each of these different types of writing has a specific name. On the HESI A², you will be asked to identify which of these categories a passage fits into:

- **NARRATIVE WRITING** tells a story (novel, short story, play).
- **INFORMATIONAL** (or **EXPOSITORY**) **WRITING** informs people (newspaper and magazine articles).
- **TECHNICAL WRITING** explains something (product manual, instructions).
- **PERSUASIVE WRITING** tries to convince the reader of something (opinion column or a blog).

Examples

One of my summer reading books was *Mockingjay*. I was captivated by the adventures of the main character and the complicated plot of the book. However, I would argue that the ending didn't reflect the excitement of the story. Given what a powerful personality the main character has, I felt like the ending didn't do her justice.

1. Which of the following best captures the author's purpose?
    A) explain the plot of the novel *Mockingjay*
    B) persuade the reader that the ending of *Mockingjay* is inferior
    C) list the novels she read during the summer
    D) explain why the ending of a novel is important

Answer:

B) is correct. The purpose of the above passage is to persuade the reader of the author's opinion of the novel *Mockingjay*, specifically that the ending did not do the main character justice. The passage's use of the verb "argue" tells us that the passage is presenting a case to the reader. The passage follows this statement with evidence—that the main character had a powerful personality.

Elizabeth closed her eyes and braced herself on the armrests that divided her from her fellow passengers. Takeoff was always the worst part for her. The revving of the engines, the way her stomach dropped as the plane lurched upward: It made her feel sick. Then, she had to watch the world fade away beneath her, getting smaller and smaller until it was just her and the clouds hurtling through the sky. Sometimes (but only sometimes) it just had to be endured. She focused on the thought of her sister's smiling face and her new baby nephew as the plane slowly pulled onto the runway.

2. Which of the following best describes the mode of the passage?

A) narrative

B) expository

C) technical

D) persuasive

Answer:

A) is correct. The passage is telling a story—we meet Elizabeth and learn about her fear of flying—so it is a narrative text. There is no factual information presented or explained, nor is the author trying to persuade the reader.

TONE

The TONE of a passage describes the author's attitude toward the topic. The tone of a text can generally be described as positive, negative, or neutral.

Table 2.1. Words That Describe Tone

POSITIVE	NEUTRAL	NEGATIVE
admiring	apathetic	accusatory
amused	candid	angry
appreciative	detached	bitter
celebratory	direct	caustic
empathetic	impartial	contemptuous
enthusiastic	pragmatic	critical
excited		disapproving
joyful		indignant
loving		malicious
optimistic		mourning
sentimental		outraged
sympathetic		pessimistic
tolerant		scathing

DICTION, or word choice, can be used to help determine the tone of a passage. Many readers make the mistake of thinking about the ideas an author puts forth and using those alone to determine particularly tone; a much better practice is to separate specific words from the text and look for patterns in connotation and emotion. By considering categories of words used by the author, the reader can discover the attitude of the author toward the subject.

Every word has not only a literal meaning but also a CONNOTATIVE MEANING, relying on the common emotions, associations, and experiences an audience might associate with that word. The following words are all synonyms: *dog, puppy, cur, mutt, canine, pet.* Two of these words—*dog* and *canine*—are neutral words, without strong associations or emotions. Two others—*pet* and *puppy*—have positive associations. The last two—cur and mutt—have negative associations. A passage that uses one pair of these words versus another pair activates the positive or negative reactions of the audience.

Example

As you can see from my latest report, my babysitting business has been really successful. The year started with a busy couple of months—several snows combined with a large number of requests for Valentine's Day services boosted our sales quite a bit. The spring months have admittedly been a bit slow, but we're hoping for a big summer once school gets out. Several clients have already put in requests for our services!

Which of the following best describes the tone of the passage?

A. sentimental

B. optimistic

C. concerned

D. detached

Answer:

B) is correct. The author ends with the note that she optimistic that sales will improve over the summer. There is no indication that she is *sentimental* about sales. She admits that sales have been slow but is not *concerned* (and thinks they will improve). The writer also takes pride in her business and is excited for the future, so she is not *detached*.

VOCABULARY

On the Reading section you may also be asked to provide definitions or intended meanings of words within passages. You may have never encountered some of these words before the test, but there are tricks you can use to figure out what they mean.

Context Clues

One of the most fundamental vocabulary skills is using the context in which a word is found to determine its meaning. Your ability to read sentences carefully is extremely helpful when it comes to understanding new vocabulary words.

Vocabulary questions on the HESI A² will usually include SENTENCE CONTEXT CLUES within the sentence that contains the word. There are several clues that can help you understand the context, and therefore the meaning of a word:

RESTATEMENT CLUES state the definition of the word in the sentence. The definition is often set apart from the rest of the sentence by a comma, parentheses, or a colon.

> Teachers often prefer teaching students with <u>intrinsic</u> motivation:
> these students have an <u>internal</u> desire to learn.
>
> The meaning of *intrinsic* is restated as *internal*.

CONTRAST CLUES include the opposite meaning of a word. Words like *but, on the other hand,* and *however* are tip-offs that a sentence contains a contrast clue.

> Janet was <u>destitute</u> after she lost her job, but her wealthy
> sister helped her get back on her feet.
>
> *Destitute* is contrasted with *wealthy*, so the definition of destitute is *poor*.

POSITIVE/NEGATIVE CLUES tell you whether a word has a positive or negative meaning.

The film was <u>lauded</u> by critics as stunning, and was nominated for several awards.

The positive descriptions *stunning* and *nominated for several awards* suggest that *lauded* has a positive meaning.

Examples

Select the answer that most closely matches the definition of the underlined word or phrase as it is used in the sentence.

1. The dog was <u>dauntless</u> in the face of danger, braving the fire to save the girl trapped inside the building.

A) difficult

B) fearless

C) imaginative

D) startled

Answer:

B) is correct. Demonstrating bravery in the face of danger would be fearless. The restatement clue (*braving*) tells you exactly what the word means.

2. Beth did not spend any time preparing for the test, but Tyrone kept a <u>rigorous</u> study schedule.

A) strict

B) loose

C) boring

D) strange

Answer:

A) is correct. The word *but* tells us that Tyrone studied in a different way from Beth, which means it is a contrast clue. If Beth did not study hard, then Tyrone did. The best answer, therefore, is choice A.

Analyzing Words

As you know, determining the meaning of a word can be more complicated than just looking in a dictionary. A word might have more than one DENOTATION, or definition, and which one the author intends can only be judged by looking at the surrounding text. For example, the word *quack* can refer to the sound a duck makes or to a person who publicly pretends to have a qualification which he or she does not actually possess.

A word may also have different CONNOTATIONS, which are the implied meanings and emotions a word evokes in the reader. For example, a cubicle is simply a walled desk in an office, but for many the word implies a constrictive, uninspiring workplace. Connotations can vary greatly between cultures and even between individuals.

Last, authors might make use of FIGURATIVE LANGUAGE, which is the use of a word to imply something other than the word's literal definition. This is often done by comparing two things. If you say *I felt like a butterfly when I got a new haircut*, the listener knows you do not resemble an insect but instead felt beautiful and transformed.

Examples

Select the answer that most closely matches the definition of the underlined word or phrase as it is used in the sentence.

1. The patient's uneven <u>pupils</u> suggested that brain damage was possible.

    A) part of the eye

    B) student in a classroom

    C) walking pace

    D) breathing sounds

    Answer:

    A) is correct. Only choice A matches both the definition of the word and context of the sentence. Choice B is an alternative definition for pupil, but does not make sense in the sentence. Both C and D could be correct in the context of the sentence, but neither is a definition of pupil.

2. Aiden examined the antique lamp and worried that he had been <u>taken for a ride</u>. He had paid a lot for the vintage lamp, but it looked like it was worthless.

    A) transported

    B) forgotten

    C) deceived

    D) hindered

    Answer:

    C) is correct. It is clear from the context of the sentence that Aiden was not literally taken for a ride. Instead, this phrase is an example of figurative language. From context clues you can figure out that Aiden paid too much for the lamp, so he was deceived.

Word Structure

You are not expected to know every word in the English language for your test; rather, you will need to use deductive reasoning to find the best definition of the word in question. Many words can be broken down into three main parts to help determine their meaning:

PREFIX — ROOT — SUFFIX

ROOTS are the building blocks of all words. Every word is either a root itself or has a root. The root is what is left when you strip away the prefixes and suffixes from a word. For example, in the word *unclear*, if you take away the prefix *un–*, you have the root *clear*.

Roots are not always recognizable words, because they often come from Latin or Greek words, such as *nat*, a Latin root meaning born. The word *native*, which means a person born in a referenced place, comes from this root; so does the word *prenatal*, meaning *before birth*. It is important to keep in mind, however, that roots do not always match the original definitions of words, and they can have several different spellings.

PREFIXES are elements added to the beginning of a word, and **SUFFIXES** are elements added to the end of the word; together they are known as affixes. They carry assigned meanings and can be attached to a word to completely change the word's meaning or to enhance the word's original meaning.

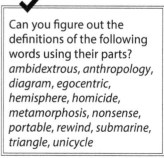

Can you figure out the definitions of the following words using their parts? *ambidextrous, anthropology, diagram, egocentric, hemisphere, homicide, metamorphosis, nonsense, portable, rewind, submarine, triangle, unicycle*

Let's use the word *prefix* itself as an example: *fix* means to place something securely and *pre–* means before. Therefore, *prefix* means to place something before or in front of. Now let's look at a suffix: in the word *feminism*, *femin* is a root which means female. The suffix *–ism* means act, practice, or process. Thus, *feminism* is the process of establishing equal rights for women.

Although you cannot determine the meaning of a word from a prefix or suffix alone, you can use this knowledge to eliminate answer choices. Understanding whether the word is positive or negative can give you the partial meaning of the word.

Table 2.2. Common Roots

ROOT	DEFINITION	EXAMPLE
ast(er)	star	asteroid, astronomy
audi	hear	audience, audible
auto	self	automatic, autograph
bene	good	beneficent, benign
bio	life	biology, biorhythm
cap	take	capture
ced	yield	secede
chrono	time	chronometer, chronic
corp	body	corporeal
crac or crat	rule	autocrat
demo	people	democracy
dict	say	dictionary, dictation
duc	lead or make	ductile, produce
gen	give birth	generation, genetics
geo	earth	geography, geometry
grad	step	graduate
graph	write	graphical, autograph
ject	throw	eject
jur or jus	law	justice, jurisdiction
juven	young	juvenile
log or logue	thought	logic, logarithm
luc	light	lucidity
man	hand	manual
mand	order	remand
mis	send	transmission
mono	one	monotone
omni	all	omnivore
path	feel	sympathy
phil	love	philanthropy
phon	sound	phonograph

ROOT	DEFINITION	EXAMPLE
port	carry	export
qui	rest	quiet
scrib or script	write	scribe, transcript
sense or sent	feel	sentiment
tele	far away	telephone
terr	earth	terrace
uni	single	unicode
vac	empty	vacant
vid or vis	see	video, vision

Table 2.3. Common Prefixes

PREFIX	DEFINITION	EXAMPLE
a– (also an–)	not, without; to, toward; of, completely	atheist, anemic, aside, aback, anew, abashed
ante–	before, preceding	antecedent, anteroom
anti–	opposing, against	antibiotic, anticlimax
belli–	warlike, combative	belligerent, antebellum
com– (also co–, col–, con–, cor–)	with, jointly, completely	combat, cooperate, collide, confide, correspond
dis– (also di–)	negation, removal	disadvantage, disbar
en– (also em–)	put into or on; bring into the condition of; intensify	engulf, embrace
hypo–	under	hypoglycemic, hypodermic
in– (also il–, im–, ir–)	not, without; in, into, toward, inside	infertile, impossible, illegal, irregular, influence, include
intra–	inside, within	intravenous, intrapersonal
out–	surpassing, exceeding; external, away from	outperform, outdoor
over–	excessively, completely; upper, outer, over, above	overconfident, overcast
pre–	before	precondition, preadolescent, prelude
re–	again	reapply, remake
semi–	half, partly	semicircle, semiconscious
syn– (also sym–)	in union, acting together	synthesis, symbiotic
trans–	across, beyond	transdermal
trans–	into a different state	translate
under–	beneath, below; not enough	underarm, undersecretary, underdeveloped

Examples

Select the answer that most closely matches the definition of the underlined word or phrase as it is used in the sentence.

1. The <u>bellicose</u> dog will be sent to training school next week.

    A) misbehaved

    B) friendly

    C) scared

    D) aggressive

    Answer:

    D) is correct. Both *misbehaved* and *aggressive* look like possible answers given the context of the sentence. However, the prefix *belli–*, which means warlike, can be used to confirm that *aggressive* is the right answer.

2. The new menu <u>rejuvenated</u> the restaurant and made it one of the most popular spots in town.

    A) established

    B) invigorated

    C) improved

    D) motivated

    Answer:

    B) is correct. All the answer choices could make sense in the context of the sentence, so it is necessary to use word structure to find the definition. The root *juven* means young and the prefix *re–* means again, so *rejuvenate* means to be made young again. The answer choice with the most similar meaning is *invigorated*, which means to give something energy.

3

VOCABULARY

The HESI A^2 vocabulary section will test your knowledge of general vocabulary as well as terms commonly used in the medical profession. The test will have the following types of questions:

- select the correct definition of a word
- infer the definition of a word used in a sentence
- select the synonym of a word

Below is a list of common medical terms and other vocabulary words that may appear on the test. Make sure to also review the lists of affixes and root words in the Reading chapter.

ABATE: become less in amount or intensity

ABBREVIATE: to shorten or abridge

ABDUCTION: the movement of a limb away from the body's midline

ABRASION: an area of the skin damaged by scraping or wearing away

ABSORB: to take in

ABSTAIN: refrain; choose to avoid or not participate

ACCESS: means of approach or admission

ACCOUNTABLE: liable or responsible

ACOUSTIC: related to sound or hearing

ACUITY: sharpness of vision or hearing; mental quickness

ADHERE: hold closely to an idea or course; be devoted

ADVERSE: harmful to one's interests; unfortunate

AMALGAM: a mixture or blend

AMBULATORY: able to walk

ANALGESIC: a drug that relieves pain

ANOMALY: something unusual

ASEPTIC: free from bacteria and other pathogens

ATTENUATE: to weaken

AUDIBLE: loud enough to be heard

BENEVOLENT: showing sympathy, understanding, and generosity

BENIGN: not harmful; not malignant

BIAS: an unfair preference or dislike

BILATERAL: having two sides

CANNULA: a thin tube inserted into the body to collect or drain fluid

CARDIAC: pertaining to the heart

CEASE: stop doing an action, discontinue

CEPHALIC: relating to the head

CHRONIC: persistent or recurring over a long time period

CO-MORBIDITY: two disorders that occur at the same time

COHORT: a group of people who are treated as a group

COLLABORATE: work together on a common project

COLLATERAL: adjoining or accompanying

COMPASSION: awareness and sympathy for the experiences and suffering of others

COMPLICATION: something intricate, involved, or aggravating

COMPLY: acquiesce to another's wish, command, etc.

COMPRESSION: pressing together

COMPROMISE: an accommodation in which both sides make concessions

CONCAVE: with an outline or surface curved inward

CONCISE: brief and compact

CONDITIONAL: dependent on something else being done

CONSISTENCY: state of being congruous; conforming to regular patterns, habits, principles, etc.

CONSTRICT: cause to shrink, cramp, crush

CONTINGENT: depending on something not certain; conditional

CONTRAINDICATION: discouragement of the use of a treatment

COPIOUS: abundant and plentiful

CULTURE: the growth of microorganisms in an artifical environment

DEFECATE: have a bowel movement

DELETERIOUS: harmful or deadly to living things

DEPRESS: weaken; sadden

DEPTH: deepness; distance measured downward, inward, or backward

DERMAL: relating to skin

DETER: to prevent or discourage

DETERIORATING: growing worse; reducing in worth; impairing

DIAGNOSIS: analysis of a present condition

DILATE: expand; make larger

DILIGENT: persistent and hardworking

DILUTE: weaken by a mixture of water or other liquid; reduce in strength

DISCRETE: separate; discontinuous

ELEVATE: raise; lift up

EMPATHY: understanding of another's feelings

ENDOGENOUS: something produced within the body

ENERVATING: causing debilitation or weakness

ENHANCE: to improve; to increase clarity

ENTERAL: relating to the small intestine

EPHEMERAL: lasting only for a short period of time

EXACERBATE: make more bitter, angry, or violent; irritate or aggravate

EXCESS: the state of being more or too much; a surplus or remainder

EXOGENOUS: something produced outside the body

EXPAND: increase in extent, bulk, or amount; spread or stretch out; unfold

EXPOSURE: the state of being exposed or open to external environments

EXTENUATING: diminish the seriousness of something

EXTERNAL: located outside of something and/or apart from something

FATAL: causing death or ruin

FATIGUE: weariness from physical or mental exertion

FLACCID: soft; flabby

FLUSHED: suffused with color; washed out with a copious flow of water

FOCAL: centered in one area

GAPING: to be open; to have a break in continuity

GASTRIC: relating to the stomach

HEMATOLOGIC: dealing with the blood

HEPATIC: relating to the liver

HYDRATION: the act of meeting body fluid demands

HYGIENE: the science that deals with the preservation of health

IMMINENT: very likely to happen

IMPAIRED: made worse, damaged, or weakened

INCIDENCE: frequency or range of occurrence; extent of effects

INCOMPATIBLE: unable to be or work together

INFECTION: tainted with germs or disease

INFLAMED: condition in which the body is inflicted with heat, swelling, and redness

INGEST: take into the body for digestion

INITIATE: set going; begin; originate

INNOCUOUS: harmless

INTACT: remaining uninjured, unimpaired, whole, or complete

INTERNAL: situated within something; enclosed; inside

INTUITIVE: to know by instinct alone

INVASIVE: being intrusive or encroaching upon

JERK: a quick, sudden movement

LABILE: unstable

LACERATION: a rough tear; an affliction

LANGUID: tired and slow

LATENT: hidden; dormant; undeveloped

LETHARGIC: not wanting to move; sluggish

LONGEVITY: having a long life

MALADY: a disease or disorder

MALAISE: a general feeling of illness or discomfort

MALIGNANT: harmful

MANIFESTATION: a demonstration or display

MUSCULOSKELETAL: pertaining to muscles and the skeleton

NEUROLOGIC: dealing with the nervous system

NEUROVASCULAR: pertaining to the nervous system and blood vessels

NEXUS: a connection or series of connections

NOVICE: a beginner; inexperienced

NUTRIENT: something affording nutrition

OBVERSE: the opposite

OCCLUDED: shut in or out; closed; absorbed

OCCULT: hidden

ORAL: spoken, not written; pertaining to the mouth

OSSIFY: to harden

OVERT: plain to the view; open

PALLIATE: to lessen symptoms without treating the underlying cause

PAROXYSMAL: having to do with a spasm or violent outburst

PATHOGENIC: causing disease

PATHOLOGY: the science of the nature and origin of disease

POSTERIOR: located in the back or rear

POTENT: wielding power; strong; effective

PRAGMATIC: concerned with practical matters and results

PRECAUTION: an act done in advance to ensure safety or benefit; prudent foresight

PREDISPOSE: give a tendency or inclination to; dispose in advance

PREEXISTING: already in place; already occurring

PRIMARY: first; earliest; most important

PRIORITY: right of precedence; order of importance

PROGNOSIS: a forecast

PRUDENT: careful and sensible; using good judgment

RATIONALE: rational basis for something; justification

RECUR: appear again; return

REGRESS: to return to a former state

RENAL: pertaining to the kidneys

RESECT: to remove or cut out

RESILIENT: quick to recover

RESPIRATION: breathing

RESTRICT: attach limitations to; restrain

RETAIN: hold or keep in possession, use, or practice

SHUNT: a tube that diverts the path of a fluid in the body

SOPORIFIC: a drug that induces sleep

STATUS: relative standing; position; condition

SUBLINGUAL: beneath the tongue

SUBTLE: understated, not obvious

SUCCUMB: to stop resisting

SUPERFICIAL: shallow in character and attitude; only concerned with things on the surface

SUPERFLUOUS: more than is needed, desired, or necessary

SUPPLEMENT: an addition to something substantially completed; to add to

SUPPRESS: restrain; abolish; repress

SYMMETRIC: similar proportion in the size or shape of something

SYMPTOM: a sign or indication of a problem or disease

SYNDROME: a set of symptoms that characterize a certain disease or condition

SYSTEMIC: affecting the whole body

THERAPEUTIC: pertaining to the curing of disease; having remedial effect

TRANSDERMAL: passing through the skin

TRANSIENT: lasting for only a short time or duration

TRANSMISSION: the act or result of sending something along or onward to a recipient or destination

TRAUMA: a bodily injury or mental shock

TRIAGE: the act of sorting or categorizing conditions and diseases in preparation for treatment

UNILATERAL: relating to only one side

VASCULAR: pertaining to bodily ducts that convey fluid

VIRUS: an agent of infection

VITAL: pertaining to life; alive; essential to existence or well-being

VOID: empty; evacuate

VOLUME: the amount of space occupied by a substance

Examples

1. What is the best definition of the word *pacify*?

A) soothe

B) transport

C) bathe

D) motivate

Answer:

A) is correct. The word root *pax* means "peace," and the suffix *–ify* means "to cause to become more." So to pacify someone means to cause that person to become more peaceful, or to soothe them.

2. What is the best definition of the word *prudent*?

A) sensible

B) inquisitive

C) terrified

D) squeamish

Answer:

A) is correct. *Prudent* means "wise or judicious." For example, a prudent decision is a wise, practical one.

3. Select the meaning of the underlined word in the sentence.

The theater's new production was a great success and received great <u>acclaim</u> from newspaper critics.

A) pity

B) praise

C) notoriety

D) interest

Answer:

B) is correct. The play was a *great success*, so critics are likely praising it.

4. What word meaning *chaotic* best fits in the sentence?

The office is organized in a _____ manner, so it's hard to find supplies quickly.

A) dangerous

B) precise

C) haphazard

D) harmonious

Answer:

C) is correct. *Haphazard* means "a lack of planning or order." For example, when a room is arranged haphazardly, it is disorganized, messy, and chaotic.

GRAMMAR

NOUNS AND PRONOUNS

NOUNS are people, places, or things. The subject of a sentence is typically a noun. For example, in the sentence *The hospital was very clean*, the subject, *hospital*, is a noun; it is a place. **PRONOUNS** stand in for nouns and can be used to make sentences sound less repetitive. Take the sentence, "Sam stayed home from school because Sam was not feeling well." The word *Sam* appears twice in the same sentence. Instead, you can use the pronoun *he* to stand in for *Sam* and say, "Sam stayed home from school because he was not feeling well."

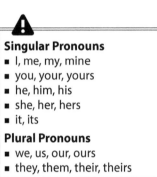

Singular Pronouns
- I, me, my, mine
- you, your, yours
- he, him, his
- she, her, hers
- it, its

Plural Pronouns
- we, us, our, ours
- they, them, their, theirs

Because pronouns take the place of nouns, they need to agree both in number and gender with the noun they replace. So, a plural noun needs a plural pronoun, and a noun referring to something feminine needs a feminine pronoun. In the first sentence in this paragraph, for example, the plural pronoun *they* replaced the plural noun *pronouns*. There will usually be several questions on the Grammar section that cover pronoun agreement, so it's good to get comfortable spotting pronouns.

> Wrong: If a student forgets their homework, they will not receive a grade.
>
> Correct: If a student forgets his or her homework, he or she will not receive a grade.

Student is a singular noun, but *their* and *they* are plural pronouns. So, the first sentence is incorrect. To correct it, use the singular pronoun *his* or *her*, or *he* or *she*.

> Wrong: Everybody will receive their paychecks promptly.
>
> Correct: Everybody will receive his or her paycheck promptly.

Everybody is a singular noun, but *their* is a plural pronoun. So, this sentence is incorrect. To correct it, use the singular pronoun *his* or *her*.

Wrong: When nurses scrub in to surgery, you should wash your hands.

Correct: When nurses scrub in to surgery, they should wash their hands.

This sentence begins in third-person perspective and then switches to second-person perspective. So, this sentence is incorrect. To correct it, use a third-person pronoun in the second clause.

Wrong: After the teacher spoke to the student, she realized her mistake.

Correct: After Mr. White spoke to his student, she realized her mistake.
(*She* and *her* refer to the student.)

Correct: After speaking to the student, the teacher realized her own mistake.
(*Her* refers to the teacher.)

This sentence refers to a teacher and a student. But whom does *she* refer to, the teacher or the student? To eliminate the ambiguity, use specific names or state more specifically who made the mistake.

Examples

I have lived in Minnesota since August, but I still don't own a warm coat or gloves.

1. Which of the following lists includes all the nouns in the sentence?

    A) coat, gloves

    B) I, coat, gloves

    C) Minnesota, August, coat, gloves

    D) I, Minnesota, August, warm, coat, gloves

    Answer:

    C) is correct. *Minnesota* and *August* are proper nouns, and *coat* and *gloves* are common nouns. *I* is a pronoun, and *warm* is an adjective that modifies *coat*.

2. In which of the following sentences do the nouns and pronouns NOT agree?

    A) After we walked inside, we took off our hats and shoes and hung them in the closet.

    B) The members of the band should leave her instruments in the rehearsal room.

    C) The janitor on duty should rinse out his or her mop before leaving for the day.

    D) When you see someone in trouble, you should always try to help them.

    Answer:

    B) is correct. *The members of the band* is plural, so it should be replaced by the plural pronoun *their* instead of the singular *her*.

VERBS

A **VERB** is the action of a sentence: it describes what the subject of the sentence is or is doing. Verbs must match the subject of the sentence in person and number, and must be in the proper tense—past, present, or future.

Person describes the relationship of the speaker to the subject of the sentence: first (I, we), second (you), and third (he, she, it, they). *Number* refers to whether the subject of the sentence is singular or plural. Verbs are conjugated to match the person and number of the subject.

> ⚠ Think of the subject and the verb as sharing a single *s*. If the subject ends with an *s*, the verb should not, and vice versa.

Table 4.1. Conjugating Verbs for Person

PERSON	SINGULAR	PLURAL
First	I jump	we jump
Second	you jump	you jump
Third	he/she/it jumps	they jump

> Wrong: The cat chase the ball while the dogs runs in the yard.
>
> Correct: The cat chases the ball while the dogs run in the yard.

Cat is singular, so it takes a singular verb (which confusingly ends with an *s*); *dogs* is plural, so it needs a plural verb.

> Wrong: The cars that had been recalled by the manufacturer was returned within a few months.
>
> Correct: The cars that had been recalled by the manufacturer were returned within a few months.

Sometimes, the subject and verb are separated by clauses or phrases. Here, the subject *cars* is separated from the verb by the relatively long phrase "that had been recalled by the manufacturer," making it more difficult to determine how to correctly conjugate the verb.

> Correct: The doctor and nurse work in the hospital.
>
> Correct: Neither the nurse nor her boss was scheduled to take a vacation.
>
> Correct: Either the patient or her parents need to sign the release forms.

When the subject contains two or more nouns connected by *and*, that subject becomes plural and requires a plural verb. Singular subjects joined by *either/or*, *neither/nor*, or *not only/but also* remain singular; when these words join plural and singular subjects, the verb should match the closest subject.

> ⚠ If the subject is separated from the verb, cross out the phrases between them to make conjugation easier.

Finally, verbs must be conjugated for tense, which shows when the action happened. Some conjugations include helping verbs like *was*, *have*, *have been*, and *will have been*.

Table 4.2. Verb Tenses

TENSE	PAST	PRESENT	FUTURE
Simple	I <u>gave</u> her a gift yesterday.	I <u>give</u> her a gift every day.	I <u>will give</u> her a gift on her birthday.
Continuous	I <u>was giving</u> her a gift when you got here.	I <u>am giving</u> her a gift; come in!	I <u>will be giving</u> her a gift at dinner.

Table 4.2. Verb Tenses (continued)

TENSE	PAST	PRESENT	FUTURE
Perfect	I had given her a gift before you got there.	I have given her a gift already.	I will have given her a gift by midnight.
Perfect continuous	Her friends had been giving her gifts all night when I arrived.	I have been giving her gifts every year for nine years.	I will have been giving her gifts on holidays for ten years next year.

Tense must also be consistent throughout the sentence and the passage. For example, the sentence *I was baking cookies and eat some dough* sounds strange. That is because the two verbs, *was baking* and *eat*, are in different tenses. *Was baking* occurred in the past; *eat*, on the other hand, occurs in the present. To make them consistent, change *eat* to *ate*.

> Wrong: Because it will rain during the party last night, we had to move the tables inside.
>
> Correct: Because it rained during the party last night, we had to move the tables inside.

All the verb tenses in a sentence need to agree both with each other and with the other information in the sentence. In the first sentence above, the tense does not match the other information in the sentence: *last night* indicates the past (*rained*), not the future (*will rain*).

Examples

1. Which of the following sentences contains an incorrectly conjugated verb?

   A) The brother and sister runs very fast.

   B) Neither Anne nor Suzy likes the soup.

   C) The mother and father love their new baby.

   D) Either Jack or Jill will pick up the pizza.

   Answer:

   A) is correct. Choice A should read "The brother and sister run very fast." When the subject contains two or more nouns connected by *and*, the subject is plural and requires a plural verb.

2. Which of the following sentences contains an incorrect verb tense?

   A) After the show ended, we drove to the restaurant for dinner.

   B) Anne went to the mall before she headed home.

   C) Johnny went to the movies after he cleans the kitchen.

   D) Before the alarm sounded, smoke filled the cafeteria.

   Answer:

   C) is correct. Choice C should read "Johnny will go to the movies after he cleans the kitchen." It does not make sense to say that Johnny does something in the past (*went to the movies*) after doing something in the present (*after he cleans*).

ADJECTIVES AND ADVERBS

ADJECTIVES provide more information about a noun in a sentence. Take the sentence, "The boy hit the ball." If you want your readers to know more about the noun *boy*, you could use an adjective to describe him: *the little boy, the young boy, the tall boy.*

ADVERBS and adjectives are similar because they provide more information about a part of a sentence. However, adverbs do not describe nouns—that's an adjective's job. Instead, adverbs describe verbs, adjectives, and even other adverbs. For example, in the sentence "The doctor had recently hired a new employee," the adverb *recently* tells us more about how the action *hired* took place.

Adjectives, adverbs, and MODIFYING PHRASES (groups of words that together modify another word) should be placed as close as possible to the word they modify. Separating words from their modifiers can create incorrect or confusing sentences.

> Wrong: Running through the hall, the bell rang and the student knew she was late.
>
> Correct: Running through the hall, the student heard the bell ring and knew she was late.

The phrase *running through the hall* should be placed next to *student*, the noun it modifies.

The suffixes *–er* and *–est* are often used to modify adjectives when a sentence is making a comparison. The suffix *–er* is used when comparing two things, and the suffix *–est* is used when comparing more than two.

> Anne is taller than Steve, but Steve is more coordinated.
>
> Of the five brothers, Billy is the funniest, and Alex is the most intelligent.

Adjectives longer than two syllables are compared using *more* (for two things) or *most* (for three or more things).

> Wrong: Of my two friends, Clara is the smartest.
>
> Correct: Of my two friends, Clara is smarter.

More and *most* should not be used in conjunction with *–er* and *–est* endings.

> Wrong: My most warmest sweater is made of wool.
>
> Correct: My warmest sweater is made of wool.

Examples

The new chef carefully stirred the boiling soup and then lowered the heat.

1. Which of the following lists includes all the adjectives in the sentence?

    A) new, boiling

    B) new, carefully, boiling

    C) new, carefully, boiling, heat

    D) new, carefully, boiling, lowered, heat

Answer:

A) is correct. *New* modifies the noun *chef*, and *boiling* modifies the noun *soup*. *Carefully* is an adverb modifying the verb *stirred*. *Lowered* is a verb, and *heat* is a noun.

2. Which of the following sentences contains an adjective error?
   A) The new red car was faster than the old blue car.
   B) Reggie's apartment is in the tallest building on the block.
   C) The slice of cake was tastier than the brownie.
   D) Of the four speeches, Jerry's was the most long.

Answer:

D) is correct. Choice D should read, "Of the four speeches, Jerry's was the longest." The word *long* has only one syllable, so it should be modified with the suffix *–est*, not the word *most*.

OTHER PARTS OF SPEECH

PREPOSITIONS express the location of a noun or pronoun in relation to other words and phrases described in a sentence. For example, in the sentence "The nurse parked her car in a parking garage," the preposition *in* describes the position of the car in relation to the garage. Together, the preposition and the noun that follow it are called a **PREPOSITIONAL PHRASE**. In this example, the prepositional phrase is *in a parking garage*.

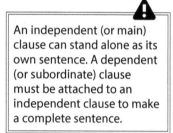

An independent (or main) clause can stand alone as its own sentence. A dependent (or subordinate) clause must be attached to an independent clause to make a complete sentence.

CONJUNCTIONS connect words, phrases, and clauses. The conjunctions summarized in the acronym FANBOYS—For, And, Nor, But, Or, Yet, So—are called **COORDINATING CONJUNCTIONS** and are used to join **INDEPENDENT CLAUSES** (clauses that can stand alone as a complete sentence). For example, in the following sentence, the conjunction *and* joins together two independent clauses:

> The nurse prepared the patient for surgery, and the doctor performed the surgery.

Other conjunctions, like *although*, *because*, and *if*, join together an independent and **DEPENDENT CLAUSE** (which cannot stand on its own). Take the following sentence:

> She had to ride the subway because her car was broken.

The clause *because her car was broken* cannot stand on its own.

INTERJECTIONS, like *wow* and *hey*, express emotion and are most commonly used in conversation and casual writing.

Examples

Choose the word that best completes the sentence.

1. Her love _____ blueberry muffins kept her coming back to the bakery every week.

   A) to

   B) with

   C) of

   D) about

   Answer:

   C) is correct. The correct preposition is *of.*

2. Christine left her house early on Monday morning, _____ she was still late for work.

   A) but

   B) and

   C) for

   D) or

   Answer:

   A) is correct. In this sentence, the conjunction is joining together two contrasting ideas, so the correct answer is *but.*

CAPITALIZATION

Capitalization questions on the HESI will ask you to spot errors in capitalization within a phrase or sentence. Below are the most important rules for capitalization you are likely to see on the test.

The first word of a sentence is always capitalized.

> We will be having dinner at a new restaurant tonight.

The first letter of a proper noun is always capitalized.

> We're going to Chicago on Wednesday.

Titles are capitalized if they precede the name they modify.

> Joe Biden, the vice president, met with President Obama.

Months are capitalized, but not the names of the seasons.

> Snow fell in March even though winter was over.

The names of major holidays should be capitalized. The word *day* is only capitalized if it is part of the holiday's name.

> We always go to a parade on Memorial Day, but Christmas day we stay home.

The names of specific places should always be capitalized. General location terms are not capitalized.

> We're going to San Francisco next weekend so I can see the ocean.

Titles for relatives should be capitalized when they precede a name, but not when they stand alone.

> Fred, my uncle, will make fried chicken, and Aunt Betty is going to make spaghetti.

Example

Which of the following sentences contains an error in capitalization?

A) My two brothers are going to New Orleans for Mardi Gras.

B) On Friday we voted to elect a new class president.

C) Janet wants to go to Mexico this Spring.

D) Peter complimented the chef on his cooking.

Answer:

C) is correct. *Spring* is the name of a season and should not be capitalized.

PHRASES

To understand what a phrase is, you have to know about subjects and predicates. The **SUBJECT** is what the sentence is about; the **PREDICATE** contains the verb and its modifiers.

> The nurse at the front desk will answer any questions you have.

The subject is *the nurse at the front desk*, and the predicate is *will answer any questions you have*.

A **PHRASE** is a group of words that communicates only part of an idea because it lacks either a subject or a predicate. Phrases are categorized based on the main word in the phrase. A **PREPOSITIONAL PHRASE** begins with a preposition and ends with an object of the preposition, a **VERB PHRASE** is composed of the main verb along with any helping verbs, and a **NOUN PHRASE** consists of a noun and its modifiers.

> Prepositional phrase: The dog is hiding <u>under the porch</u>.
>
> Verb phrase: The chef <u>wanted to cook</u> a different dish.
>
> Noun phrase: <u>The big red barn</u> rests beside <u>the vacant chicken house</u>.

Example

Identify the type of phrase underlined in the following sentence.

David, <u>smelling the fresh bread baking,</u> smiled as he entered the kitchen.

A) prepositional phrase

B) noun phrase

C) verb phrase

D) verbal phrase

Answer:

D) is correct. The phrase is a verbal phrase modifying the noun *David*. It begins with the word *smelling*, derived from the verb *to smell*.

CLAUSES

CLAUSES contain both a subject and a predicate. They can be either independent or dependent. An INDEPENDENT (or main) CLAUSE can stand alone as its own sentence.

> The dog ate her homework.

Dependent (or subordinate) clauses cannot stand alone as their own sentences. They start with a subordinating conjunction, relative pronoun, or relative adjective, which will make them sound incomplete.

> <u>Because</u> the dog ate her homework

A sentence can be classified as simple, compound, complex, or compound-complex based on the type and number of clauses it has.

Table 4.3. Types of Clauses

SENTENCE TYPE	NUMBER OF INDEPENDENT CLAUSES	NUMBER OF DEPENDENT CLAUSES
simple	1	0
compound	2 or more	0
complex	1	1 or more
compound-complex	2 or more	1 or more

A SIMPLE SENTENCE consists of one independent clause. Because there are no dependent clauses in a simple sentence, it can be a two-word sentence, with one word being the subject and the other word being the verb, such as *I ran*. However, a simple sentence can also contain prepositions, adjectives, and adverbs. Even though these additions can extend the length of a simple sentence, it is still considered a simple sentence as long as it does not contain any dependent clauses.

> Simple: San Francisco in the springtime is one of my favorite places to visit.

Although the sentence is lengthy, it is simple because it contains only one subject and one verb (*San Francisco* and *is*), modified by additional phrases.

COMPOUND SENTENCES have two or more independent clauses and no dependent clauses. Usually a comma and a coordinating conjunction (the FANBOYS: For, And, Nor, But, Or, Yet, and So) join the independent clauses, though semicolons can be used as well.

> On the test you will have to both identify and construct different kinds of sentences.

> Compound: The game was canceled, but we will still practice on Saturday.

This sentence is made up of two independent clauses joined by a conjunction (*but*), so it is compound.

COMPLEX SENTENCES have one independent clause and at least one dependent clause. The two clauses will be joined by a subordinating conjunction.

> Complex: I love listening to the radio in the car because I can sing along.

The sentence has one independent clause (*I love...car*) and one dependent (*because I... along*), so it is complex.

COMPOUND-COMPLEX SENTENCES have two or more independent clauses and at least one dependent clause. Compound-complex sentences will have both a coordinating and a subordinating conjunction.

> I wanted to get a dog, but I have a fish because my roommate is allergic to pet dander.

This sentence has three clauses: two independent (*I wanted...dog* and *I have a fish*) and one dependent (*because my...dander*), so it is compound-complex.

Examples

1. Which of the following choices is a simple sentence?

   A) Elsa drove while Erica navigated.

   B) Betty ordered a fruit salad, and Sue ordered eggs.

   C) Because she was late, Jenny ran down the hall.

   D) John ate breakfast with his mother, brother, and father.

   Answer:

   D) is correct. Choice D contains one independent clause with one subject and one verb. Choices A and C are complex sentences because they each contain both a dependent and independent clause. Choice B contains two independent clauses joined by a conjunction and is therefore a compound sentence.

2. Which of the following sentences is a compound-complex sentence?

   A) While they were at the game, Anne cheered for the home team, but Harvey rooted for the underdogs.

   B) The rain flooded all of the driveway, some of the yard, and even part of the sidewalk across the street.

   C) After everyone finished the test, Mr. Brown passed a bowl of candy around the classroom.

   D) All the flowers in the front yard are in bloom, and the trees around the house are lush and green.

   Answer:

   A) is correct. Choice A is a compound-complex sentence because it contains two independent clauses and one dependent clause. Despite its length, choice B is a simple sentence because it contains only one independent clause. Choice C is a complex sentence because it contains one dependent clause and one independent clause. Choice D is a compound sentence; it contains two independent clauses.

PUNCTUATION

The basic rules for using the major punctuation marks are given in Table 4.4.

Table 4.4. How to Use Punctuation

PUNCTUATION	USED FOR	EXAMPLE
period	ending sentences	Periods go at the end of complete sentences.
question mark	ending questions	What's the best way to end a sentence?
exclamation point	ending sentences that show extreme emotion	I'll never understand how to use commas!
comma	joining two independent clauses (always with a coordinating conjunction)	Commas can be used to join clauses, but they must always be followed by a coordinating conjunction.
	setting apart introductory and nonessential words and phrases	Commas, when used properly, set apart extra information in a sentence.
	separating items in a list	My favorite punctuation marks include the colon, semicolon, and period.
semicolon	joining together two independent clauses (never used with a conjunction)	I love exclamation points; they make sentences seem so exciting!
colon	introducing a list, explanation, or definition	When I see a colon I know what to expect: more information.
apostrophe	forming contractions	It's amazing how many people can't use apostrophes correctly.
	showing possession	Parentheses are my sister's favorite punctuation; she finds commas' rules confusing.
quotation marks	indicating a direct quote	I said to her, "Tell me more about parentheses."

Examples

1. Which of the following sentences contains an error in punctuation?

   A) I love apple pie! John exclaimed with a smile.
   B) Jennifer loves Adam's new haircut.
   C) Billy went to the store; he bought bread, milk, and cheese.
   D) Alexandra hates raisins, but she loves chocolate chips.

   Answer:

   A) is correct. Choice A should use quotation marks to set off a direct quote: *"I love apple pie!" John exclaimed with a smile.*

2. Which punctuation mark correctly completes the sentence?
   Sam, why don't you come with us for dinner_

   A) .
   B) ;
   C) ?
   D) :

Answer:

C) is correct. The sentence is a question, so it should end with a question mark.

COMMONLY CONFUSED WORDS

The HESI will include questions that ask you to choose between **HOMOPHONES**, words that are pronounced the same but have different meanings. *Bawl* and *ball*, for example, are homophones: they sound the same, but the first means to cry, and the second is a round toy. You may also have to choose from a set of words with similar meanings, such as *bring/take*, *farther/further*, and *fewer/less*.

Commonly confused words include:

- **ACCEPT:** agree
  EXCEPT: not including

- **ALOUD:** said out loud
  ALLOWED: able to

- **BARE:** uncovered
  BEAR: the large animal; to carry

- **BRAKE:** to stop
  BREAK: to damage or interrupt

- **BRING:** toward the speaker (*bring to me*)
  TAKE: away from the speaker (*take away from me*)

- **DIE:** to no longer be alive
  DYE: to artificially change color

- **EFFECT:** result (a noun)
  AFFECT: to change (a verb)

- **FARTHER:** a measurable distance (*the house farther up the road*)
  FURTHER: more or greater (*explain further what you mean*)

- **FEWER:** a smaller amount of something plural (*fewer chairs*)
  LESS: a smaller amount of something that can't be counted (*less water*)

- **FLOUR:** used for cooking
  FLOWER: grows out of the ground

- **HEAL:** to get better
  HEEL: the back part of the foot

- **HOLE:** an opening
  WHOLE: all of something

- **INSURE:** to have insurance (*I need to insure my car.*)
  ENSURE: to make sure something happens (*She ensured that the dog found a good home.*)

- **LOSE:** to fail to win; to not be able to find something
  LOOSE: relaxed; not firmly in place

- **MEAT**: the flesh of an animal
  MEET: to see someone
- **MORNING**: the start of the day
  MOURNING: grieving
- **PATIENCE**: tolerating annoyances
  PATIENTS: people receiving medical care
- **PEACE**: not at war
  PIECE: a part of something
- **POOR**: having very little money
  POUR: to dispense from a container
- **PRINCIPAL**: the leader or administrative head of a school
  PRINCIPLE: a strongly held belief
- **RAIN**: precipitation
  REIN: a strap that controls an animal
  REIGN: to rule over
- **RIGHT**: correct; a legal entitlement
  RITE: a ritual
  WRITE: to put words on paper
- **STAIR**: used to get from one floor to another
  STARE: a long, fixed look
- **SUITE**: a set of rooms
  SWEET: the taste associated with sugar
- **THEIR**: belonging to them (*they brought their luggage*)
  THERE: a place (*the luggage is over there*)
  THEY'RE: they are (*they're looking for the luggage*)
- **THROUGH**: to go in one side and out of the other
  THREW: tossed (past tense of *throw*)
- **WEAR**: to put on (*I'll wear my new dress.*)
  WHERE: to question about place (*Where is the door?*)
- **YOUR**: belonging to you (*your car*)
  YOU'RE: you are (*you're going to need a new car*)

Examples

Select the best word for the blank in the following sentences.

1. Our school's _____ will decide whether Aaron will be expelled.

   A) principle

   B) principal

   C) students

   D) teachers

Answer:

B) is correct. The *principal* is the administrative head of a school; a *principle* is a strongly held belief. *Students* and *teachers* would be grammatically correct, but *principal* fits the context of the sentence better.

2. The nurse has three _____ to see before lunch.

   A) patents

   B) patience

   C) patients

   D) patiences

Answer:

C) is correct. *Patients* is the correct spelling and the correct homophone. *Patients* are people in a hospital and *patience* is the ability to avoid getting upset in negative situations.

5

BIOLOGY

PROPERTIES OF WATER

The two hydrogen atoms and single oxygen atom that comprise water (H_2O) are held together by covalent bonds. These atoms do not share electrons equally, however. Oxygen attracts electrons more strongly than hydrogen atoms; therefore, oxygen carries a partial negative charge, while the hydrogen atoms carry partial positive charges. This type of covalent bond is called a **POLAR BOND**, which makes water a polar molecule. When the negative end of one polar molecule binds to a hydrogen atom on another polar molecule, a **HYDROGEN BOND** forms.

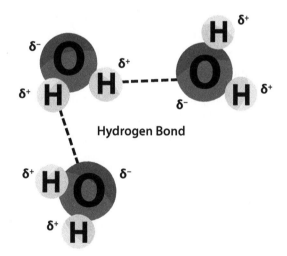

Figure 5.1. Hydrogen Bonds of Water

Although an individual hydrogen bond is a weak chemical bond, water contains many hydrogen bonds. Together, these bonds give water the properties that make it essential for life. Polar molecules, for instance, are attracted to each other; **COHESION** is the attraction between two water molecules. Cohesion creates the high **SURFACE TENSION** of water, which is the force that allows certain insects to stride across the surface of a pond or lake and organizes biomolecules into cellular structures like membranes and organelles. Water molecules are also very attracted to other types of molecules, a property called **ADHESION**. This property allows water to "climb" against gravity via **CAPILLARY ACTION**.

Hydrogen bonds also influence the **SPECIFIC HEAT** of water. Water molecules are held tightly together by hydrogen bonds, which means that a lot of energy is needed to heat water; therefore, water heats slowly but also maintains its temperature longer.

Lastly, water is often referred to as the "universal solvent" because its polarity allows it to dissolve other polar substances, such as salts. However, nonpolar substances, such as oils, will not dissolve in water.

Example

Which of the following properties of water causes water droplets to form beads on surfaces, such as on a leaf?

A. adhesion

B. specific heat

C. surface tension

D. ability to dissolve substances

Answer:

C is correct. Surface tension pulls together the molecules on the surface of water, forcing them to form a sphere, or bead.

BIOLOGICAL MACROMOLECULES

ORGANIC compounds are those that contain carbon. These compounds, such as glucose, triacylglycerol, and guanine, are used in day-to-day metabolic processes. Many of these molecules are **POLYMERS** formed from repeated smaller units called **MONOMERS**. **INORGANIC** compounds are those that do not contain carbon. These make up a very small fraction of mass in living organisms and are usually minerals such as potassium, sodium, and iron.

There are several classes of organic compounds commonly found in living organisms. These biological molecules include carbohydrates, proteins, lipids, and nucleic acids, which, when combined, make up more than 95 percent of non-water material in living organisms.

Carbohydrates

CARBOHYDRATES, also called sugars, are molecules made of carbon, hydrogen, and oxygen. Sugars are primarily used in organisms as a source of energy: they can be catabolized (broken down) to create energy molecules such as adenosine triphosphate (ATP) or nicotinamide adenine dinucleotide (NAD⁺), providing a source of electrons to drive cellular processes.

Glucose: $C_6H_{12}O_6$

Figure 5.2. A Carbohydrate

The monomer of carbohydrates is the **MONOSACCHARIDE**, a sugar with the formula $C_nH_{2n}O_n$. Glucose, for example, is the monosaccharide $C_6H_{12}O_6$. Simple sugars like glucose can bond together to form polymers called **POLY-SACCHARIDES**. Some polymers of glucose include starch, which is used to store excess sugar, and cellulose, which is a support fiber responsible in part for the strength of plants.

Lipids

LIPIDS are compounds primarily composed of carbon and hydrogen with only a small percentage of oxygen. Lipids contain a **HEAD**, usually formed of glycerol or phosphate, and a **TAIL**, which is a hydrocarbon chain. The composition of the head, whether it is a carboxylic acid functional group, a phosphate group, or some other functional group, is usually polar, meaning it is hydrophilic. The tail is composed of carbon and hydrogen and is usually nonpolar, meaning it is hydrophobic.

The combined polarity of the lipid head and the non-polarity of the lipid tail are unique features of lipids critical to the formation of the phospholipid bilayer in the cell membrane. The fatty acid tails are all pointed inward, and the heads are pointed outward. This provides a semipermeable membrane that allows a cell to separate its contents from the environment.

The **SATURATION** of a lipid describes the number of double bonds in the tail of the lipid. The more double bonds a lipid tail has, the more unsaturated the molecule is, and the more bends there are in its structure. As a result, unsaturated fats (like oils) tend to be liquid at room temperature, whereas saturated fats (like lard or butter) are solid at room temperature.

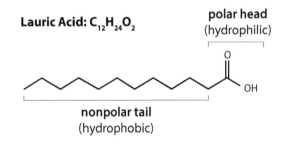

Lauric Acid: $C_{12}H_{24}O_2$

polar head (hydrophilic)

nonpolar tail (hydrophobic)

Figure 5.3. A Lipid (Lauric Acid)

Proteins

PROTEINS are large molecules that play an important role in almost every cellular process in the human body. They act as catalysts, transport molecules across membranes, facilitate DNA replication, and regulate the cell cycle, including mitosis and meiosis.

Proteins are composed of a chain of **AMINO ACIDS**. The sequence of amino acids in the chain determines the protein's structure and function. Each amino acid is composed of three parts:

- Amino group ($-NH_2$): The amino group is found on all amino acids.
- Carboxyl group ($-COOH$): The carboxyl group is found on all amino acids.
- R group: The R group is a unique functional group that is different for each amino acid.

There are twenty-two amino acids used to produce proteins. It is not necessary to know each amino acid, but it is important to know that sequences of these amino acids form proteins, and that each amino acid has a unique R-functional group.

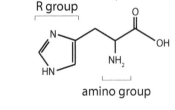

Histidine

carboxyl group

R group

OH

NH_2

amino group

Figure 5.4. An Amino Acid (Histidine)

Nucleic Acids

NUCLEIC ACIDS, which include DNA and RNA, store all information necessary to produce proteins. These molecules are built using smaller molecules called **NUCLEOTIDES**, which are composed of a 5-carbon sugar, a phosphate group, and a nitrogenous base.

DNA is made from four nucleotides: adenine, guanine, cytosine, and thymine. Together, adenine and guanine are classified as **PURINES**, while thymine and cytosine are classified as **PYRIMIDINES**. These nucleotides bond together in pairs; the pairs are then bonded together in a chain to create a double helix shape with the sugar as the outside and the nitrogenous base on the inside. In DNA, adenine and thymine always bond together, as do guanine and cytosine. In RNA, thymine is replaced by a nucleotide called uracil, which bonds with adenine. RNA also differs from DNA in that it often exists as a single strand.

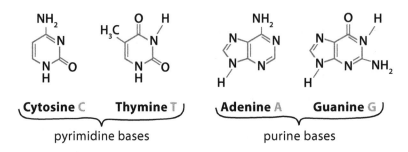

Figure 5.5. DNA Nucleotides

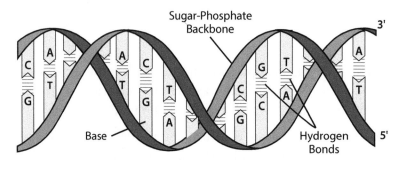

Figure 5.6. DNA Double Helix

The individual strands of DNA are directional, meaning it matters in which direction the DNA is read. The two ends of a DNA strand are called the 3' end and the 5' end, and these names are included when describing a section of DNA, as shown below:

5'-ATGAATTGCCT-3'

For two complementary strands of DNA, one end starts at 5', and the other starts at 3':

5'-ATGAATTGCCT-3'

3'-TACTTAACGGA-5'

This naming convention is needed to understand the direction of DNA replication and where the enzymes bind during the process.

Examples

1. Which of the following polymers is created by joining amino acids?

    A) DNA

    B) lipid

    C) protein

    D) carbohydrate

    Answer:

    C) is correct. Proteins are built by joining amino acids.

2. Which of the following nucleotides is NOT found in DNA?

    A) adenine

    B) uracil

    C) thymine

    D) cytosine

    Answer:

    B) is correct. Uracil is a nucleotide found in RNA, not DNA.

3. Which of the following compounds is NOT created by joining monosaccharides?

    A) glycogen

    B) starch

    C) cellulose

    D) guanine

    Answer:

    D) is correct. Guanine is a nucleic acid, not a polysaccharide.

THE BASICS OF THE CELL

The CELL is the smallest unit of life that can reproduce on its own. All higher organisms are composed of cells, which are specialized to perform the many processes that keep organisms alive and allow them to reproduce.

Parts of the Cell

Although the cell is the smallest unit of life, there are many small bodies, called ORGAN-ELLES, which exist in the cell. These organelles are required for the many processes that take place inside a cell.

- The MITOCHONDRIA are the organelles responsible for making ATP within the cell. Mitochondria have several layers of membranes used to assist the electron transport chain. This pathway uses energy provided by molecules such as glucose or fat (lipid) to generate ATP through the transfer of electrons.

- A **VACUOLE** is a small body used to transfer materials within and out of the cell. It has a membrane of its own and can carry things such as cell wastes, sugars, or proteins.

- The **NUCLEUS** of a eukaryotic cell contains all of its genetic information in the form of DNA. In the nucleus, DNA replication and transcription occur. In the eukaryotic cell, after transcription, the mRNA is exported out of the nucleus into the cytosol for use.

- The **ENDOPLASMIC RETICULUM** (ER) is used for translation of mRNA into proteins and for the transport of proteins out of the cell. The rough endoplasmic reticulum has many ribosomes attached to it, which function as the cell's machinery in transforming RNA into protein. The smooth endoplasmic reticulum is associated with the production of fats and steroid hormones.

- A **RIBOSOME** is a small two-protein unit that reads mRNA and, with the assistance of transport proteins, creates an amino acid.

- The **GOLGI APPARATUS** collects, packages, and distributes the proteins produced by ribosomes.

- **CHLOROPLASTS** are plant organelles where the reactions of photosynthesis take place.

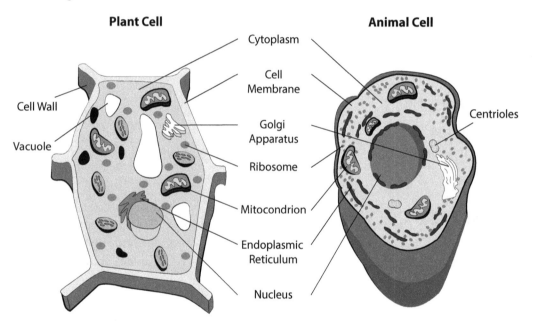

Figure 5.7. Plant and Animal Cell Organelles

Cell Membrane

The **CELL MEMBRANE** surrounds the cell and controls what enters and leaves. It is composed of compounds called **PHOSPHOLIPIDS** that consist of an alkane tail and a phospho-group head. The alkane lipid tail is hydrophobic, meaning it will not allow water to pass through, and the phosphate group head is hydrophilic, which allows water to pass through. The arrangement of these molecules forms a bilayer, which has a hydrophobic middle layer. In this manner, the cell is able to control the import and export of various substances into the cell.

In addition to the phospholipid bilayer, the cell membrane often includes proteins, which perform a variety of functions. Some proteins are used as receptors, which allow the cell to interact with its surroundings. Others are **TRANSMEMBRANE PROTEINS**, meaning they cross the entire membrane. These types of proteins are usually channels that allow the transportation of molecules into and out of the cell.

Membrane proteins are also used in cell-to-cell interaction. This includes functions such as cell-cell joining or recognition, in which a cell membrane protein contacts a protein from another cell. A good example of this is the immune response in the human body. Due to the proteins found on the cell membrane of antigens, immune system cells can contact, recognize, and attempt to remove them.

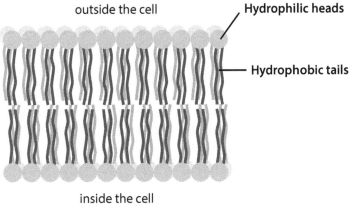

Figure 5.8. Cell Membrane Bilayer

Membrane Transport

A cell needs to be able to both import and export vital substances across the membrane while at the same time preventing harmful substances from entering the cell. Two major classes of transportation allow this process to occur: active transport and passive transport.

ACTIVE TRANSPORT uses ATP to accomplish one of two tasks: it can move a molecule against the concentration gradient (from low concentration to high), or it can be used to import or export a bulky molecule, such as a sugar or a protein, across the cell membrane. Active transport requires the use of proteins and energy in the form of ATP. The ATP produced by the cell binds to the proteins in the cell membrane and is hydrolyzed, producing the energy required to change the conformational structure of the protein. This change in the structure of the protein allows the protein to funnel molecules across the cell membrane.

PASSIVE TRANSPORT does not require energy and allows molecules such as water to passively diffuse across the cell membrane. Facilitated diffusion is a form of passive transport that does not require energy but does require the use of proteins located on the cell membrane. These transport proteins typically have a "channel" running through the core of a protein specific to a certain type of molecule. For example, a transport protein for sodium only allows sodium to flow through the channel.

Tonicity

The balance of water in the cell is one of the most important regulatory mechanisms for the cell. Water enters or exits the cell through a process called **OSMOSIS**. This movement of water does not usually require energy, and the movement is regulated by a factor called tonicity.

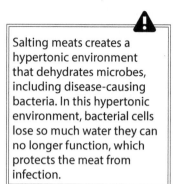

Salting meats creates a hypertonic environment that dehydrates microbes, including disease-causing bacteria. In this hypertonic environment, bacterial cells lose so much water they can no longer function, which protects the meat from infection.

TONICITY is the concentration of solutes in the cell. Solutes can be salt ions, such as sodium or chlorine, or other molecules, such as sugar, amino acids, or proteins. The difference in tonicity between the cell and its outside environment governs the transportation of water into and out of the cell. For example, if there is a higher tonicity inside the cell, then water will enter the cell. If there is a higher tonicity outside the cell, the water will leave the cell. This is due to a driving force called the CHEMIOSMOTIC POTENTIAL, which attempts to make tonicity equal across a membrane.

There are three terms used to describe a cell's tonicity:

- When a cell is in an ISOTONIC environment, the same concentration of solutes exists inside and outside the cell. There will be no transport of water in this case.

- When a cell is in a HYPERTONIC environment, the concentration of solutes outside the cell is higher than that inside the cell. The cell will lose water to the environment and shrivel. This is what happens if a cell is placed into a salty solution.

- When a cell is in a HYPOTONIC environment, the concentration of solutes outside the cell is lower than that inside the cell. The cell will absorb water from the environment and swell, becoming turgid.

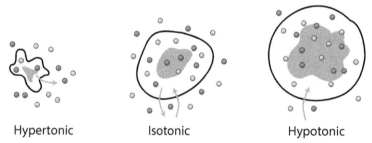

Hypertonic   Isotonic   Hypotonic

Figure 5.9. Tonicity

Cell Interactions

With the vast number of cells in living organisms (an estimated 100 trillion in the human body), how do they all interact and talk with one another? Cells are able to communicate with one another through cell signaling, which occurs via chemical signals excreted by the cell. It is also possible to have direct cell-to-cell communication through protein receptors located in the cell membrane. Important signaling molecules include CYCLIC AMP, which is best known for its function in the signaling cascade when epinephrine binds to a cell, and NEUROTRANSMITTERS such as dopamine and serotonin, among many others.

LOCAL, or DIRECT, SIGNALING is a signal that occurs between cells that are either right next to each other or within a few cells' distance. This communication can occur by two methods. First, GAP JUNCTIONS exist between the membranes of two cells that can allow signaling molecules to directly enter the cells. Second, the receptors on the membrane can bind with other cells that have membrane receptors to communicate.

The primary chemical used in long-range, or endocrine, signaling is called a **HORMONE**. In humans and animals, hormones are produced by organs and cells in the endocrine system such as the testes, hypothalamus, and pituitary glands. These hormones, once released, can travel throughout the organism through the circulatory system (blood). The hormones can then bind to other cells that have the appropriate receptor and cause a signal to start inside the cell.

One example of long-range signaling in the human body is the production of insulin by the pancreas. Insulin spreads through the body via the blood, and when it binds to an insulin receptor on a cell, the cell begins to take in more glucose. This process is called long-range signaling because insulin is produced by cells in only one location (the pancreas) but is able to affect nearly all other cells in the body.

An example of long-distance signaling in plants is the production of ethylene, a ripening chemical. It can be present in the air or can diffuse through cell walls, and the production of ethylene by one plant can produce a chain reaction that causes nearby plants to also start ripening.

Examples

1. The Golgi apparatus is responsible for which of the following tasks?

    A) protein synthesis

    B) intracellular and extracellular transport

    C) storage and replication of DNA

    D) production of ATP

    Answer:

    B) is correct. The Golgi apparatus packages and transports proteins produced on the endoplasmic reticulum.

2. Which of the following structures is embedded in the cell membrane to facilitate the movement of molecules across the membrane?

    A) proteins

    B) ATP

    C) glucose

    D) lipids

    Answer:

    A) is correct. Proteins embedded in the cell membrane are integral to many cell functions, including active transport and some types of passive transport.

3. A student places a cell with a 50 mM intracellular ion content into a solution containing a 20 mM ion content. Which of the following will happen in this system?

    A) Water will move out of the cell, decreasing the size of the cell.

    B) Water will move into the cell, increasing the size of the cell.

    C) Ions will move into the cell.

    D) There will be no movement of water or ions across the cell membrane.

Answer:

B) is correct. The concentration of ions is higher inside the cell than outside, so water will move into the cell from the environment, increasing the size of the cell.

4. Which of the following substances cannot travel across a cell membrane without the use of energy?

   A) water

   B) potassium

   C) sodium

   D) glucose

Answer:

D) is correct. A glucose molecule is too large to pass through the cell membrane without the help of specialized proteins.

BIOCHEMICAL PATHWAYS

Organisms use chains of chemical reactions called BIOCHEMICAL PATHWAYS to acquire, store, and use energy. The molecule most commonly used to store energy is ADENOSINE TRIPHOSPHATE (ATP). When a phosphate group (Pi) is removed from ATP (creating ADENOSINE DIPHOSPHATE (ADP)), energy is released. This energy is harnessed by the cell to perform processes such as transport, growth, and replication.

Cell also transfer energy using the molecules NICOTINAMIDE ADENINE DINUCLEOTIDE PHOSPHATE (NADPH) and NICOTINAMIDE ADENINE DINUCLEOTIDE (NADH). These molecules are generally used to carry energy-rich electrons during the process of creating ATP.

Photosynthesis

The sun powers nearly all biological systems on this planet. Plants, along with some bacteria and algae, harness the energy of sunlight and transform it into chemical energy through the process of PHOTOSYNTHESIS.

Inside each chloroplast are stacks of flat, interconnected sacs called THYLAKOIDS. Within the membrane of each thylakoid sac are light-absorbing pigments called CHLOROPHYLL.

In the light-dependent reactions of photosynthesis, light penetrates the chloroplast and strikes the chlorophyll. The energy in the sunlight excites electrons, boosting them to a higher energy level. These excited electrons then cascade through the ELECTRON TRANSPORT CHAIN, creating energy in the form of ATP and NADPH. This reaction also splits water to release O_2.

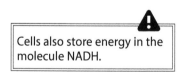
Cells also store energy in the molecule NADH.

The ATP and NADPH created by the light-dependent stage of photosynthesis enters the CALVIN CYCLE, which uses the energy to produce the carbohydrate glucose ($C_6H_{12}O_6$). The carbon needed for this reaction comes from atmospheric CO_2.

The balanced chemical equation for photosynthesis is:

$$6CO_2 + 6H_2O \rightarrow C_6H_{12}O_6 + 6O_2$$

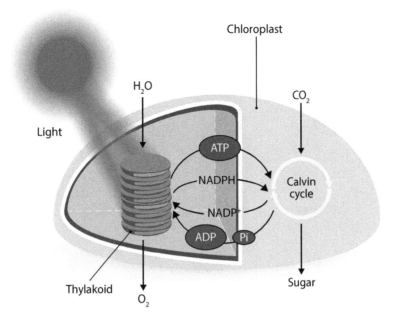

Figure 5.10. Photosynthesis

Example

All of the following molecules are used in the Calvin Cycle EXCEPT

A. O_2

B. CO_2

C. ATP

D. NADPH

Answers:

A. is correct. O_2 is released during the light-dependent stage of photosynthesis and is not used during the Calvin Cycle. The other choices are all used during the Calvin Cycle to produce glucose.

Cellular Respiration

In **CELLULAR RESPIRATION**, food molecules such as glucose are broken down, and the electrons harvested from these molecules are used to make ATP. The first stage of cellular respiration is an **ANAEROBIC** (does not require oxygen) process called **GLYCOLYSIS**. Glycolysis takes place in the cytoplasm of a cell and transforms glucose into two molecules of pyruvate. In the process, two molecules of ATP and two molecules of NADH are produced.

Under anaerobic conditions, pyruvate is reduced to acids and sometimes gases and/or alcohols in a process called **FERMENTATION**. However, this process is less efficient than aerobic cellular respiration and produces only two ATP.

Under aerobic conditions, pyruvate enters the second stage of cellular respiration—the **KREBS CYCLE**. The Krebs cycle takes place in the mitochondria, or tubular organelles, of a eukaryotic cell. Here, pyruvate is oxidized completely to form six molecules of carbon dioxide (CO_2). This set of reactions also produces two more molecules of ATP, ten molecules of NADH, and two molecules of $FADH_2$ (an electron carrier).

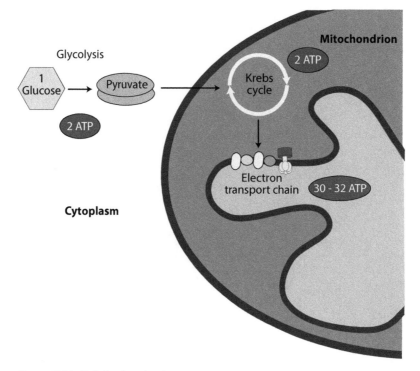

Figure 5.11. Cellular Respiration

The electrons carried by NADH and $FADH_2$ are transferred to the **ELECTRON TRANSPORT CHAIN**, where they cascade through carrier molecules embedded in the inner mitochondrial membrane. Oxygen is the final electron receptor in the chain; it reacts with these electrons and hydrogen to form water. This sequential movement of electrons drives the formation of a proton (H^+) gradient, which is used by the enzyme ATP synthase to produce ATP. The electron transport chain produces 30 to 32 molecules of ATP.

The balanced chemical equation for cellular respiration is:

$$C_6H_{12}O_6 + 6O_2 \rightarrow 6CO_2 + 6H_2O$$

Example

Which of the following stages of cellular respiration produces the largest number of ATP molecules?

A) glycolysis

B) fermentation

C) Krebs cycle

D) electron transport chain

Answer:

D) is correct. The electron transport chain produces 30 to 32 molecules of ATP made during cellular respiration. The other choices each produce only two molecules of ATP.

THE CELL CYCLE

The cell cycle is the process cells go through as they live, grow, and divide to produce new cells. The cell cycle can be divided into four primary phases:

1. G1 phase: growth phase one
2. S phase: DNA replication
3. G2 phase: growth phase two
4. Mitotic phase: The cell undergoes mitosis and splits into two cells.

Together, the G1, S, and G2 phases are known as INTERPHASE. During these phases, which usually take up 80 to 90 percent of the total time in a cell cycle, the cell is growing and conducting normal cell functions.

> ⚠️
> **The Cell Cycle**
> Go Sally Go, Make Children!
> ■ Growth phase 1
> ■ DNA Synthesis
> ■ Growth phase 2
> ■ Mitosis
> ■ Cytokinesis

Mitosis

The process of cell division is called MITOSIS. When a cell divides, it needs to make sure that each copy of the cell has a roughly equal amount of the necessary elements, including DNA, proteins, and organelles. In multicellular organisms, mitosis occurs in somatic (body) cells that contain a pair of homologous chromosomes. The two resulting daughter cells will have identical genetic material.

Interphase

Prophase

Metaphase

Anaphase

Telophase and Cytokinesis

Two daughter cells

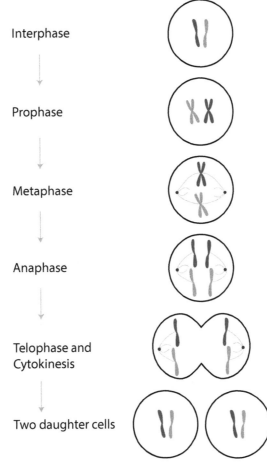

Figure 5.12. Mitosis

The mitotic phase is separated into five substages:

- Prophase: In prophase, the DNA in the cell winds into chromatin, and each pair of duplicated chromosomes becomes joined. The mitotic spindle, which pulls apart the chromosomes later, forms and drifts to each end of the cell.

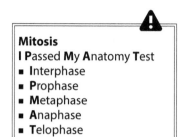

Mitosis
I **P**assed **M**y **A**natomy **T**est
- Interphase
- Prophase
- Metaphase
- Anaphase
- Telophase

- Prometaphase: In this phase, the nuclear membrane, which holds the DNA, dissolves, allowing the chromosomes to come free. The chromosomes now start to attach to microtubules linked to the centrioles.

- Metaphase: The centrioles, with microtubules attached to the chromosomes, are now on opposite sides of the cell. The chromosomes align in the middle of the cell, and the microtubules begin contracting.

- Anaphase: In anaphase, the chromosomes move to separate sides of the cell, and the cell structure begins to lengthen, pulling apart as it goes.

- Telophase and Cytokinesis: In this last part of the cell cycle, the cell membrane splits, and two new daughter cells are formed. The nucleolus, containing the DNA, re-forms.

Meiosis

Meiosis is cellular division that creates gametes (sex cells). The dividing cell starts with a set of homologous chromosomes ($2n$), but the four resulting daughter cells will each have only one set of chromosomes ($1n$). There are two consecutive stages of meiosis known as Meiosis I and Meiosis II. These two stages are further broken down into four stages each.

Meiosis I

1. Prophase I: The chromosomes condense, using histone proteins, and become paired. Microtubules attach to the chromosomes and centrioles and begin to align them in the middle of the cell.

2. Metaphase I: The chromosomes align in the middle of the cell and begin to pull apart from one another.

3. Anaphase I: The homologous chromosomes separate and move toward opposite sides of the cell.

4. Telophase I: The cells separate, and each cell now has one copy each of a homologous chromosome.

Meiosis II

1. Prophase II: A spindle forms and aligns the chromosomes. No crossing-over occurs.

2. Metaphase II: The chromosomes again align at the metaphase plate.

3. Anaphase II: The sister chromatids pull apart to opposite ends of the cell.

4. Telophase II: The cell splits apart, resulting in four unique daughter cells.

Examples

1. A scientist takes DNA samples from a cell culture at two different times, each sample having the same cell count. In the first sample, he finds that there is 6.5 pg of DNA, whereas in the second sample, he finds that there is 13 pg of DNA. Which stage of the cell cycle is the first sample in?

   A) interphase G1

   B) interphase S

   C) interphase G2

   D) mitotic phase

   Answer:

   A) is correct. During the G1 phase of interphase, the cell has not replicated its DNA. During the other three phases listed, the cell would have replicated its DNA, doubling the amount of DNA in the cell.

2. At the end of which phase of mitosis are chromosomes first clearly visible under a light microscope?

   A) interphase

   B) prophase

   C) metaphase

   D) anaphase

   Answer:

   B) is correct. During prophase, the DNA replicated during interphase condenses into chromosomes, which are clearly visible under a light microscope.

NUCLEIC ACIDS

The Structure of DNA

A cell has a lot of DNA: even the smallest human cell contains a copy of the entire human genome. In human cells, this copy of the genome is nearly two meters in length—quite long, considering the average cell is only 100 μm in diameter.

In the nucleus, DNA is organized around proteins called HISTONES; together, this protein and DNA complex is known as CHROMATIN. During interphase, chromatin is usually arranged loosely to allow access to DNA. During mitosis, however, DNA is tightly packaged into units called CHROMOSOMES. When DNA has replicated, the chromosome is composed of two CHROMATIDS joined together at the CENTROMERE.

Each somatic cell is DIPLOID ($2n$), meaning it has two sets of homologous chromosomes, one from each parent. For example, humans have twenty-three pairs of chromosomes, for a total of forty-six chromosomes. Gametes (sex cells) have only one set of chromosomes, so a human sex cell has twenty-three chromosomes. Cells with one set of chromosomes are referred to as HAPLOID ($1n$).

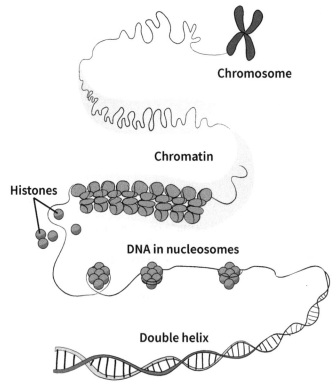

Figure 5.13. Structure of DNA

DNA Replication

DNA REPLICATION is the process by which a copy of DNA is created in a cell. During DNA replication, three steps will occur. The first step is **INITIATION**, in which an initiator protein binds to regions of DNA known as origin sites. Once the initiation protein has been bound, the DNA polymerase complex will be able to attach. At this point, the enzyme helicase unwinds DNA into two separate single strands.

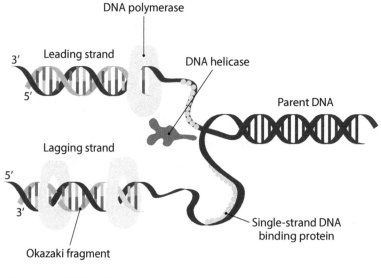

Figure 5.14. DNA replication

During the next step, **ELONGATION**, new strands of DNA are created. Single-strand binding proteins (SSBs) will bind to each strand of the DNA. Then, DNA polymerase will attach and start replicating the strands by synthesizing a new, complementary strand. DNA polymerase reads the DNA in the 3' to 5' direction, meaning the new strand is synthesized in the 5' to 3' direction. This creates a problem, because the DNA can only be read in the 3' to 5' direction on one strand, known as the **LEADING STRAND**. The **LAGGING STRAND**, which runs from 5' to 3', has to be synthesized piece by piece in chunks called **OKAZAKI FRAGMENTS**. The breaks between these fragments are later filled in by DNA ligase.

The last step in the process of DNA replication is **TERMINATION**. After DNA polymerase completes the copying process, the replication forks meet, and the process is terminated. There is one catch to this: because the DNA polymerase enzyme can never read or replicate the very end of a strand of DNA, every time a full chromosome is replicated, a small part of DNA is lost at the end. This piece of DNA is usually noncoding and is called a **TELOMERE**. The shortening of the telomeres is the reason why replication can occur only a limited number of times in somatic cells before DNA replication is no longer possible.

Table 5.1. Important Enzymes in DNA Replication

DNA Helicase	This unwinds a section of DNA to create a segment with two single strands.
DNA Polymerase	DNA polymerase I is responsible for synthesizing Okazaki fragments. DNA polymerase III is responsible for the primary replication of the 5' to 3' strand.
DNA Ligase	Ligase fixes small breaks in the DNA strand and is used to seal the finished DNA strands.
DNA Telomerase	In some cells, DNA telomerase lengthens the telomeres at the end of each strand of DNA, allowing it to be copied additional times.

Transcription and Translation

The "message" contained in DNA and RNA is encoded in the nucleotides. Each amino acid is represented by a set of three base pairs in the nucleotide sequence called a **CODON**. There are sixty-four possible codons (4 × 4 × 4), which means many of the twenty-two amino acids are coded for with more than one codon. There are also three stop codons, which instruct the ribosome to stop processing the mRNA.

The processing of information stored in DNA to produce a protein takes place in two stages: transcription and translation. In transcription, an mRNA copy of the DNA is created. In translation, the mRNA strand is read by a ribosome to create an amino acid chain, which is folded into a protein.

DNA **TRANSCRIPTION** is the process of making messenger RNA (mRNA) from a DNA strand. The steps for DNA transcription are similar to those of DNA replication, although different enzymes are used. The DNA strand provides a template for RNA polymerase: the DNA is first unwound, and then RNA polymerase makes a complementary transcript of the DNA sequence, called mRNA.

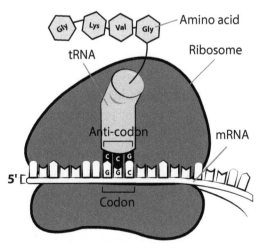

Figure 5.15. Translation

The **TRANSLATION** process converts the mRNA transcript into a useable protein. This process occurs in a ribosome, which lines up the mRNA so it can bind to the appropriate tRNA (transfer RNA). Each tRNA includes an amino acid and an **ANTICODON**, which matches to the complementary codon on the mRNA. When the tRNA is in place, a bond is formed between the growing amino acid strand and the new amino acid brought by the tRNA.

The translation process stops when a stop codon is reached in the sequence. These codons activate a protein called a release factor, which binds to the ribosome. The ribosome, which is made of two proteins, will split apart after the release factor binds. This releases the newly formed amino acid chain.

Mutations

The DNA sequence can sometimes undergo a **MUTATION**, which is a change in the base-pair sequence of the DNA strand. A mutation can be benign, or silent, meaning it has no effect, or it can cause a change in the protein structure.

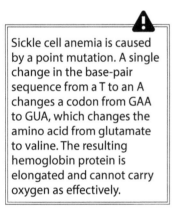

How would the consequences of a mutation in a gamete cell be different from those resulting from a mutation in a somatic cell?

Sickle cell anemia is caused by a point mutation. A single change in the base-pair sequence from a T to an A changes a codon from GAA to GUA, which changes the amino acid from glutamate to valine. The resulting hemoglobin protein is elongated and cannot carry oxygen as effectively.

One way a gene can be changed permanently is through a **POINT MUTATION**, where a single base in the sequence of a gene changes. This can happen through a single base substitution, insertion, or deletion. If one base (or a few bases) in the sequence changes, this is called a **BASE SUBSTITUTION**. An **INSERTION** occurs when one base (or a few bases) is added to the sequence, and a deletion occurs when one nucleotide (or a few nucleotides) is lost from the sequence.

Adding or removing nucleotides from a stretch of DNA changes the total amount of DNA, which can influence how the gene is read by RNA polymerase and, ultimately, by ribosomes. This type of mutation is called a **FRAME-SHIFT MUTATION**. Occasionally, two breaks may occur in a chromosome, and the fragment that breaks away flips around and reattaches. This type of mutation is called a **CHROMOSOME INVERSION**.

Many mutations will not result in any change in the protein sequence at all. For example, if the sequence CCG mutated to CCA, there would be no change, because the codon produced by both sequences corresponds to the amino acid glycine.

Gene Regulation

An important part of understanding metabolism is learning how genes are activated and deactivated. Studying gene expression and regulation is easier in bacteria due to their simple genomes and the simplicity of extracting their plasmids. Although human gene regulation is becoming more thoroughly understood, the vast complexity of the human metabolism and number of genes makes it difficult to get a full picture of all the interactions.

To understand gene regulation, it is necessary to understand the structure of the genetic code. Proteins are not produced from a single gene; instead, a set of genes, called an **OPERON**, is required. The operon includes a **PROMOTER**, which initiates transcription; an **OPERATOR**, to which an enzyme can bind to regulate transcription; and the protein coding sequence.

Either negative or positive regulation is used to control the operon. In negative regulation, a gene will be expressed unless a repressor becomes attached. In positive regulation, genes are expressed only when an activator attaches to initiate expression.

In addition to interactions with the operon, the expression of DNA can be controlled by modifications to the chromatin. Because the location of the promoters in the chromatin sequence greatly affects access to the gene, expression can be regulated by managing how tightly bound the chromatin is in the nucleus. Modifications to histone proteins, small amino acid structures found only in eukaryotic cell nuclei, can also inhibit or allow access to DNA.

Examples

1. Which of the following sequences is the complementary segment of this section of DNA: 5' AAGCCCTATAC 3'?

   A) 3' UUCGGGAUAUG 5'

   B) 3' TTCGGGATATG 5'

   C) 3' GTATAGGGCTT 5'

   D) 3' GUAUAGGGCUU 5'

   Answer:

   B) is correct. This sequence correctly matches each nucleotide, has the correct orientation, and does not contain the nucleotide uracil (which is found in RNA).

2. Which of the following describes why small sections of DNA are lost during replication?

   A) The sections of DNA between Okazaki fragments cannot be recovered.

   B) DNA polymerase cannot replicate the end of the DNA strand.

   C) DNA cannot be read in the 5' to 3' direction.

   D) The initiator proteins bind to only one strand of DNA.

   Answer:

   B) is correct. DNA polymerase cannot replicate the end of a DNA strand, so that section of the DNA is lost during replication.

3. At an ACU codon, the amino acid threonine will be inserted in the polypeptide. Which of the following anticodons would be found on the tRNA molecule that carries threonine?

   A) ACU

   B) UCA

   C) TGA

   D) UGA

   Answer:

   D) is correct. Anticodons and codons are complementary: the complement of the codon ACU is the anticodon UGA.

Genetics

GENETICS is the study of genes and how they are passed down to offspring. Before the discovery of genes, there were many theories about how traits are passed to offspring. One of the dominant theories in the nineteenth century was blending inheritance, which stated that the genetic material from the parents would mix to form that of the children in the same way that two colors might mix.

The idea was eventually displaced by the current theory, which is based on the concept of a GENE, which is a region of DNA that codes for a specific protein. Multiple versions of the same gene, called ALLELES, account for variation in a population.

During sexual reproduction, offspring receive a single copy of every gene from each parent. These two genes may be identical, making the individual HOMOZYGOUS, or they may be different, making the individual HETEROZYGOUS for that gene. In a heterozygous individual, the genes do not blend; instead they act separately, with one often being completely or partially suppressed.

> Natural selection acts on an organism's phenotype, not its genotype. Only alleles that affect an organism's fitness will be selected for or against.

An organism's GENOTYPE is its complete genetic code. PHENOTYPE is an organism's observable characteristics, such as height, eye color, skin color, and hair color. Although the genotype of two different people might be different, each person could have the same phenotype, depending on which alleles are dominant or recessive. For example, the two types of roses Rr and RR are both red, meaning they have the same phenotype. However, they have a different genotype, with one rose type being heterozygous and the other being homozygous.

Mendel's Laws

The idea that individual genes are passed down from parents to their children was conceived by **GREGOR MENDEL**. Mendel used various plants to test his ideas, but his best-known work is with pea plants.

Mendel became an Augustinian monk at the age of twenty-one. He studied briefly at the University of Vienna and, after returning to the monastery, started work on breeding plants. During the course of his work, he discovered that the plants had heritable features, meaning features that were passed from parent to offspring. Because of the short generation time of peas, Mendel started working on identifying the traits that could be passed on in the pea plant. He tracked two characteristics: pea flower color and pea shape. From this, he found that the traits were independent of one another, meaning that the pea's flower color in no way affected the pea shape.

> If an organism is described as true-breeding for a specific trait, it is homozygous for that trait and will pass it on to its offspring.

During the course of his work, Mendel came up with three laws to describe genetic inheritance: the law of segregation, the law of independent assortment, and the law of dominance. The LAW OF SEGREGATION states that genes come in allele pairs (if the organism is diploid, which most are) and that each parent can pass only a single allele down to its child. Thus, for a pair of alleles in a gene, one comes from the father, and one comes from the mother in sexual reproduction. The law of segregation also states that the alleles must separate during the course of meiosis so that only one is given to each gamete.

The **LAW OF INDEPENDENT ASSORTMENT** states that genes responsible for different traits are passed on independently. Thus, there is not necessarily a correlation between two genes. For example, if a mother is tall and has brown hair, she might pass on her genes for tallness to her child, but perhaps not the ones for brown hair. This law can be seen in the use of the Punnett square, in which gene alleles are separated to determine inheritance.

Lastly, the **LAW OF DOMINANCE** states that some alleles are dominant and some are recessive. Dominant alleles will mask the behavior of recessive ones. For example, red might be dominant in a rose, and white might be recessive. Thus, if a homozygous red rose mates with a homozygous white rose, all of their offspring will be red. Although the white gene allele will be present, it will not be expressed.

> ⚠️
> When writing the genetic information for a genotype, the dominant allele is written as a capital letter (A), while the recessive is written as a lowercase (a). A homozygous genotype can be AA or aa, and a heterozygous genotype will be Aa.

Monohybrid and Dihybrid Crosses

A **GENETIC CROSS** is a method in genetic experimentation in which a scientist intentionally breeds two individual parent organisms in order to produce an offspring that carries genetic material from both parents. The pair of parents is called the parental generation, or **P GENERATION**. The offspring of this initial breeding is known as the first filial generation, or **F1 GENERATION**. If the F1 generation is intentionally bred as well, the offspring of this generation is known as the second filial generation, or **F2 GENERATION**. This pattern of naming continues on as more generations are bred during experimentation.

The purpose of these genetic crosses is to isolate and study traits as they are passed through the generations. In **MONOHYBRID** crosses, the P generation is selected based on one particular trait—one parent possesses the dominant trait, while the other possesses the recessive trait. For example, in one of his pea experiments, Mendel selectively bred one plant with the dominant yellow seed trait with another plant that had the recessive green seed trait. The parent with the dominant trait can have a genotype that is either homozygous (YY) or heterozygous (Yy), while the parent with the recessive trait has a homozygous genotype (yy).

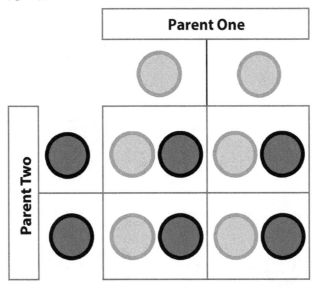

Figure 5.16. Punnett Square: Monohybrid Cross of Seed Color

The phenotype of the resulting F1 generation can be predicted using a **Punnett square**. This diagram determines the probability that an offspring will inherit a particular genotype. For monohybrid crosses, the Punnett square has only four possible combinations for a genotype, each with a 25 percent chance of occurring.

The probability that a certain genotype combination will occur is the Punnett ratio. For example, if two heterozygous yellow pea plants (Yy) are crossed, the Punnett square shows that there is a 3/4 probability that the offspring will be yellow and a 1/4 probability the offspring will be green. This gives this monohybrid cross a Punnett ratio of 3:1.

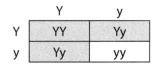

	Y	y
Y	YY	Yy
y	Yy	yy

Figure 5.17. Punnet Square: Monohybrid Cross of Seed Color

If the parent with the dominant yellow seed trait has a homozygous trait of YY, then there is a 100 percent chance that the F1 generation will express the yellow seed trait. How does this change if the YY parent instead has a Yy genotype?

In a **dihybrid cross**, the P generation is selected for two traits that differ between the two parents. One of Mendel's pea experiments included the dihybrid cross of a P generation that bred one parent with the two dominant traits (yellow and smooth) with a parent that had two recessive traits (green and wrinkled). The resulting Punnett square displays sixteen possible combinations of genotypes for these two traits. The Punnett ratio for this is 9:3:3:1 because there is a:

- 9/16 probability that the offspring will be yellow and smooth
- 3/16 probability that the offspring will be yellow and wrinkled

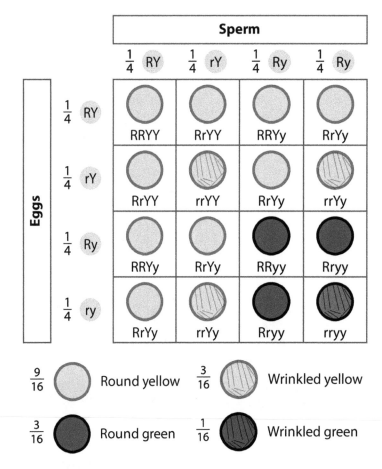

Figure 5.18. Punnett Square: Dihybrid Cross of Seed Color and Shape

- 3/16 probability that the offspring will be green and smooth
- 1/16 probability that the offspring will be green and wrinkled

Non-Mendelian Genetics

Mendel's laws apply to traits that are controlled by only one gene that has two possible alleles with a dominant/recessive relationship. Many traits do not fit these qualifications and will show inheritance patterns that are different from what Mendelian genetics would predict.

GENE LINKAGE occurs with genes that are situated close together on a chromosome and thus are more likely to be inherited together. Tracking the frequency of linked genes being transmitted together can help researchers determine the physical relationship between genes. All genes have a 50 percent chance of being inherited with any other gene. Genes that are paired with another gene more than 50 percent of the time are more likely to be linked; the higher the percentage, the closer the genes are in distance to one another.

SEX-LINKED genes are located on the **SEX CHROMOSOME** of each individual. All females have two **X CHROMOSOMES**, while all males have both an **X** and a **Y CHROMOSOME**. Genes that are located on the Y chromosome result in traits that are expressed only in the males of a species. Because females have two X chromosomes (and thus carry two alleles), the dominant allele will express itself for X-linked traits. Males, however, have only one allele for every X gene. As a result, the trait will be expressed regardless of whether it is dominant or recessive.

Non-Mendelian inheritance patterns can also be seen when alleles do not have a binary dominant/recessive relationship. The appearance of two dominant alleles creates an effect called **CODOMINANCE**, in which both dominant genes are expressed in the individual. This effect is responsible for the human blood type AB, as the gene for blood types A and B are both dominant.

> Color blindness and hemophilia are both X-linked disorders: they are carried by females but appear more frequently in males.

INCOMPLETE DOMINANCE occurs when one allele is not completely dominant over the other. For example, if the flower color red is incompletely dominant over the color white, offspring with both alleles will have pink flowers (a blend of red and white).

Introduction of Genetic Variation

Sexual reproduction introduces genetic variation into each generation. During meiosis, the **INDEPENDENT ASSORTMENT** of chromosomes gives each gamete a unique subset of genes from the parent. When a gamete combines with another to form a zygote, the result is a genetically unique organism that has a different gene composition from either of the parents.

The process of meiosis also introduces genetic variation during **CROSSING-OVER**, which occurs in prophase I when homologous chromosomes pair along their lengths. Each gene on each chromosome becomes aligned with its sister gene. When crossing-over occurs, a DNA sequence is broken and crisscrossed, creating a new chromatid with pieces of each of the original homologous chromosomes.

RANDOM FERTILIZATION, the random pairing of sperm and egg, also produces genetic variation. Organisms produce millions of gametes, so no matter how many times a pair breeds, it is next to impossible to get two children that have the same genotype (except identical twins).

Examples

1. In a certain plant, having the dominant allele R results in bright-red seeds, and the recessive allele r results in pale-pink seeds. In the first generation, a scientist crosses a true-breeding RR plant with a recessive rr plant. The F1 plant is then crossed with itself, resulting in the F2 generation. In the F2 generation, what percentage of the plants will have bright-red seeds?

   A) 25 percent

   B) 50 percent

   C) 75 percent

   D) 100 percent

   Answer:

   C) is correct. Use Punnett squares to find the result of each cross. The F1 generation will all have the genotype Rr:

F1	R	R
r	Rr	Rr
r	Rr	Rr

   In the F2 generation, 75 percent of the plants will carry the dominant R allele:

F2	R	r
R	RR	Rr
r	Rr	rr

2. Which of the following statements describes the expression of X-linked traits?

   A) X-linked traits are expressed more often in men.

   B) X-linked traits are expressed more often in women.

   C) X-linked traits are expressed equally in men and women.

   D) X-linked traits are expressed only in men who carry the dominant allele.

   Answer:

   A) is correct. X-linked traits are expressed more often in men because they carry only one copy of the gene and so will express the gene whether the allele is dominant or recessive.

3. Which of the following is NOT a way that meiosis increases genetic variation?

   A) creating haploid sex cells that will be randomly fertilized

   B) allowing for the exchange of genetic material between chromosomes

   C) increasing the probability of mutations in the nucleotide sequence of DNA

   D) sorting each set of homologous chromosomes independently

   Answer:

   C) is correct. Meiosis does not increase the probability of mutations. Mutations are caused by environmental factors (such as radiation) or mistakes in DNA replication.

6

CHEMISTRY

THE STRUCTURE OF THE ATOM

The ATOM is the basic building block of all physical matter. It is composed of three subatomic particles: protons, electrons, and neutrons. A PROTON is a positively charged subatomic particle with a mass of approximately 1.007 atomic mass units. The number of protons in an atom determines which ELEMENT it is. For example, an atom with one proton is hydrogen, and an atom with twelve protons is carbon.

A NEUTRON is a non-charged subatomic particle with a mass of approximately 1.008 atomic mass units. The number of neutrons in an atom does not affect its chemical properties but will influence its rate of radioactivity. Both protons and neutrons are found in the center, or NUCLEUS, of the atom.

Lastly, an ELECTRON is a negatively charged subatomic particle with a mass of approximately 0.00055 atomic mass units. The number of electrons in an atom, in conjunction with the protons, determines the atom's charge. An atom with more protons than electrons

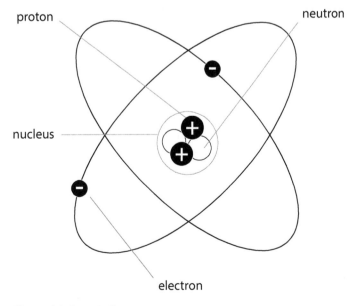

Figure 6.1. Atomic Structure

is a positive CATION, and an atom with more electrons than protons is a negative ANION. Cations and anions are collectively referred to as IONS.

While electrons are often depicted as orbiting the nucleus like a planet orbits the sun, they're actually arranged in cloud-like areas called SHELLS. The shells closest to the nucleus have the lowest energy and are filled first. The high-energy shells farther from the nucleus only fill with electrons once lower-energy shells are full.

The outermost electron shell of an atom is its VALENCE SHELL. The electrons in this shell are involved in chemical reactions. Atoms are most stable when their valence shell is full (usually with eight electrons), so the atom will lose, gain, or share electrons to fill its valence shell.

Examples

1. Which of the following subatomic particles are found in the nucleus of an atom?

A) protons only

B) electrons only

C) protons and neutrons only

D) protons, electrons, and neutrons

Answer:

C) is correct. The nucleus of an atom includes protons and neutrons. Electrons orbit around the nucleus.

2. What is the charge of an atom with five protons and seven electrons?

A) 12

B) −12

C) 2

D) −2

Answer:

D) is correct. The total charge of an atom is calculated by the difference of the number of protons and electrons: 5 − 7 = −2.

THE PERIODIC TABLE OF ELEMENTS

The **PERIODIC TABLE** is a table used to organize and characterize the various elements. The table was first proposed by Dmitri Mendeleev in 1869, and a similar organization system is still used today. In the table, each column is called a GROUP, and each row is called a PERIOD. Elements in the same column have similar electron configurations and the same number of electrons in their valence shells.

Reading the Periodic Table

Each cell in the table includes the symbol for the element, which is a letter or set of letters; for example, C for carbon and Fe for iron. The number at the top of each cell in the table is the ATOMIC NUMBER. This represents the number of protons in the element.

1	2	3	4	5	6	7	8	9	10	11	12	13	14	15	16	17	18
1 **H** Hydrogen 1.008																	2 **He** Helium 4.0026
3 **Li** Lithium 6.941	4 **Be** Beryllium 9.0122											5 **B** Boron 10.81	6 **C** Carbon 12.011	7 **N** Nitrogen 14.007	8 **O** Oxygen 15.999	9 **F** Fluorine 18.998	10 **Ne** Neon 20.180
11 **Na** Sodium 22.990	12 **Mg** Magnesium 24.305											13 **Al** Aluminum 26.982	14 **Si** Silicon 28.085	15 **P** Phosphorus 30.974	16 **S** Sulfur 32.06	17 **Cl** Chlorine 35.45	18 **Ar** Argon 39.948
19 **K** Potassium 39.098	20 **Ca** Calcium 40.078	21 **Sc** Scandium 44.956	22 **Ti** Titanium 47.867	23 **V** Vanadium 50.942	24 **Cr** Chromium 51.996	25 **Mn** Maganese 54.938	26 **Fe** Iron 55.845	27 **Co** Cobalt 58.933	28 **Ni** Nickel 58.963	29 **Cu** Copper 63.546	30 **Zn** Zinc 65.38	31 **Ga** Gallium 69.723	32 **Ge** Germanium 72.64	33 **Es** Arsenic 74.922	34 **Se** Selenium 78.971	35 **Br** Bromine 79.904	36 **Kr** Krypton 83.798
37 **Rb** Rubidium 85.468	38 **Sr** Strontium 87.62	39 **Y** Yttrium 88.906	40 **Zr** Zirconium 91.224	41 **Nb** Niobium 92.906	42 **Mo** Molybdenum 254	43 **Tc** Technetium 98	44 **Ru** Ruthenium 101.07	45 **Rh** Rhodium 102.91	46 **Pd** Palladium 106.42	47 **Ag** Silver 107.87	48 **Cd** Cadmium 112.41	49 **In** Indium 114.82	50 **Sn** Tin 118.71	51 **Sb** Antimony 121.76	52 **Te** Tellurium 127.60	53 **I** Iodine 126.90	54 **Xe** Xenon 121.29
55 **Cs** Caesium 132.91	56 **Ba** Barium 137.33	57-71	72 **Hf** Hafnium 178.49	73 **Ta** Tantalum 183.84	74 **W** Tungsten 183.84	75 **Re** Rhenium 186.21	76 **Os** Osmium 190.23	77 **Ir** Iridium 192.22	78 **Pt** Platinum 195.08	79 **Au** Gold 196.97	80 **Hg** Mercury 200.59	81 **Tl** Thallium 204.38	82 **Pb** Lead 207.2	83 **Bi** Bismuth 208.98	84 **Po** Polonium 209	85 **At** Astatine 210	86 **Rn** Radon 222
87 **Fr** Francium 223.020	88 **Ra** Radium 226	89-103	104 **Rf** Rutherfordium 267	105 **Db** Dubnium 268	106 **Sg** Seaborgium 271	107 **Bh** Bohrium 272	108 **Hs** Hassium 277	109 **Mt** Meitnerium 276	110 **Ds** Darmstadtium 281	111 **Rg** Roentgenium 280	112 **Cn** Copernicium 285	113 **Uut** Ununtrium Unknown	114 **Fl** Flerovium 254	115 **Uup** Ununpentium Unknown	116 **Lv** Livermorium 291	117 **Uus** Ununseptium Unknown	118 **Uuo** Ununoctium Unknown

Lanthanide	57 **La** Lanthanium 138.905	58 **Ce** Cerium 140.12	59 **Pr** Praseodymium 140.91	60 **Nd** Neodymium 144.24	61 **Pm** Promethium 144.913	62 **Sm** Samarium 150.36	63 **Eu** Europium 151.96	64 **Gd** Gadolinium 157.25	65 **Tb** Terbium 158.93	66 **Dy** Dysprosium 152.50	67 **Ho** Holmium 154.930	68 **Er** Erbium 167.259	69 **Tm** Thulium 168.934	70 **Yb** Ytterbium 173.065	71 **Lu** Lutetium 174.967
Actinide	89 **Ac** Actinium 227.028	90 **Th** Thorium 232.038	91 **Pa** Protactinium 231.036	92 **U** Uranium 238.029	93 **Np** Neptunium 237.048	94 **Pu** Plutonium 244.064	95 **Am** Americium 243.061	96 **Cm** Curium 247.070	97 **Bk** Berkelium 247.070	98 **Cf** Californium 251.080	99 **Es** Einsteinium 254	100 **Fm** Fermium 257.095	101 **Md** Mendelevium 258.1	102 **No** Nobelium 259.101	103 **Lr** Lawrencium 262

Key: Atomic Number / **Symbol** / Name / Atomic Mass

Alkaline Metal | Alkaline Earth Metals | Transition Metal | Basic Metal | Metalloid | Nonmetal | Halogen | Noble Gas | Lanthanide | Actinide

Figure 6.2. The Periodic Table of the Elements

The number below the element symbol is the ATOMIC MASS, which represents the total mass of the element (atomic mass – atomic number = # of neutrons).

Because atoms of the same element can have different numbers of neutrons, elements have no single standard atomic mass. Instead, the atomic mass is the weighted average of all commonly found species of the element. For this reason, it is almost never a whole number. For example, a small amount of carbon actually has an atomic mass of 13, possessing seven neutrons instead of the usual six, giving carbon an atomic mass of 12.011. Atoms of the same element with different numbers of neutrons are called ISOTOPES.

> ⚠ Many elemental symbols are derived from the Latin names for elements. For example, the symbol for gold is Au, from its Latin name, *Aurum*.

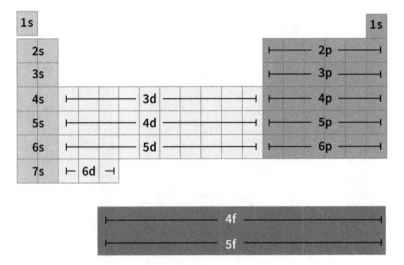

Figure 6.3. Reading the Periodic Table

Groups of Elements

Below are the important properties of the groups in the periodic table of elements.

GROUP 1 (THE ALKALI METALS): The elements in group 1 are all silvery metals that are soft and can be easily crushed or cut. They all possess a single valence electron, meaning they easily form +1 cations and are highly reactive. Because these metals are so reactive, they are not usually found in their pure form but instead are found as ionic compounds.

> ⚠ You do not need to memorize all of these properties, but you should be able to recognize the general similarities of a group's chemical properties.

GROUP 2 (THE ALKALI EARTH METALS): The elements in group 2 are also silvery metals that are soft. These metals contain two valence electrons, so they are not as reactive as those in group 1. However, they are still highly reactive: they form +2 cations and are found in ionic compounds.

GROUPS 3 – 12 (THE TRANSITION METALS): The elements from groups 3 to 12 are the transition metals and are all capable of conducting electricity (some better than others). Because their valence electrons are in *d* orbitals, their electron configurations are complex, and they form many different compounds and bonds. Transition metals are moderately reactive and malleable and can conduct electricity due to the capability of gaining and losing many electrons in their outer electron shell.

GROUPS 13 AND 14 (SEMI-METALLIC): The elements in groups 13 and 14 are semi-metallic. They have moderate conductivity and are very soft. Elements in group 13 have three valence electrons, and elements in group 14 have four, allowing for five and four bonds, respectively.

GROUP 15: This group is characterized by a shift from the top of this group (gases) to the bottom (semi-metallic). This group has five valence electrons and can form three bonds. The semi-metallic elements, such as arsenic and antimony, can react in specific circumstances but are generally not considered reactive.

GROUP 16: This group is also characterized by a shift from gases at the top of the group to semi-metallic at the bottom. This group has six valence electrons and is quite reactive. The need to obtain only two more electrons to fill the valence shell means that these elements are electronegative and typically form an anion with a charge of –2. As a result, these elements are reactive and tend to bond with the alkali or alkali earth metals.

GROUP 17 (HALOGENS): The halogens are all gases, and all contain seven electrons in their valence shell. They are extremely reactive, much like the alkali metals. Due to their reactivity and gaseous form at room temperature, they are often hazardous to humans. Inhaling chlorine or fluorine, for example, is usually deadly. The halogens will react in order to obtain a single additional electron to fill their valence shell and typically have a charge of –1.

GROUP 18 (THE NOBLE GASES): The noble gases have a full valence shell. Because their electron orbitals are already full, the noble gases are largely unreactive, except for a few rare exceptions. The heavier noble gases (xenon and radon) can sometimes react with other species under high temperature and pressure conditions.

Trends in the Periodic Table

Some element properties can be predicted based on the placement of the element on the periodic table.

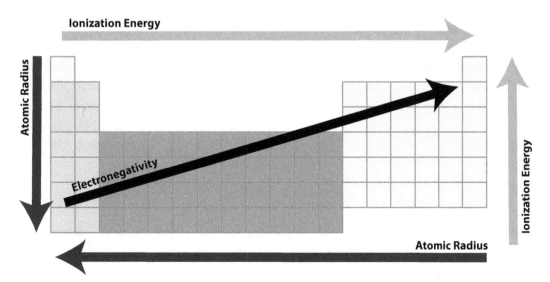

Figure 6.4. Trends in the Periodic Table

- **ATOMIC RADIUS**, the distance from the center of the atom to its outermost electron shell, increases from right to left and top to bottom on the periodic table.
- **ELECTRONEGATIVITY** measures how strongly an atom attracts electrons. In general, electronegativity increases from left to right and bottom to top on the periodic table with fluorine being the most electronegative element.
- **IONIZATION ENERGY**, a measure of how much energy is required to remove an electron from an atom, increases from lower left to top right.

Examples

1. Which of the following elements is an alkali metal?

   A) sodium

   B) oxygen

   C) neon

   D) iron

   Answer:

   A) is correct. Sodium (Na) is in group 1, the alkali metals.

2. Which of the following lists the elements carbon, fluorine, oxygen, and nitrogen in order of increasing electronegativity?

   A) $C < N < O < F$

   B) $F < N < O < C$

   C) $F < O < N < C$

   D) $C < N < F < O$

   Answer:

   A) is correct. Electronegativity increases across a period (row). From left to right, the order of the elements is $C < N < O < F$.

CHEMICAL BONDING

Molecules and Compounds

Atoms can exist on their own or bound together. When two or more atoms are held together by chemical bonds, they form a **MOLECULE**. If the molecule contains more than one type of atom, it is a **COMPOUND**. Molecules and compounds form the smallest unit of a substance—for example, if water (H_2O) is broken down into hydrogen and oxygen atoms, it no longer has the unique properties of water. Molecules and compounds always have the same ratio of elements. Water, for example, always has two hydrogens for every one oxygen.

Intramolecular Forces

A chemical bond is a force that holds two atoms together. There are three primary types of bonds: ionic, covalent, and metallic.

In an IONIC BOND, one atom has lost electrons to the other, which results in a positive charge on one atom and a negative charge on the other atom. The bond is then a result of the electrostatic interaction between these positive and negative charges. For example, in the compound sodium chloride, sodium has lost an electron to chlorine, resulting in a positive charge on sodium and a negative charge on chlorine.

In a COVALENT BOND, electrons are shared between two atoms; neither atom completely loses or gains an electron. This can be in the form of one pair of shared electrons (a single bond), two pairs (a double bond), or three pairs of electrons shared (triple bond). In diatomic oxygen gas, for example, the two oxygen molecules share two sets of electrons.

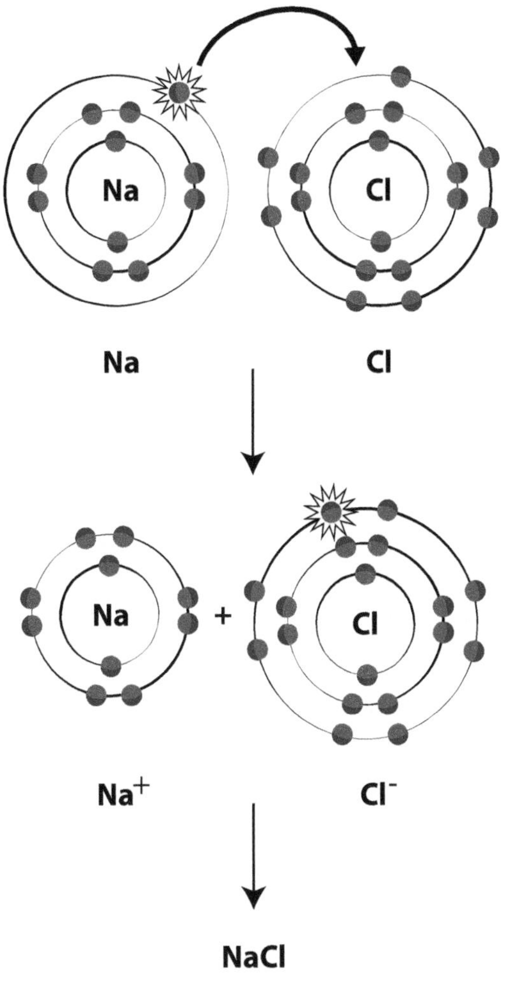

> Water is often called the universal solvent because its strong dipole allows it to dissolve most polar and ionic compounds. Nonpolar substances, such as oil, will not dissolve in water because they have no charge to interact with water's dipole.

Covalent bonds are often depicted using Lewis diagrams, in which an electron is represented by a dot, and a shared pair of electrons is represented by a line.

Electrons within a covalent bond are not always shared equally. More electronegative atoms, which exert a strong pull on the electrons, will hold onto the electrons longer than less electronegative atoms. For example, oxygen is more electronegative than hydrogen, so in H_2O (water), both oxygens have a slight negative charge, and the hydrogen has a slight positive charge. This imbalance is called POLARITY, and the small charge, a DIPOLE.

Note that there is a commonality between these two types of bonding. In both ionic and covalent bonding types, the bond results in each atom having a full valence shell of electrons. When bonding, atoms seek to find the most stable electron configuration. In the majority of cases, this means filling the valence shell of the atom either through the addition or removal of electrons.

Figure 6.5. The Ionic Bond in Table Salt (NaCl)

METALLIC BONDS are created when metals form tightly packed arrays. Valence electrons are not attached to a particular atom and instead float freely among the positive metallic cations. This "sea" of electrons creates a strong bond that has high electrical and thermal conductivity.

Water: H₂O

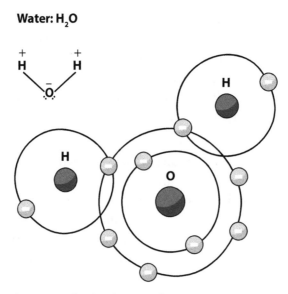

Figure 6.6. The Covalent Bond in Water (H₂O)

Intermolecular Forces

What causes water to stick together, forming a liquid at room temperature but a solid at lower temperatures? Why do we need more heat and energy to increase the temperature of water compared to other substances? The answer is **INTERMOLECULAR FORCES**: attractive or repulsive forces that occur between molecules. These are different from ionic and covalent bonds, which occur within a molecule.

The force of attraction between hydrogen and an extremely electronegative atom, such as oxygen or nitrogen, is known as a **HYDROGEN BOND**. For example, in water (H_2O), oxygen atoms are attracted to the hydrogen atoms in nearby molecules, creating hydrogen bonds. These bonds are significantly weaker than the chemical bonds that involve sharing or transfer of electrons, and they have only 5 to 10 percent of the strength of a covalent bond.

Despite its relative weakness, hydrogen bonding is quite important in the natural world; it has major effects on the properties of water and ice and is important biologically with regard to proteins and nucleic acids as well as the DNA double-helix structure.

VAN DER WAALS FORCES are electrical interactions between two or more molecules or atoms. They are the weakest type of intermolecular attraction, but their net effect can be quite strong. There are two major types of van der Waals forces. The **LONDON DISPERSION FORCE** is a temporary force that occurs when electrons in two adjacent atoms form spontaneous, temporary dipoles due to the positions the atoms are occupying. This is the weakest intermolecular force, and it does not exert a force over long distances.

The second type of van der Waals force is **DIPOLE-DIPOLE INTERACTIONS**, which are the result of two dipolar molecules interacting with each other. This interaction occurs when the partial positive dipole in one molecule is attracted to the partial negative dipole in the other molecule.

Examples

1. Which of the following bonds is the most polar?

A) H—C

B) H—O

C) H—F

D) H—N

Answer:

C) is correct. Fluorine is more electronegative than carbon (C), oxygen (O), or nitrogen (N). In the bond with hydrogen, it will pull the shared electrons more strongly, creating the bond with the highest polarity.

2. Which of the following elements is most likely to form an ionic bond?

A) argon

B) calcium

C) copper

D) nitrogen

Answer:

B) is correct. Calcium is an alkaline earth metal and easily forms a +2 cation, which in turn forms an ionic bond with an anion. Argon is a noble gas and does not form bonds, and copper is a metal that forms metallic bonds. Nitrogen most often forms covalent bonds.

PHYSICAL AND CHEMICAL PROPERTIES

Substances, whether they are composed of individual atoms or molecules, all have unique properties that are grouped into two categories: physical and chemical. A change in a **PHYSICAL PROPERTY** (called a physical change) results only in a change of the physical structure, not in the chemical composition of a reactant. For example, a change of state is a physical reaction. A physical property may be identified just by observing, touching, or measuring the substance in some way.

A change in a **CHEMICAL PROPERTY** is one in which the molecular structure or composition of the compound has been changed. Chemical properties cannot be identified simply by observing a material. Rather, the material must be engaged in a chemical reaction in order to identify its chemical properties.

Physical and chemical properties are often influenced by intramolecular and intermolecular forces. For example, substances with strong hydrogen bonds will have higher boiling points.

Table 6.1. Physical and Chemical Properties

PHYSICAL PROPERTIES	CHEMICAL PROPERTIES
temperature	heat of combustion
color	flammability
mass	toxicity

Table 6.1. Physical and Chemical Properties (continued)

PHYSICAL PROPERTIES	CHEMICAL PROPERTIES
viscosity	chemical stability
density	enthalpy of formation

Example

Which of the following describes a physical change?

A)   Water becomes ice.

B)   Batter is baked into a cake.

C)   A firecracker explodes.

D)   An acid is neutralized with a base.

Answer:

A) is correct. When water changes states, its chemical composition does not change. Once water becomes ice, the ice can easily turn back into water.

STATES OF MATTER

A STATE (also called a phase) is a description of the physical characteristics of a material. There are four states: solid, liquid, gas, and plasma.

- A SOLID is a dense phase characterized by close bonds between all molecules in the solid; solids have a definite shape and volume.
- A LIQUID is a fluid phase characterized by loose bonds between molecules in the liquid; liquids have an indefinite shape but a definite volume.
- A GAS is a very disperse phase characterized by the lack of, or very weak, bonds between molecules; gases have both an indefinite shape and volume.
- The PLASMA phase occurs when a substance has been heated and pressurized past its critical point, resulting in a new phase that has liquid and gas properties.

A substance will change phase depending on the temperature and pressure. As temperature increases, the phase will progress from solid to liquid to gas. As pressure increases, the opposite is true, and the phase will progress from gas to liquid to solid.

✔

The "smoke" released from dry ice is solid CO_2 sublimating into a gas. Can you think of other everyday examples of phase changes?

These phase changes have specific names, as shown below. Note that reciprocal changes will involve the same amount of energy; however, moving from a less to a more energetic state uses energy, while moving from a more to a less energetic state will release energy.

Table 6.2. Phase Changes

NAME	FROM	TO	OCCURS AT	ENERGY CHANGE
evaporation	liquid	gas	boiling point	uses energy
condensation	gas	liquid	boiling point	releases energy
melting	solid	liquid	freezing point	uses energy

NAME	FROM	TO	OCCURS AT	ENERGY CHANGE
freezing	liquid	solid	freezing point	releases energy
sublimation	solid	gas	---	uses energy
deposition	gas	solid	---	releases energy

PHASE DIAGRAMS are used to show the relationships between phases, temperature, and pressure for a particular substance. In the phase diagram, there are two points that are interesting to note. At the TRIPLE POINT, all three phases exist together, and at the CRITICAL POINT, the substance enters the plasma phase.

The boiling point and freezing point of a molecule are related to its structure. There are three important factors that contribute to boiling and freezing points:

1. Strength of intermolecular forces: the greater the intermolecular force, the greater the boiling point of the substance will be.

2. Molecule size: as the molecule becomes larger, the boiling point of the molecule typically increases.

3. Molecule branching: as more branch points are present in the molecule, the molecule's boiling point will decrease.

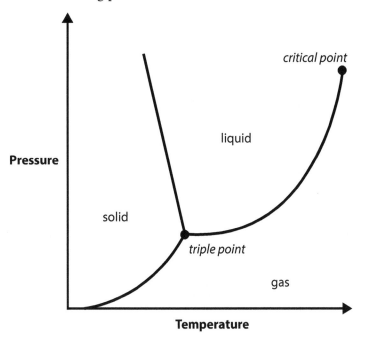

Figure 6.7. Phase Diagram

Methane has a molecular weight of 16 grams per mole, and water has a molecular weight of 18 grams per mole. Neither molecule is branched. As a result, factors 2 and 3 (as listed above), are not relevant. However, water has a boiling point of 100°C, while methane has a boiling point of –164°C.

This large difference is a result of intermolecular forces. Water is a highly polar molecule that has strong intermolecular forces. On the other hand, methane is an uncharged, nonpolar molecule with next to no intermolecular forces. Thus, the energy required to break the bonds between water molecules, and cause the phase change from liquid to vapor, is much greater than that for the methane molecule.

Examples

1. Which of the following is likely to have the highest number of molecules?

   A) 1 liter of gaseous CO_2

   B) 1 liter of liquid CO_2

   C) 1 liter of solid CO_2

   D) 1 liter of a mix of solid and gaseous CO_2

Answer:

C) is correct. Molecules are more closely packed together in a solid than in a liquid or gas. So, 1 L of solid CO_2 would have more molecules than 1 L of gaseous or liquid CO_2.

2. Which of the following terms describes the phase change from liquid to solid?

   A) evaporation

   B) deposition

   C) melting

   D) freezing

Answer:

D) is correct. Freezing is the change from liquid to solid, as when liquid water freezes to form solid ice.

ACIDS AND BASES

The Definition of Acids and Bases

In general, an ACID can be defined as a substance that produces hydrogen ions (H^+) in solution, while a BASE produces hydroxide ions (OH^-). Acidic solutions, which include common liquids like orange juice and vinegar, share a set of distinct characteristics: they have a sour taste and react strongly with metals. Bases, such as bleach and detergents, will taste bitter and have a slippery texture.

> What acidic and basic solutions do you handle on a daily basis?

There are a number of different technical definitions for acids and bases, including the Arrhenius, Brønsted-Lowry, and Lewis acid definitions.

- The **ARRHENIUS** definition: An acid is a substance that produces H^+ hydrogen ions in aqueous solution. A base is a substance that produces hydroxide ions OH^- in aqueous solution.

- The **BRØNSTED-LOWRY** definition: An acid is anything that donates a proton H^+, and a base is anything that accepts a proton H^+.

- The **LEWIS** definition: An acid is anything able to accept a pair of electrons, and a base is anything that can donate a pair of electrons.

Measuring the Strength of Acids and Bases

The **pH** of a solution is a measure of the acidity or basicity of the solution. It is found by taking the negative log of the concentration of hydrogen ions, making pH an exponential scale:

$$pH = -\log[H^+]$$

The pH scale runs from 0 to 14 with a low pH being more acidic and a high pH being more basic. A pH of 7 is that of water with no dissolved ions and is considered neutral.

Strong acids and bases will dissolve completely in solution, while weak acids and bases will only partially dissolve. Thus, strong acids and bases will have high or low pH values, respectively, and weak acids and bases will have pH values closer to 7.

pH scale

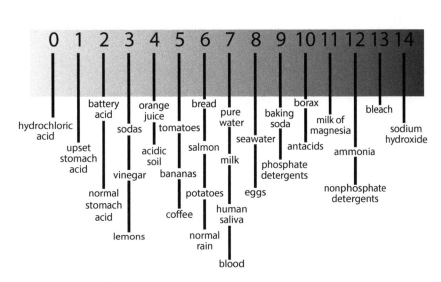

Figure 6.8. pH Scale

Table 6.3. Strong Acids and Bases

	HCl	Hydrochloric acid
	HNO_3	Nitric acid
Strong acids	H_2SO_4	Sulfuric acid
	$HClO_4$	Perchloric acid
	HBr	Hydrobromic acid
	HI	Hydroiodic acid
	LiOH	Lithium hydroxide
	NaOH	Sodium hydroxide
	KOH	Potassium hydroxide
Strong bases	$Ca(OH)_2$	Calcium hydroxide
	$Ba(OH)_2$	Barium hydroxide
	$Sr(OH)_2$	Strontium hydroxide

Acid Base Reactions

Acids and bases react with each other in solution to produce a salt and water: a process called NEUTRALIZATION. As a result of this reaction, if an equal amount of strong acid is mixed with an equal amount of strong base, the pH will remain at 7. For example, mixing hydrochloric acid and sodium hydroxide yields sodium chloride (a salt) and water, as shown below:

$$HCl + Na(OH) \rightarrow H_2O + NaCl$$

Examples

1. Which of the following acids is a strong acid?

   A) HClO

   B) HBr

   C) HF

   D) HN_3

   Answer:

   B) is correct. Hydrobromic acid (HBr) is one of the strong acids.

2. Which of the following best describes a substance with a pH of 12?

   A) very acidic

   B) slightly acidic

   C) neutral

   D) very basic

   Answer:

   D) is correct. Substances with a pH higher than 7 are basic. The pH scale goes up to 14, meaning a pH of 12 is very basic.

SOLUTIONS

In chemistry, the term MIXTURE describes a set of two or more substances that have been mixed together but are not chemically joined together. In a HOMOGENEOUS mixture, the substances are evenly distributed; in a HETEROGENEOUS mixture, the substances are not evenly distributed.

✔

Are the following mixtures homogeneous or heterogeneous? lemonade, concrete, air, trail mix, salt water

A SOLUTION is a specific type of homogeneous mixture in which all substances share the same basic properties and generally act as a single substance. In a solution, a SOLUTE is dissolved in a SOLVENT. For example, in salt water, salt is the solute and water is the solvent. The opposite process, in which a compound comes out of the solution, is called PRECIPITATION.

The CONCENTRATION of a solution—the amount of solute versus the amount of solvent—can be measured in a number of ways. Usually it is given as a ratio of solute to solvent in the relevant units. Some of these include:

- moles per volume (e.g., moles per liter)—also called MOLARITY
- moles per mass (e.g., moles per kilogram)—also called MOLALITY

- mass per volume (e.g., grams per liter)
- volume per volume (e.g., milliliter per liter)
- mass per mass (e.g., milligrams per gram)

Solubility

Solubility is a measure of how much solute will dissolve into a solvent. When a solution contains the maximum amount of solute possible, it is called a **SATURATED SOLUTION**. A solution with less solute is **UNSATURATED**, and a solution with more solute than can normally be dissolved in that solvent is **SUPERSATURATED**.

There are many factors that can affect the solubility of a compound, including temperature and pressure. Generally, solubility increases with temperature (although there are some compounds whose solubility will decrease with an increase in temperature). The relationship between solubility and temperature is shown in a solubility curve.

Another factor affecting solubility is the **COMMON ION EFFECT**, which occurs in solutions with two compounds that share a

Decompression sickness, also called *the bends*, is an ailment that afflicts divers who come to the surface too quickly. The high pressure deep in the ocean allows more gas to be dissolved in the fluid inside the diver's body. A quick drop in pressure (rising to the surface quickly) will lower the solubility of the gas, causing the gas to come out of solution and form bubbles inside the diver's body.

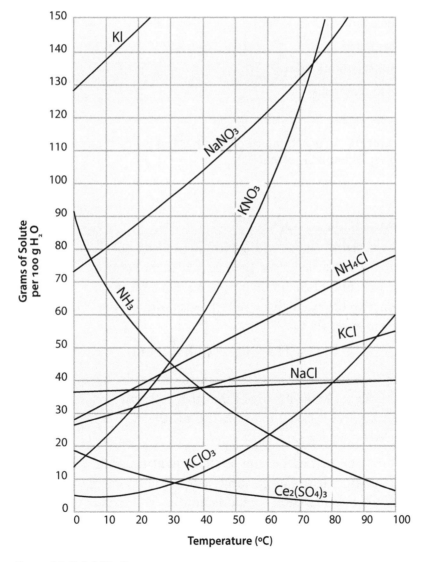

Figure 6.9. Solubility Curve

common ion. When the two compounds are mixed into a solvent, the presence of the common ion reduces the solubility of each compound. For example, NaCl and $MgCl_2$ share the common ion of chlorine. When they are mixed in a solution, the maximum saturation of the chlorine ion in water will be reached before the saturation of either sodium or magnesium is reached. This causes a reduction in the overall solubility.

Examples

1. In a carbonated soda, carbon dioxide is dissolved in water. Which of the following terms describes the water in this mixture?

A) common ion

B) solvent

C) solute

D) precipitant

Answer:

B) is correct. The water is the solvent in which the solute (carbon dioxide) is dissolved.

2. Which of the following terms describes a solution in which more solvent can be dissolved?

A) unsaturated

B) saturated

C) supersaturated

D) homogeneous

Answer:

A) is correct. An unsaturated solution has less solute than can be dissolved in the given amount of solvent.

CHEMICAL REACTIONS

In a **CHEMICAL REACTION**, one set of chemical substances, called the **REACTANTS**, is transformed into another set of chemical substances, called the **PRODUCTS**. This transformation is described in a chemical equation with the reactants on the left and products on the right. In the equation below, methane (CH_4) reacts with oxygen (O_2) to produce carbon dioxide (CO_2) and water (H_2O).

$$CH_4 + 2O_2 \rightarrow CO_2 + 2H_2O$$

When a reaction runs to **COMPLETION**, all the reactants have been used up in the reaction. If one reactant limits the use of the other reactants (i.e., if one reactant is used up before the others), it is called the **LIMITING REACTANT**. The **YIELD** is the amount of product produced by the reaction.

A chemical reaction that uses energy is **ENDOTHERMIC**, while a reaction that releases energy is **EXOTHERMIC**. Generally, creating bonds requires energy, and breaking bonds releases energy. Whether a reaction is endothermic or exothermic depends on the specific energy requirements of the bonds being broken and made in the reaction.

Processes can also be described as being endothermic or exothermic. For example, boiling water to form vapor is an endothermic process because it requires energy. Freezing liquid water to form ice is an exothermic process because it releases energy.

Balancing Equations

The integer values placed before the chemical symbols are the COEFFICIENTS that describe how many molecules of that substance are involved in the reaction. These values are important because in a chemical reaction, there is a conservation of mass. The inputs, or reactant mass, must equal the outputs, or products.

In order to BALANCE AN EQUATION, you'll need to add the coefficients necessary to match the atoms of each element on both sides. In the reaction below, the numbers of bromine (Br) and nitrate ions (NO_3^-) do not match up:

> ⚠ Always balance H and O last when balancing chemical equations.

$$CaBr_2 + NaNO_3 \rightarrow Ca(NO_3)_2 + NaBr$$

To balance the equation, start by adding a coefficient of 2 to the products to balance the bromine:

$$CaBr_2 + NaNO_3 \rightarrow Ca(NO_3)_2 + 2NaBr$$

There are now 2 sodium ions on the right, so another 2 need to be added on the left to balance it:

$$CaBr_2 + 2NaNO_3 \rightarrow Ca(NO_3)_2 + 2NaBr$$

Notice that adding this 2 also balances the nitrate ions, so the equation is now complete.

Types of Reactions

There are five main types of chemical reactions. In a SYNTHESIS REACTION, two reactants combine to form a single product. A DECOMPOSITION REACTION is the opposite of a synthesis reaction and involves a single reactant breaking down into several products.

In a displacement reaction, one ion takes the place of another in a compound. SINGLE-DISPLACEMENT reactions include a free ion taking the place of the ion in a compound. In a DOUBLE-DISPLACEMENT reaction, ions in two different compounds switch places.

Finally, in a COMBUSTION REACTION, a fuel (usually an alkane or carbohydrate) will react with oxygen to form carbon dioxide and water. Combustion reactions also produce heat.

The five types of chemical reactions are summarized in Table 6.4.

Table 6.4. Types of Reactions

TYPE OF REACTION	GENERAL FORMULA	EXAMPLE REACTION
Synthesis	$A + B \rightarrow C$	$2H_2 + O_2 \rightarrow 2H_2O$
Decomposition	$A \rightarrow B + C$	$2H_2O_2 \rightarrow 2H_2O + O_2$
Single displacement	$AB + C \rightarrow A + BC$	$CH_4 + Cl_2 \rightarrow CH_3Cl + HCl$
Double displacement	$AB + CD \rightarrow AC + BD$	$CuCl_2 + 2AgNo_3 \rightarrow Cu(NO_3)_2 + 2AgCl$
Combustion	$C_xH_yO_z + O_2 \rightarrow CO_2 + H_2O$	$2C_8H_{18} + 25O_2 \rightarrow 16CO_2 + 18H_2O$

Oxidation and Reduction Reactions

An oxidation and reduction reaction (often called a redox reaction) is one in which there is an exchange of electrons. The species that loses electrons is OXIDIZED, and the species that gains electrons is REDUCED. The species that loses electrons is also called the REDUCING AGENT, and the species that gains electrons is the OXIDIZING AGENT.

The movement of electrons in a redox reaction is analyzed by assigning each atom in the reaction an OXIDATION NUMBER (or state) that corresponds roughly to that atom's charge. (The actual meaning of the oxidation number is much more complicated.) Once all the atoms in a reaction have been assigned an oxidation number, it is possible to see which elements have gained electrons and which elements have lost electrons. The basic rules for assigning oxidation numbers are given in the table below.

Table 6.5. Assigning Oxidation Numbers

SPECIES	EXAMPLE	OXIDATION NUMBER
Elements in their free state and naturally occurring diatomic elements	$Zn(s)$, O_2	0
Monoatomic ions	Cl^-	−1
Oxygen in compounds	H_2O	−2
Hydrogen in compounds	HCl	+1
Alkali metals in a compound	Na	+1
Alkaline earth metals in a compound	Mg	+2

RULES		
The oxidation numbers on the atoms in a neutral compound sum to zero.	NaOH	Na: +1; O: −2; H: +1 $1 + -2 + 1 = 0$
The oxidation numbers of the atoms in an ion sum to the charge on that ion.	SO_3^{-2}	S: +4; O: −2 $4 + (-2)(3) = -2$

Examples

1. Which of the following types of reactions is shown below?

   $Pb(NO_3)_2 + K_2CrO_4 \rightarrow PbCrO_4 + 2\ KNO_3$

   A) combustion

   B) decomposition

   C) double-displacement

   D) single-replacement

   Answer:

   C) is correct. In the reaction, the Pb and K exchange their anions in a double-displacement reaction.

2. Which of the following equations is a balanced equation?

   A) $2KClO_3 \rightarrow KCl + 3O_2$

   B) $KClO_3 \rightarrow KCl + 3O_2$

   C) $2KClO_3 \rightarrow 2KCl + 3O_2$

   D) $6KClO_3 \rightarrow 6KCl + 3O_2$

Answer:

C) is correct. In this equation, there are equal numbers of each type of atom on both sides (2 K atoms, 2 Cl atoms, and 6 O atoms).

3. Which of the following substances is reduced in the reaction shown below?

$$Fe_2O_3 + 3CO \rightarrow 2Fe + 3CO_2$$

A) Fe

B) O

C) CO

D) CO_2

Answer:

A) is correct. Fe has an oxidation number of +3 in the compound Fe_2O_3 and an oxidation number of 0 on its own as Fe. Because Fe lost three electrons (to go from +3 to 0), it was reduced.

STOICHIOMETRY

STOICHIOMETRY uses the relative quantities of the molecules in a chemical equation to calculate the amount of reactants used or products made in a reaction. The basic unit of stoichiometry is the MOLE, which is the amount of an element or compound that contains 6.022×10^{23} atoms or molecules.

The coefficients in a chemical equation represent the number of moles participating in the reaction. For example, the combustion of methane (shown below) requires 1 mole of methane to react with 2 moles of oxygen. This reaction then produces 1 mole of carbon dioxide and 2 moles of water.

$$CH_4 + 2\,O_2 \rightarrow CO_2 + 2\,H_2O$$

Stoichiometry problems are worked using dimensional analysis (or railroad tracks), which requires three basic steps:

1. Identify the given or initial value.

2. Add conversion factors that will leave the desired units when cancelled.

3. Multiply across the top and across the bottom, and then divide.

☐ If 0.4 mol of CH_4 reacts completely with oxygen, how many moles of water are produced?

0.4 mol CH_4	2 mol H_2O	= 0.8 mol H_2O
	1 mol CH_4	

☐ How many moles of O_2 are needed to produce 5 moles of CO_2?

5 mol CO_2	2 mol O_2	= 10 mol O_2
	1 mol CO_2	

Example

In the reaction $2\,BiCl_3 + 3\,H_2S \rightarrow Bi_2S_3 + 6\,HCl$, how many moles of $BiCl_3$ are required to produce 18 moles of HCl?

A) 2

B) 3

C) 6

D) 18

Answer:

C) is correct. Set up railroad tracks using the conversion factor given by the chemical equation:

18 mol HCl	2 mol BiCl$_3$	18 × 2	= **6 moles**
	6 mol HCl	6	

NUCLEAR CHEMISTRY

In a chemical reaction, such as combustion or acid-base neutralization, it is only the number of electrons in an atom that changes—the nucleus remains unaffected. Conversely, in a **NUCLEAR REACTION**, changes occur in an atom's nucleus, affecting the number of protons, neutrons, or both. In a nuclear reaction, unstable atoms called **RADIOISOTOPES** spontaneously emit particles and energy.

In **ALPHA DECAY**, atoms emit **ALPHA (α) PARTICLES**, which contain two protons and two neutrons. Alpha particles are written as $^4_2\alpha$ or ^4_2He because they are identical to a helium nucleus. They have a high ionization power (100 times higher than beta particles and 10,000 times higher than gamma radiation), meaning they have the potential to cause severe damage to biological tissue. However, their penetrating power is low: they can only travel a few centimeters through the air, and they cannot penetrate even thin surfaces.

Beta decay releases **BETA (β) PARTICLES**, which have the charge of an electron but can be thought of as fast-moving electrons emitted by the nucleus. Beta particles are written as $^0_{-1}e$ or $^0_{-1}\beta$, so the resulting element will have a higher atomic number. They have a low ionization power (about 1/100th the power of an alpha particle) but are highly penetrative (100 times more than alpha particles).

⚠

A **radioactive series** is a sequence of nuclear reactions that create a stable nucleus from a previously unstable one. There are three naturally occurring radioactive sequences: thorium-232 to lead-208, uranium-235 to lead-207, and uranium-238 to lead-206.

GAMMA (γ) RADIATION consists of high-energy, short wavelength photons that are often released with other radioactive particles during decay. They are written as $^0_0\gamma$ and do not change the number of protons or neutrons in the atom. Their penetrating power is greater than alpha and beta particles, but their ionization power is much lower.

The time it takes for substances to decay varies widely—some radioisotopes decay completely in only a few seconds, while others decay over millions of years. The time it takes for half of a radioactive sample to decay is that substance's **HALF-LIFE** (h or $t_{\frac{1}{2}}$). The equation for half-life is written as:

$$A = A_0 \left(\frac{1}{2}\right)^{\frac{t}{h}}$$

where A is the final amount, A_0 is the initial amount, t is the time, and h is the half-life.

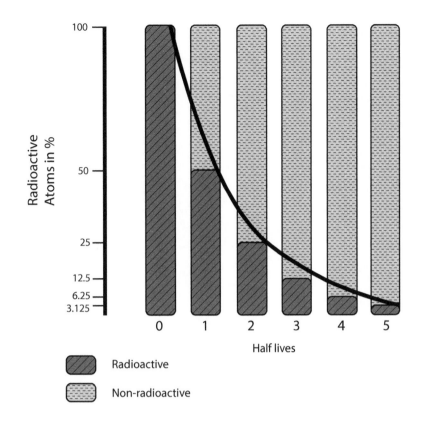

Figure 6.10. Half-Life Decay

Example

The half-life of iodine-131 is 8 days. How much of a 120 g sample of iodine-131 will remain after 24 days?

A) 0 g

B) 15 g

C) 30 g

D) 60 g

Answer:

B) is correct. Use the half-life equation:

$$A = A_0\left(\frac{1}{2}\right)^{\frac{t}{h}} = (120\text{ g})\left(\frac{1}{2}\right)^{\frac{24}{8}} = (120\text{ g})\left(\frac{1}{2}\right)^{3} = (120\text{ g})\left(\frac{1}{8}\right) = \textbf{15 g}$$

7

ANATOMY AND PHYSIOLOGY

TERMINOLOGY

Directional Terms

Anatomical science uses common terms to describe spatial relationships, often in pairs of opposites. These terms generally refer to the position of a structure in an organism that is upright with respect to its environment (e.g., in its typical orientation while moving forward).

How would you use anatomical terms to describe the relative positions of the heart and lungs?

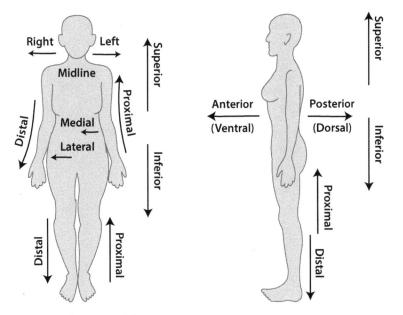

Figure 7.1. Directional Terms

Table 7.1. Directional Terms

TERM	DEFINITION
superior	toward the head, or toward the upper body region
inferior	toward the lower body region
anterior (ventral)	on the belly or front side of the body
posterior (dorsal)	on the buttocks or back side of the body
proximal	near the trunk or middle part of the body
distal	farthest away from the point of reference
medial	close to the midline of the body
lateral	away from the midline of the body

Body Cavities

The internal structure of the human body is organized into compartments called CAVITIES, which are separated by membranes. There are two main cavities in the human body: the dorsal cavity and the ventral cavity (both named for their relative positions).

The DORSAL CAVITY is further divided into the CRANIAL CAVITY, which holds the brain, and the SPINAL CAVITY, which surrounds the spine. The two sections of the dorsal cavity are continuous. Both sections are lined by the MENINGES, a three-layered membrane that protects the brain and spinal cord.

The VENTRAL CAVITY houses most of the body's organs. It also can be further divided into smaller cavities. The THORACIC CAVITY holds the heart and lungs, the ABDOMINAL CAVITY holds the digestive organs and kidneys, and the PELVIC CAVITY holds the bladder and reproductive organs. Both the abdominal and pelvic cavities are enclosed by a membrane called the PERITONEUM.

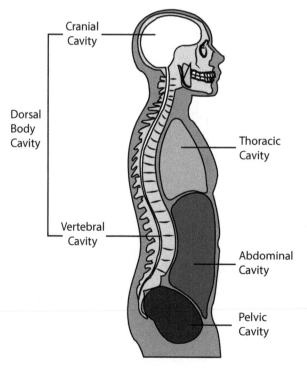

Figure 7.2. Body Cavities

Examples

1. Which of the following terms describes the location of the wrist relative to the elbow?

   A) distal

   B) proximal

   C) anterior

   D) posterior

   Answer:

   A) is correct. The wrist is distal, or farther from the trunk, than the elbow.

2. Which of the following cavities holds the ovaries?

   A) ventral

   B) thoracic

   C) abdominal

   D) pelvic

   Answer:

   D) is correct. The pelvic cavity holds the reproductive organs, which, in females, include the ovaries.

THE CIRCULATORY SYSTEM

The **CIRCULATORY SYSTEM** circulates nutrients, gases, wastes, and other substances throughout the body. This system includes the blood, which carries these substances; the heart, which powers the movement of blood; and the blood vessels, which carry the blood.

The Pulmonary and Systemic Loops

The circulatory system includes two loops. In the **PULMONARY LOOP**, deoxygenated blood is carried from the heart to the lungs, where gas exchange takes place. The newly oxygenated blood then travels back to the heart. In the **SYSTEMIC LOOP**, oxygenated blood is pushed out of the heart and travels through larger blood vessels until it reaches the capillaries, where gas exchange takes place. The deoxygenated blood is then carried back to the heart by veins, and the process starts again. A healthy resting heart can pump around five liters per minute through this cycle.

The veins of the stomach and intestines do not carry blood directly to the heart. Instead, they divert it to the liver (through the hepatic portal vein) so that the liver can store sugar, remove toxins, and process the products of digestion.

CONTINUE

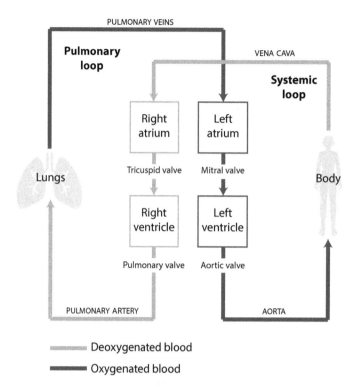

Pulmonary loop

VENA CAVA

Systemic loop

Right atrium

Left atrium

Lungs

Tricuspid valve

Mitral valve

Body

Right ventricle

Left ventricle

Pulmonary valve

Aortic valve

PULMONARY ARTERY

AORTA

Deoxygenated blood

Oxygenated blood

Figure 7.3. The Path of Blood in the Circulatory System

The Heart

The circulatory system relies on the **HEART**, a cone-shaped muscular organ that is no bigger than a closed fist. The heart must pump the blood low in oxygen to the lungs; once the blood is in the lungs, it is oxygenated and returned to the heart. The heart then pumps the oxygenated blood through the whole body.

The cavity that holds the heart is called the **PERICARDIAL CAVITY**. It is filled with serous fluid produced by the pericardium, which is the lining of the pericardial cavity. The serous fluid acts as a lubricant for the heart. It also keeps the heart in place and empties the space around the heart.

The heart wall has three layers:

- **EPICARDIUM**: the protective outermost layer of the heart composed of connective tissue.
- **MYOCARDIUM**: the middle layer of the heart that contains the cardiac muscular tissue. It performs the pumping function to circulate blood.
- **ENDOCARDIUM**: the smooth innermost layer that keeps the blood from sticking to the inside of the heart.

The heart wall is uneven because some parts of the heart—like the atria—do not need a lot of muscle power to perform their duties. Other parts, like the ventricles, require a thicker muscle to pump the blood.

There are four **CHAMBERS** in the heart: the right and left atria, and the right and left ventricles. The **ATRIA** (plural for *atrium*) are smaller than the ventricles, and they have thin walls, as their function is to receive blood from the lungs and the body and pump it to the ventricles. The **VENTRICLES** have to pump the blood to the lungs and the rest of the body, so they are larger and have thicker walls. The left half of the heart, which is responsible for pumping the blood through the body, has a thicker wall than the right half, which pumps the deoxygenated blood to the lungs.

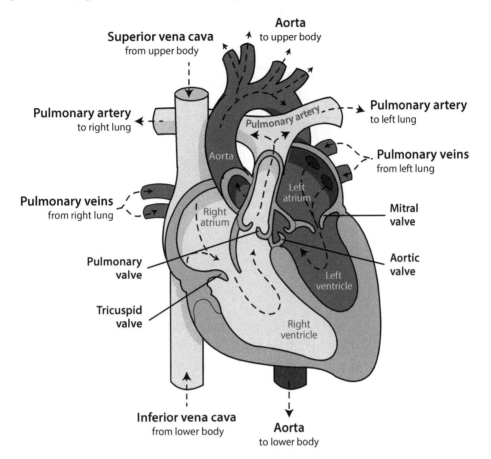

Figure 7.4. The Heart

The heart has one-way valves allowing the blood to flow in only one direction. The valves that keep the blood from going back into the atria from the ventricles are called the ATRIOVENTRICULAR VALVES, and the valves that keep the blood from going back into the ventricles from the arteries are called the SEMILUNAR VALVES.

The Heart Valves
Try Pulling My Aorta
- Tricuspid
- Pulmonary
- Mitral
- Aorta

The pumping function of the heart is made possible by two groups of cells that set the heart's pace and keep it well-coordinated: the sinoatrial and the atrioventricular node. The SINOATRIAL NODE sets the pace and signals the atria to contract. The ATRIOVENTRICULAR NODE picks up the signal from the sinoatrial node, and this signal tells the ventricles to contract.

The Blood Vessels

The BLOOD VESSELS carry the blood from the heart throughout the body and then back. They vary in size depending on the amount of the blood that needs to flow through them. The hollow part in the middle, called the LUMEN, is where the blood actually flows. The vessels are lined with endothelium, which is made out of the same type of cells as the endocardium and serves the same purpose—to keep the blood from sticking to the walls and clotting.

ARTERIES are blood vessels that transport the blood away from the heart. They work under a lot more pressure than the other types of blood vessels; hence, they have a thicker, more muscular wall, which is also highly elastic. The smaller arteries are usually more muscular, while the larger are more elastic.

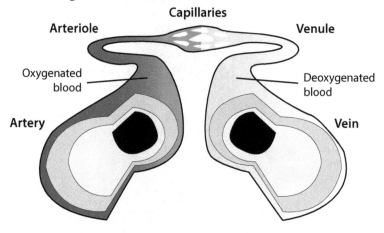

Figure 7.5. Blood Vessels

The largest artery in the body is called the **AORTA**. It ascends from the left ventricle of the heart, arches to the back left, and descends behind the heart. Narrower arteries that branch off of main arteries and carry blood to the capillaries are called **ARTERIOLES**. The descending part of the aorta carries blood to the lower parts of the body, except for the lungs. The lungs get blood through the **PULMONARY ARTERY** that comes out of the right ventricle.

The arching part of the aorta (called the **AORTIC ARCH**) branches into three arteries: the brachiocephalic artery, the left common artery, and the left subclavian artery. The **BRA-CHIOCEPHALIC ARTERY** carries blood to the brain and head; it further divides into the right subclavian artery, which brings the blood to the right arm. The **LEFT COMMON CAROTID ARTERY** carries blood to the brain; the **LEFT SUBCLAVIAN ARTERY** carries blood to the left arm.

The **DESCENDING AORTA** bends away from the aortic arch and carries blood to the abdomen and lower body. At the fourth lumbar vertebra, the descending aorta splits into the two **ILIAC ARTERIES**, which further divide into the **INTERNAL** and **EXTERNAL ILIAC ARTERIES**. These vessels bring blood to the pelvis and legs.

VEINS are blood vessels that bring the blood from the body back to the heart. As they do not work under the same pressure as the arteries, they are much thinner and not as muscular or elastic. The veins also have a number of one-way valves that stop the blood from going back through them.

> The pulmonary veins are the only veins in the human body that carry oxygenated blood.

Veins use inertia, muscle work, and gravity to get the blood to the heart. Thin veins that connect to the capillaries are called **VENULES**. The lungs have their own set of veins: the **LEFT** and **RIGHT SUPERIOR** and **INFERIOR PULMONARY VEINS**. These vessels enter the heart through the left atrium.

The two main veins are called the superior vena cava and the inferior vena cava. The **SUPERIOR VENA CAVA** ascends from the right atrium and connects to the head and neck, delivering the blood supply to these structures. The superior vena cava also connects to the arms via both the subclavian and brachiocephalic veins. The **INFERIOR VENA CAVA** descends from the right atrium, carrying the blood from the lumbar veins, gonadal veins, hepatic veins, phrenic veins, and renal veins.

CAPILLARIES are the smallest blood vessels, and the most populous in the body. They can be found in almost every tissue. They connect to arterioles on one end and the venules on the other end. Also, capillaries carry the blood very close to the cells and thus enable cells to exchange gases, nutrients, and cellular waste. The walls of capillaries have to be very thin for this exchange to happen.

The Blood

BLOOD is the medium for the transport of substances throughout the body. There are four to five liters of this liquid connective tissue in the human body. Blood is comprised of red blood cells, hemoglobin, white blood cells, platelets, and plasma.

Also called ERYTHROCYTES, RED BLOOD CELLS (RBCs) are produced inside the red bone marrow and transport oxygen. HEMOGLOBIN (HGB) is a red pigment found in the red blood cells, and it is rich in iron and proteins, which both allow these cells to transport the oxygen. RBCs also have a biconcave shape, which means they are round and thinner in the middle. This shape gives them a larger surface area, making them more effective.

The blood also contains many immune system components, including white blood cells (or LEUKOCYTES). PLATELETS, also called THROMBOCYTES, circulate in the blood and are vital for blood clotting. They are formed in the red bone marrow and serve many functions in the body.

Finally, PLASMA is the liquid part of blood, and it forms 55 percent of the total blood volume. Plasma consists of up to 90 percent water, as well as proteins, including antibodies and albumins. Other substances circulating in the blood plasma include glucose, nutrients, cell waste, and various gases.

Examples

1. Which of the following layers of the wall of the heart contains cardiac muscles?

    A) myocardium only

    B) epicardium only

    C) endocardium only

    D) myocardium and epicardium only

    Answer:

    A) is correct. The myocardium is the muscular layer of the heart that contains cardiac muscle.

2. The blood from the left ventricle goes to

    A) the left atria.

    B) the vena cava.

    C) the aorta.

    D) the lungs.

    Answer:

    D) is correct. The left ventricle pumps deoxygenated blood from the heart to the lungs.

3. The blood vessels that carry the blood from the heart are called

A) veins.

B) venules.

C) capillaries.

D) arteries.

Answer:

D) is correct. Blood leaves the heart in arteries.

THE RESPIRATORY SYSTEM

The human body needs oxygen in order to function. The **RESPIRATORY SYSTEM** is responsible for intake of this gas. This system is also in charge of removing carbon dioxide from the body, an equally important function. The respiratory system can be divided into two sections: the upper respiratory tract and the lower respiratory tract.

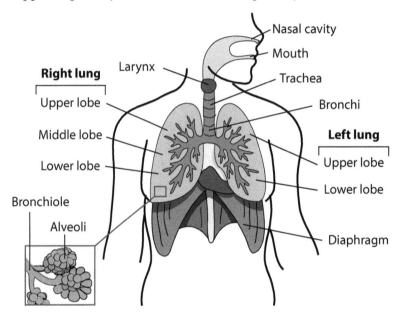

Figure 7.6. The Respiratory System

The Upper Respiratory Tract

The **UPPER RESPIRATORY TRACT** consists of the nose, nasal cavity, olfactory membranes, mouth, pharynx, epiglottis, and the larynx.

The **NOSE** is the primary body part for air intake and removing carbon dioxide. The nose itself is made out of bone, cartilage, muscle, and skin, and it serves as a protector of the hollow space behind it called the **NASAL CAVITY**. The nasal cavity is covered with hair and mucus, which together serve an important function—they stop contaminants from the outside. Common contaminants include dust, mold, and other particles. The nasal cavity prevents the contaminants from entering further into the respiratory system; it also warms and moisturizes air.

The nose and the nasal cavity also contain OLFACTORY MEMBRANES, which are small organs responsible for our sense of smell. They are located on the top of the nasal cavity, just under the bridge of the nose.

We can also breathe through the MOUTH, although it is not the primary breathing opening. The mouth does not perform as well when it comes to the three functions of the primary opening (filtering, moisturizing, and warming of air). However, the mouth does have advantages over the nose when it comes to breathing, including its larger size and proximity to the lungs.

The next part of the respiratory system is the THROAT, which is also called the PHARYNX. The pharynx is a smooth, muscular structure lined with mucus and divided into three regions: the nasopharynx, the oropharynx, and the laryngopharynx.

Air comes in through the nose and then passes through the NASOPHARYNX, which is also where the Eustachian tubes from the middle ears connect with the pharynx. The air then enters the OROPHARYNX, which is where air from the mouth enters the pharynx; this is the same passageway used for transporting food when eating. Both air and food also pass through the LARYNGOPHARYNX, where these substances are diverted into different systems.

The EPIGLOTTIS is responsible for ensuring that air enters the trachea and food enters the esophagus. The epiglottis is a flap made of elastic cartilage, which covers the opening of one passageway to allow the air or food to go into the other one. When you breathe, the epiglottis covers the opening of the esophagus, and when you swallow, it protects the opening of the trachea.

The LARYNX is the part of the airway that sits between the pharynx and the trachea. It is also called the *voice box*, because it contains mucus membrane folds (vocal folds) that vibrate when air passes through them to produce sounds. The larynx is made out of three cartilage structures: the epiglottis, the thyroid cartilage (also called the Adam's apple), and the cricoid cartilage, a ring-shaped structure that keeps the larynx open.

The Lower Respiratory Tract

The LOWER RESPIRATORY TRACT consists of the trachea, bronchi, lungs, and the muscles that help with breathing.

The lower respiratory tract begins with the TRACHEA, also known as the *windpipe*. The trachea stretches between the larynx and the bronchi. As its name suggests, the windpipe resembles a pipe, and its flexibility allows it to follow various head and neck movements. The trachea is made out of fibrous and elastic tissues, smooth muscle, and about twenty cartilage rings.

The inner lining of the windpipe is composed of epithelial tissue, which contains mucus-producing cells called GOBLET CELLS, as well as cells that have small, hair-like fringes. These structures, called CILIA, allow air to pass through the windpipe, where it is further filtered by the mucus. The fringes also help to move mucus up the airways and out, keeping the air passage clear.

Connecting to the trachea are the BRONCHI. The PRIMARY BRONCHI, consisting of many *C*-shaped cartilage rings, branch into the secondary bronchi. Two branches extend from the left primary bronchi, and three branches extend from the right, corresponding to the number of lobes in the lungs.

The **SECONDARY BRONCHI** contain less cartilage and have more space between the rings. The same goes for the **TERTIARY BRONCHI**, which are extensions of the secondary bronchi as they divide throughout the lobes of the lungs. Like the trachea, the bronchi are lined with epithelium that contains goblet cells and cilia.

BRONCHIOLES branch from the tertiary bronchi. They contain no cartilage at all; rather, they are made of smooth muscle and elastic fiber tissue, which allows them to be quite small yet still able to change their diameter. For example, when the body needs more oxygen, they expand, and when there is a danger of pollutants entering the lungs, they constrict.

Bronchioles end with **TERMINAL BRONCHIOLES**, which connect them with **ALVEOLI**, which is where the gas exchange happens. Alveoli are small cavities located in alveolar sacs and surrounded by capillaries. The inner surface of alveoli is coated with **ALVEOLAR FLUID**, which plays a vital role in keeping the alveoli moist, the lungs elastic, and the thin wall of the alveoli stable. The wall of the alveoli is made out of alveolar cells and the connective tissue that forms the respiratory membrane where it comes into contact with the wall of the capillaries.

The **LUNGS** themselves are two spongy organs that contain the bronchi, bronchioles, alveoli, and blood vessels. The lungs are contained in the rib cage, and are surrounded by the pleura, a double-layered membrane consisting of the outer **PARIETAL PLEURA** and the inner **VISCERAL PLEURA**. Between the layers of the pleura is a hollow space called the **PLEURAL CAVITY**, which allows the lungs to expand.

> ⚠
> In anatomy, the terms *right* and *left* are used with respect to the subject, not the observer.

The lungs are wider at the bottom, which is referred to as the **BASE**, and they are narrower at the top part, which is called the **APEX**. The lungs are divided into **LOBES**, with the larger lung (the right one) consisting of three lobes, and the smaller lung (the left lung) consisting of two lobes.

Respiration

The muscles that play a major role in respiration are the diaphragm and the intercostal muscles. The **DIAPHRAGM** is a structure made of skeletal muscle, and it is located under the lungs, forming the floor of the thorax. The **INTERCOSTAL MUSCLES** are located between the ribs. The **INTERNAL INTERCOSTAL MUSCLES** help with breathing out (expiration) by depressing the ribs and compressing the thoracic cavity; the **EXTERNAL INTERCOSTAL MUSCLES** help with breathing in (inspiration).

Breathing in and out is also called **PULMONARY VENTILATION**. The two types of pulmonary ventilation are inhalation and exhalation.

During **INHALATION** (also called inspiration), the diaphragm contracts and moves a few inches toward the stomach, making more space for the lungs to expand. This movement pulls the air into the lungs. The external intercostal muscles also contract to expand the rib cage and pull more air into the lungs. The lungs are now at a lower pressure than the atmosphere, (called negative pressure), which causes air to come into the lungs until the pressure inside the lungs and the atmospheric pressure are the same.

During **EXHALATION** (expiration), the diaphragm and the external intercostal muscles relax, and the internal intercostal muscles contract. This causes the thoracic cavity to become smaller and the pressure in the lungs to climb higher than the atmospheric pressure, which moves air out of the lungs.

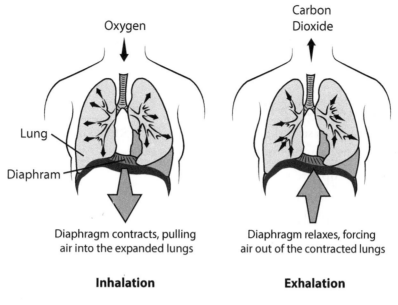

Figure 7.7. Pulmonary Ventilation

Types of Breathing

In shallow breathing, around 0.5 liters of air is circulated, a capacity called TIDAL VOLUME. During deep breathing, a larger amount of air is moved, usually three to five liters, a volume known as VITAL CAPACITY. The abdominal, as well as other muscles, are also involved in breathing in and out during deep breathing.

EUPNEA is a term for the breathing our body does when resting, which consists of mostly shallow breaths with an occasional deep breath. The lungs are never completely without air—around a liter of air is always present in the lungs.

Examples

1. Which of the following is the opening in the throat through which air passes after it enters the mouth?

   A) nasopharynx

   B) oropharynx

   C) laryngopharynx

   D) larynx

   Answer:

   B) is correct. Air that enters through the mouth passes through the oropharynx to reach the larynx.

2. During respiration, the epiglottis prevents air from entering which of the following organs?

   A) bronchi

   B) pharynx

   C) larynx

   D) esophagus

Answer:

D) is correct. The epiglottis covers the esophagus during respiration so that air does not enter the digestive track.

THE SKELETAL SYSTEM

The skeletal system plays several roles in the body. The bones and joints that make up the skeletal system are responsible for:

- providing support and protection
- allowing movement
- generating blood cells
- storing fat, iron, and calcium
- guiding the growth of the entire body

Generally, the skeleton can be divided into two parts: the axial skeleton and the appendicular skeleton. The **AXIAL SKELETON** consists of eighty bones placed along the body's midline axis and grouped into the skull, ribs, sternum, and vertebral column. The **APPENDICULAR SKELETON** consists of 126 bones grouped into the upper and lower limbs and the pelvic and pectoral girdles. These bones anchor muscles and allow for movement.

Bone Components

On the cellular level, the bone consists of two distinctively different parts: the matrix and living bone cells. The **BONE MATRIX** is the nonliving part of the bone, which is made out of water, collagen, protein, calcium phosphate, and calcium carbonate crystals. The **LIVING BONE CELLS (OSTEOCYTES)** are found at the edges of the bones and throughout the bone matrix in small cavities. Bone cells play a vital part in the growth, development, and repair of bones, and can be used for the minerals they store.

Looking at a cross section of a bone, you can see that it is made out of layers. These include the **PERIOSTEUM**, which is the topmost layer of the bone, acting as a layer of connective tissue. The periosteum contains collagen fibers that anchor the tendons and the muscles; it also holds the stem and the osteoblast cells that are necessary for growth and repair of the bones. Nervous tissue, nerve endings, and blood vessels are also present in the periosteum.

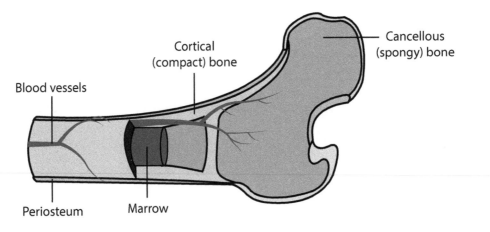

Figure 7.8. The Structure of Bone

Under the periosteum is a layer of COMPACT BONE, which gives the bone its strength. Made out of mineral salts and collagen fibers, it also contains many cavities where osteocytes can be found. CANCELLOUS (SPONGY) BONE is found under the compact bone at the ends of long bones and in vertebrae. This layer of bone is less dense than compact bone but includes a much larger surface area, making it ideal for exchange. The functional unit of cancellous bone is the TRABECULA, which holds red bone marrow and provides structural support.

Bone Cell Processes

New bone is formed by osteoblasts during OSSIFICATION. This process occurs in fetal development and is ongoing as bones grow and repair themselves. OSTEOCLASTS, another type of bone cell, are responsible for breaking down bone tissue. They are located on the surface of bones and help balance the body's calcium levels by degrading bone to release stored calcium.

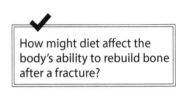

How might diet affect the body's ability to rebuild bone after a fracture?

Inside the red bone marrow, which is located in the medullar cavity of the bones, a process called HEMATOPOIESIS occurs. In the process, white and red blood cells are made from stem cells. The amount of the red bone marrow declines at the end of puberty, as a significant part of it is replaced by the yellow bone marrow.

The Five Types of Bones

The LONG BONES make up the major bones of the limbs. They are longer than they are wide, and they are responsible for most of our height. The long bones can be divided in two regions: the EPIPHYSES, located at the ends of the bone, and DIAPHYSIS, located in the middle. The middle of the diaphysis contains a hollow medullary cavity, which serves as storage for bone marrow.

The SHORT BONES are roughly as long as they are wide, and are generally cube shaped or round. Short bones in the body include the carpal bones of the wrist and tarsal bones of the foot. The FLAT BONES do not have the medullary cavity because they are thin and usually thinner on one end region. Flat bones in the body include the ribs, the hip bones, and the frontal, the parietal, and the occipital bones of the skull. The IRREGULAR BONES are those bones that do not fit the criteria to be classified as long, short, or flat bones. The vertebrae and the sacrum, among others, are irregular bones.

There are only two SESAMOID BONES that are actually counted as proper bones: the patella and the pisiform bone. Sesamoid bones are formed inside the tendons located across the joints, and apart from the two mentioned, they are not present in all people.

The Skull

Composed of twenty-two bones, the SKULL protects the brain and the sense organs for vision, hearing, smell, taste, and balance. The skull has only one movable joint; this joint connects it with the MANDIBLE, or the *jaw bone*, which is the only movable bone of the skull. The other twenty-one bones are fused together.

The upper part of the skull is known as the CRANIUM, which protects the brain, while the lower and frontal parts of the skull form the facial bones. Located just under the mandible, and not a part of the skull, is the HYOID BONE. The hyoid is the only bone in the body that is not attached to any other bone. It helps keep the trachea open and anchors the tongue muscles.

Other bones closely connected to, but not part of the skull, are the **AUDITORY OSSICLES**: the malleus, incus, and stapes. These bones play an important role in hearing.

The Vertebral Column

The **VERTEBRAL COLUMN**, or the spine, begins at the base of the skull and stretches through the trunk down the middle of the back to the coccyx. It supports the weight of the upper body and protects the spinal cord. It is made up of twenty-four vertebrae, plus the **SACRUM** and the **COCCYX** (the *tailbone*). These twenty-four vertebrae are divided into three groups:

- the **CERVICAL**, or the neck vertebrae (seven bones)
- the **THORACIC**, or the chest vertebrae (twelve bones)
- the **LUMBAR**, or the lower back vertebrae (five bones)

Furthermore, each vertebra has its own name, which is derived from the first letter of the group to which it belongs (for example, *L* for lumbar vertebrae). The letter is placed first, followed by a number (the first of the lumbar vertebrae is thus called *L1*).

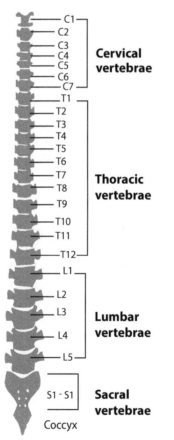

Figure 7.9. The Vertebral Column

The Ribs and the Sternum

The ribs and the sternum are the bones that form the rib cage of the thoracic region. The **STERNUM**, also known as the *breastbone*, is a thin bone along the midline of the thoracic region. Most of the ribs are connected to this bone via the COSTAL CARTILAGE, a thin band of cartilage.

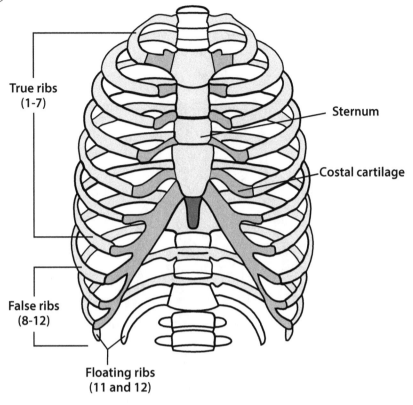

True ribs
(1-7)

Sternum

Costal cartilage

False ribs
(8-12)

Floating ribs
(11 and 12)

Figure 7.10. The Ribs

The human skeleton has twelve pairs of RIBS. On the back side, they are attached to the thoracic vertebrae. On the front, the first seven of them attach directly to the sternum, the next three attach to the cartilage between the seventh rib and the sternum, and the remaining two do not attach to the sternum at all. These ribs protect the kidneys, not the lungs and heart. The first seven ribs are known as the *true ribs*, and the rest are known as *false ribs*. Together, these bones form the THORACIC CAGE, which supports and protects the heart and lungs.

The Appendicular Skeleton

The upper limbs, which belong to the APPENDICULAR SKELETON, are connected with the axial skeleton by the PECTORAL GIRDLE. The pectoral girdle is formed from the left and right CLAVICLE and SCAPULA. The scapula and the HUMERUS, the bones of the upper arm, form the ball and socket of the shoulder joint. The upper limbs also include the ULNA, which forms the elbow joint with the humerus, and the RADIUS, which allows the turning movement at the wrist.

The WRIST JOINT is formed out of the forearm bones and the eight CARPAL bones, which themselves are connected with the five METACARPALS. Together, these structures form the bones of the hand. The metacarpals connect with the fingers. Each finger is composed of three bones called PHALANGES, except the thumb, which only has two phalanges.

The lower limbs are connected to the axial skeleton by the PELVIC GIRDLE, which includes the left and right hip bones. The hip joint is formed by the hip bone and the

FEMUR, which is the largest bone in the body. On its other end, the femur forms the knee joint with the PATELLA (the kneecap) and the TIBIA, which is one of the bones of the lower leg.

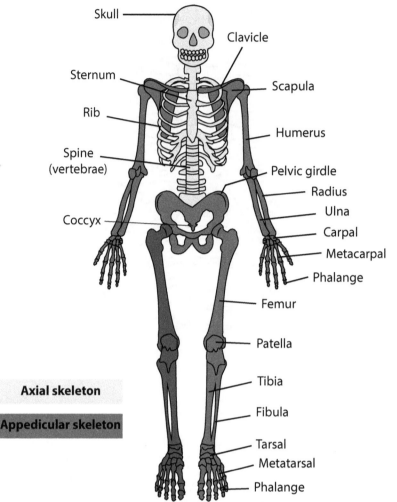

Figure 7.11. The Axial and Appendicular Skeletons

Of the two lower leg bones, the TIBIA is the larger, and it carries the weight of the body. The FIBULA, the other leg bone, serves mostly to anchor the muscle. Together, these two bones form the ankle joint with a foot bone called the TALUS. The talus is one of seven tarsal bones that form the back part of the foot and the heel. They connect to the five long METATARSALS, which form the foot itself and connect to the toes. Each toe is made out of three phalanges, except the big toe, which has only two phalanges.

The Joints

The JOINTS, also known as *articulations*, are where the bones come into contact with each other, with cartilage, or with teeth. There are three types of joints: synovial, fibrous, and cartilaginous joints.

The SYNOVIAL JOINTS feature a small gap between the bones that is filled with synovial fluid, which lubricates the joint. They are the most common joints in the body, and they allow the most movement. **FIBROUS JOINTS**, found where bones fit tightly together, permit little to no movement. These joints also hold teeth in their sockets. In a **CARTILAGINOUS JOINT**, two bones are held together by cartilage; these joints allow more movement than fibrous joints but less than synovial ones.

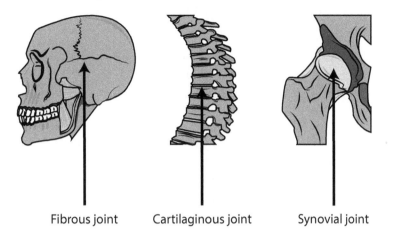

Figure 7.12. Types of Joints

Examples

1. Stem cells are found in which of the following tissues?

    A) red bone marrow

    B) periosteum

    C) compact bones

    D) bone matrix

    Answer:

    A) is correct. Stem cells are found in red bone marrow.

2. Which of the following parts of the skeletal system is formed from long bones?

    A) limbs

    B) thoracic cage

    C) skull

    D) vertebral column

    Answer:

    A) is correct. Long bones are the main bones composing the arms and legs.

THE MUSCULAR SYSTEM

Movement is the main function of the **MUSCULAR SYSTEM**; muscles are attached to the bones in our bodies and allow us to move our limbs. They also work in the heart, blood vessels, and digestive organs, where they facilitate movement of substances through the body. In addition to movement, muscles also help support the body's posture and create heat. There are three types of muscle: visceral, cardiac, and skeletal.

Visceral Muscle

VISCERAL MUSCLE is the weakest type of muscle. It can be found in the stomach, intestines, and blood vessels, where it helps contract and move substances through them. We cannot consciously control visceral muscle—it is controlled by the unconscious part of the brain. That's why it is sometimes referred to as *involuntary muscle*.

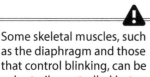

Some skeletal muscles, such as the diaphragm and those that control blinking, can be voluntarily controlled but usually operate involuntarily.

Visceral muscle is also called SMOOTH MUSCLE because of its appearance under the microscope. The cells of the visceral muscle form a smooth surface, unlike the other two types of muscle.

Cardiac Muscle

CARDIAC MUSCLE is only found in the heart; it makes the heart contract and pump blood through the body. Like visceral muscle, cardiac muscle cannot be voluntarily controlled. Unlike visceral muscle, however, the cardiac muscle is quite strong.

Cardiac muscle is composed of individual muscle cells called CARDIOMYOCYTES that are joined together by INTERCALATED DISCS. These discs allow the cells in cardiac muscle to contract in sync. When observed under a microscope, light and dark stripes are visible in the muscle: this pattern is caused by the arrangement of proteins.

Skeletal Muscle

The last type of muscle is SKELETAL MUSCLE, which is the only type of muscle that contracts and relaxes by voluntary action. Skeletal muscle is attached to the bone by tendons. Tendons are formed out of connective tissue rich in collagen fibers.

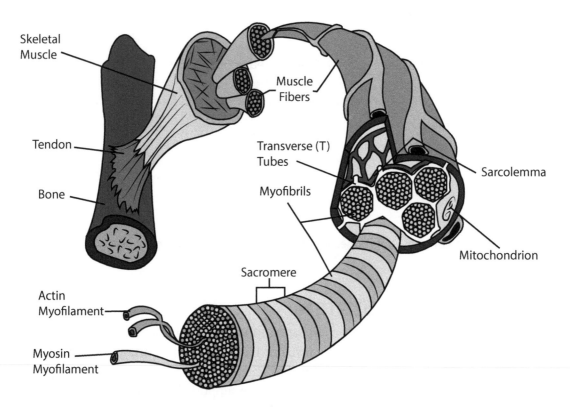

Figure 7.13. The Structure of Skeletal Muscle

Skeletal muscle is made out of cells that are lumped together to form fiber structures. These fibers are covered by a cell membrane called the SARCOLEMMA, which serves as a conductor for electrochemical signals that tell the muscle to contract or expand. The TRANSVERSE TUBES, which are connected to the sarcolemma, transfer the signals deeper into the middle of the muscle fiber.

Calcium ions, which are necessary for muscle contraction, are stored in the SARCOPLASMIC RETICULUM. The fibers are also rich in MITOCHONDRIA, which act as power stations fueled by sugars and provide the energy necessary for the muscle to work. Muscle fibers are mostly made out of MYOFIBRILS, which do the actual contracting. Myofibrils are in turn made out of protein fibers arranged into small subunits called SARCOMERES.

Muscle contraction is explained by the SLIDING FILAMENT THEORY. When the sarcomere is at rest, the thin filaments containing ACTIN are found at both ends of the muscle, while the thick filaments containing MYOSIN are found at the center. Myosin filaments contain "heads," which can attach and detach from actin filaments. The myosin attaches to actin and pulls the thin filaments to the center of the sarcomere, forcing the thin filaments to slide inward and causing the entire sarcomere to shorten, or contract, creating movement. The sarcomere can be broken down into zones that contain certain filaments.

- The **Z-LINE** separates the sarcomeres: a single sarcomere is the distance between two Z-lines.
- The **A-BAND** is the area of the sarcomere in which thick myosin filaments are found and does not shorten during muscular contraction.
- The **I-BAND** is the area in the sarcomere between the thick myosin filaments in which only thin actin filament is found.
- The **H-ZONE** is found between the actin filaments and contains only thick myosin filament.

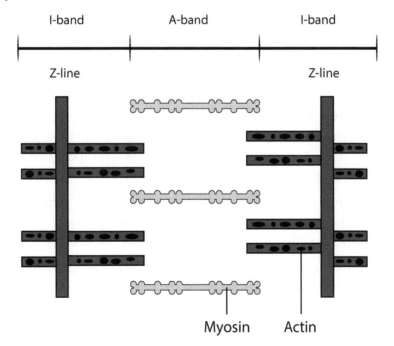

Figure 7.14. Sliding Filament Theory

Skeletal muscle can be divided into two types, according to the way it produces and uses energy. **TYPE I** fibers contract slowly and are used for stamina and posture. They produce energy from sugar using aerobic respiration, making them resistant to fatigue. **TYPE II** muscle fibers contract more quickly. Type IIA fibers are found in the legs, and are weaker and show more endurance than Type IIB fibers, which are found mostly in the arms.

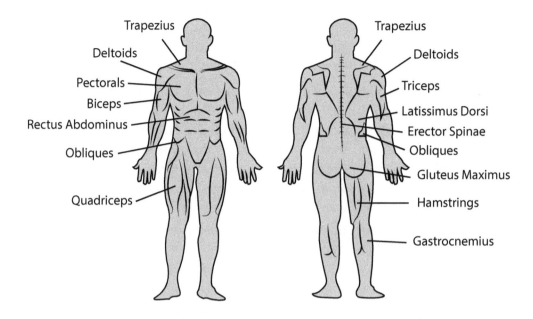

Figure 7.15. Important Skeletal Muscles

Skeletal muscles work by contracting. This shortens the length in their middle part, called the *muscle belly*, which in turn pulls one bone closer to another. The bone that remains stationary is called the **ORIGIN**. The other bone, the one that is actually moving toward the other, is called the **INSERTION**.

Skeletal muscles usually work in groups. The muscle mainly responsible for the action is called the **AGONIST**, and it is always paired with another muscle that does the opposite action, called the **ANTAGONIST**. For example, the biceps are the agonist when the elbow is flexed—they contract to pull the lower arm up. The triceps are the antagonist and remain relaxed. When the elbow is extended, the opposite is true—the triceps are the agonist and the biceps are the antagonist.

Other muscles that support the agonist include **SYNERGISTS**, which are found near the agonist, attach to the same bones, stabilize the movement, and reduce unnecessary movement. **FIXATORS** are other support muscles that keep the origin stable.

There are several different ways to name the more than 600 skeletal muscles found in the human body. Muscles can be named according to:

- the region of the body in which they are located (e.g., transverse abdominis)
- number of origins (e.g., biceps)
- bones to which they are attached (e.g., occipitofrontalis)
- function (e.g., flexor)
- relative size (e.g., gluteus maximus)

Motor Neurons and Contractions

The neurons that control muscles are called MOTOR NEURONS. Motor neurons control a number of muscle cells that together are called the MOTOR UNIT. The number of cells in the motor unit is larger in big muscles that need more strength, like those in the arms and legs. In small muscles where precision is more important than strength, like the muscles in fingers and around the eyes, the number of cells in motor units is smaller.

When signaled by motor neurons, muscles can contract in several different ways:

- Isotonic muscle contractions produce movement.
- Isometric muscle contractions maintain posture and stillness.
- Muscle tone is naturally occurring constant semi-contraction of the muscle.
- Twitch contraction is a short contraction caused by a single, short nerve impulse.
- Temporal summation is a phenomenon in which a few short impulses delivered over time build up the muscle contraction in strength and duration.
- Tetanus is a state of constant contraction caused by many rapid short impulses.

Muscle Metabolism

There are two ways muscles get energy: through aerobic respiration, which is most effective, and through LACTIC ACID FERMENTATION, which is a type of anaerobic respiration. The latter is less effective and it only happens when blood cannot get into the muscle due to very strong or prolonged contraction.

In both these methods, the goal is to produce ADENOSINE TRIPHOSPHATE (ATP) from glucose. ATP is the most important energy molecule for our bodies. During its conversion to ADENOSINE DIPHOSPHATE (ADP), energy is released.

Muscles also use other molecules to help in the production of energy. MYOGLOBIN stores oxygen, allowing muscles to use aerobic respiration even when there is no blood coming into the muscles. CREATINE PHOSPHATE creates ATP by giving its phosphate group to the energy-depleted adenosine diphosphate. Lastly, muscles use GLYCOGEN, a large molecule made out of several glucose molecules, which helps muscles make ATP.

When it runs out of energy, a muscle goes into a state called MUSCLE FATIGUE. This means it contains little to no oxygen, ATP, or glucose, and that it has high levels of lactic acid and ADP. When a muscle is fatigued, it needs more oxygen to replace the oxygen used up from myoglobin sources, and to rebuild its other energy supplies.

Examples

1. Which of the following types of muscle is found in blood vessels?

   A) cardiac muscle

   B) visceral muscle

   C) Type I muscle fibers

   D) Type II muscle fibers

   Answer:

   B) is correct. Blood is moved through blood vessels by visceral, or smooth, muscle that cannot be voluntarily controlled.

2. Which of the following processes are performed by myofibrils?

A) sugar storage

B) electrochemical communication

C) lactic acid fermentation

D) muscle contractions

Answer:

D) is correct. Myofibrils are the muscle fibers that contract.

THE NERVOUS SYSTEM

The **NERVOUS SYSTEM** consists of the brain, the spinal cord, the nerves, and the sensory organs. This system is responsible for gathering, processing, and reacting to information from both inside and outside of the body. It is divided into two parts: the central nervous system and the peripheral nervous system. The **CENTRAL NERVOUS SYSTEM** (**CNS**) is made of the brain and spinal cord and is responsible for processing and storing information, as well as deciding on the appropriate action and issuing commands.

The **PERIPHERAL NERVOUS SYSTEM** (**PNS**) is responsible for gathering information, transporting it to the CNS, and then transporting commands from the CNS to the appropriate organs. Sensory organs and nerves do the gathering and transporting of information, while the efferent nerves transport the commands.

Nervous System Cells

The nervous system is mostly made out of nervous tissue, which in turn consists of two classes of cells: neurons and neuralgia. **NEURONS** are the nerve cells. They can be divided into several distinct parts. The **SOMA** is the body of the neuron; it contains most of the cellular organelles. **DENDRITES** are small, treelike structures that extend from the soma. Their main responsibility is to carry information to the soma, and sometimes away from it. Also extending from the soma is the long, thin **AXON**. There is usually one axon per soma, but the axon can branch out farther. It is responsible for sending information from the soma, rarely to it. Lastly, the places where two neurons meet, or where they meet other types of cells, are called **SYNAPSES**.

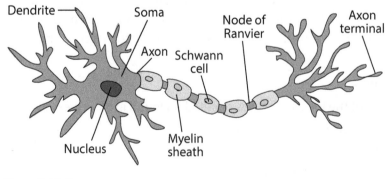

Figure 7.16. Neuron

NEUROGLIA are the maintenance cells for neurons. Neurons are so specialized that they almost never reproduce. Therefore, they need the neuroglial cells, a number of which surround every neuron, to protect and feed them. Neuroglia are also called the GLIAL CELLS.

In the peripheral nervous system, the primary glial cell is a SCHWANN CELL. Schwann cells secrete a fatty substance called MYELIN that wraps around the neuron and allows much faster transmission of the electrical signal the neuron is sending. Gaps in the myelin sheath are called NODES OF RANVIER.

Protecting the Central Nervous System (CNS)

The CNS consists of the brain and spinal cord. Both are placed within cavities in protective skeletal structures: the brain is housed in the cranial cavity of the skull, and the spinal cord is enclosed in the vertebral cavity in the spine. The BRAIN serves as the control system for the nervous system, while the SPINAL CORD carries signals and processes some reflexes to stimuli.

Since the organs that form the CNS are vital to our survival, they are also protected by two other important structures: the meninges and the cerebrospinal fluid. The MENINGES are a protective covering of the CNS made up of three distinct layers. The first is the DURA MATER, which, as its name suggests, is the most durable, outer part of the meninges. It is made out of collagen fibers—rich and thick connective tissue—and it forms a space for the cerebrospinal fluid around the CNS.

Next is the ARACHNOID MATER, which is the thin lining on the inner side of the dura mater. It forms many tiny fibers that connect the dura mater with the next layer, the PIA MATER, which is separated from the arachnoid mater by the SUBARACHNOID SPACE. The pia mater directly covers the surface of the brain and spinal cord, and it provides sustenance to the nervous tissue through its many blood vessels.

The subarachnoid space is filled with CEREBROSPINAL FLUID (CSF), a clear fluid formed from blood plasma. CSF can also be found in the ventricles (the hollow spaces in the brain) and in the central canal (a cavity found in the middle of the spinal cord).

As the CNS floats in the cerebrospinal fluid, it appears lighter than it really is. This is especially important for the brain, because the fluid keeps it from being crushed by its own weight. The floating also protects the brain and the spinal cord from shock—like sudden movements and trauma. Additionally, the CSF contains the necessary chemical substance for the normal functioning of the nervous tissue, and it removes the cellular waste from the neurons.

The Brain

The nervous tissue that makes up the brain is divided into two classes. The GRAY MATTER, which consists mostly of interneurons that are unmyelinated, is the tissue where the actual processing of signals happens. It is also where the connections between neurons are made. The WHITE MATTER, which consists mostly of myelinated neurons, is the tissue that conducts signals to, from, and between the gray matter regions.

The brain can be divided into three distinct parts: the forebrain (prosencephalon), the midbrain (mesencephalon), and the hindbrain (rhombencephalon).

The **FOREBRAIN** is broken down into two more regions: the cerebrum and the diencephalon. The **CEREBRUM** is the outermost and largest part of the brain. It is divided through the middle by the longitudinal fissure into the left and the right hemisphere, each of which is further divided into four lobes: the frontal, parietal, temporal, and occipital. The two hemispheres are connected by a bundle of white matter called the **CORPUS CALLOSUM**.

The surface of the cerebrum, called the **CEREBRAL CORTEX**, is made out of gray matter with characteristic **SULCI** (grooves) and **GYRI** (bulges). The cerebral cortex is where the actual processing happens in the cerebrum: it is responsible for the higher brain functions like thinking and using language.

The **DIENCEPHALON** is a structure formed by the thalamus, hypothalamus, and the pineal gland. The **THALAMUS**, composed of two gray matter masses, routes the sensory signals to the correct parts of the cerebral cortex. The hypothalamus and the pineal gland are both endocrine glands.

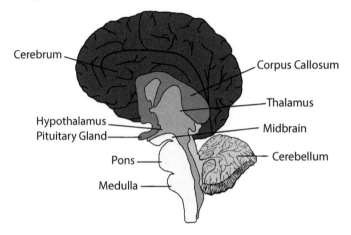

Figure 7.17. The Brain

The **MIDBRAIN** is the topmost part of the brain stem. It is involved in reflex reactions to visual and auditory information, muscle movement, reward-seeking, and learning.

The **HINDBRAIN** consists of the brain stem and the cerebellum. The brain stem is further broken down into the medulla oblongata and the pons. The **MEDULLA OBLONGATA** is mostly made out of white matter, but it also contains gray matter that processes involuntary body functions like blood pressure, level of oxygen in the blood, and reflexes like sneezing. The **PONS** is in charge of transporting signals to and from the cerebellum, and between the upper regions of the brain, the medulla, and the spinal cord.

The **CEREBELLUM** looks like a smaller version of the cerebrum—it has two spheres and is wrinkled. The cerebellum's role is to control and coordinate complex muscle activities; it also helps maintain posture and balance.

Peripheral Nervous System (PNS)

The nerves that form the **PERIPHERAL NERVOUS SYSTEM** (**PNS**) are made of bundled axons whose role is to carry signals to and from the spinal cord and the brain. A single axon, covered with a layer of connective tissue called the **ENDONEURIUM**, bundles with other axons to form **FASCICLES**. These are covered with another sheath of connective tissue called the **PERINEURIUM**. Groups of fascicles wrapped together in another layer of connective tissue, the **EPINEURIUM**, form a whole nerve.

There are five types of peripheral nerves.

1. **EFFERENT NEURONS** (also called motor neurons) signal effector cells in muscles and glands to react to stimuli.

2. **AFFERENT NEURONS** (also called sensory neurons) take in information from inside and outside the body through the sensory organs and receptors.

3. **INTERNEURONS** transmit information to the CNS where it is evaluated, compared to previously stored information, stored or discarded, and used to make a decision (a process called integration).

4. **SPINAL NERVES**—thirty-one pairs in total—extend from the side of the spinal cord. They exit the spinal cord between the vertebrae, and they carry information to and from the spinal cord and the neck, the arms, the legs, and the trunk. Spinal nerves are grouped and named according to the region they originate from: eight pairs of cervical, twelve pairs of thoracic, five pairs of lumbar, five pairs of sacral, and one pair of coccygeal nerves.

5. **CRANIAL NERVES**—twelve pairs in total—extend from the lower side of the brain. They are identified by their number, and they connect the brain with the sensory organs, head muscles, neck and shoulder muscles, the heart, and the gastrointestinal track.

The Divisions of the Peripheral Nervous System

The PNS is divided into two parts based on our ability to exert conscious control. The part of the PNS we can consciously control is the **SOMATIC NERVOUS SYSTEM** (**SNS**), which stimulates the skeletal muscles. The **AUTONOMIC NERVOUS SYSTEM** (**ANS**) cannot be consciously controlled; it stimulates the visceral and cardiac muscle, as well as the glandular tissue.

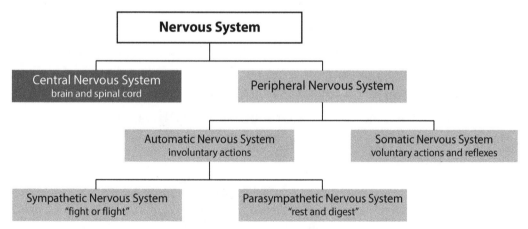

Figure 7.18. Divisions of the Nervous System

The ANS itself is further divided into the sympathetic, parasympathetic, and enteric nervous systems. The **SYMPATHETIC NERVOUS SYSTEM** forms the *fight-or-flight* reaction to stimuli like emotion, danger, and exercise. It increases respiration and heart rate, decreases digestion, and releases stress hormones. The **PARASYMPATHETIC NERVOUS SYSTEM** is responsible for stimulating activities that occur when the body is at rest, including digestion and sexual arousal.

The *fight-or-flight* reaction includes accelerated breathing and heart rate, dilation of blood vessels in muscles, release of energy molecules for use by muscles, relaxation of the bladder, and slowing or stopping movement in the upper digestive tract.

Lastly, the ENTERIC NERVOUS SYSTEM is responsible for the digestive system and its processes. This system works mostly independently from the CNS, although it can be regulated through the sympathetic and parasympathetic systems.

Examples

1. Which of the following parts of a neuron is responsible for carrying information away from the cell?

   A) soma

   B) axon

   C) dendrite

   D) myelin

   Answer:

   B) is correct. The axon carries information away from the soma, or body of the cell.

2. Which of the following neurons signals muscles to contract?

   A) efferent neuron

   B) afferent neurons

   C) interneurons

   D) efferent and afferent neurons

   Answer:

   A) is correct. Efferent neurons signal muscles to contract.

THE DIGESTIVE SYSTEM

The DIGESTIVE SYSTEM is a system of organs in the body that is responsible for the intake and processing of food and the removal of food waste products. The digestive system ensures that the body has the nutrients and the energy it needs to function.

The digestive system includes the GASTROINTESTINAL (GI) TRACT, which consists of the organs through which food passes on its way through the body:

1. oral cavity
2. pharynx
3. esophagus
4. stomach
5. small intestines
6. large intestines

Throughout the digestive system there are also organs that have a role in processing food, even though food does not pass through them directly. These include the teeth, tongue, salivary glands, liver, gallbladder, and pancreas.

The Mouth

The digestive system begins with the **ORAL CAVITY**, also known as the **MOUTH**. The mouth contains other organs that play a role in digestion. The **TEETH** are small organs that cut and grind food. They are located on the edges of the mouth, are made out of dentin, which is a substance that resembles bone, and are covered by enamel. The teeth are very hard organs, and each of them has its own blood vessels and nerves, which are located in the matter that fills the tooth, called the pulp.

Also in the mouth is the **TONGUE**, which is a muscle located behind the teeth. The tongue contains the taste buds and moves food around the mouth as it is processed by the teeth. It then moves food toward the pharynx in order to swallow. The **SALIVARY GLANDS**, located around the mouth, produce saliva. There are three pairs of salivary glands, and the saliva they produce lubricates and digests carbohydrates.

The Pharynx

The **PHARYNX** is a tube that enables the passage of food and air further into the body. This structure performs two functions. The pharynx needs the help of the epiglottis, which allows food to pass to the esophagus by covering the opening of the larynx, a structure that carries air into the lungs. When you need to breathe in, the esophagus is closed, so the air passes only into the larynx.

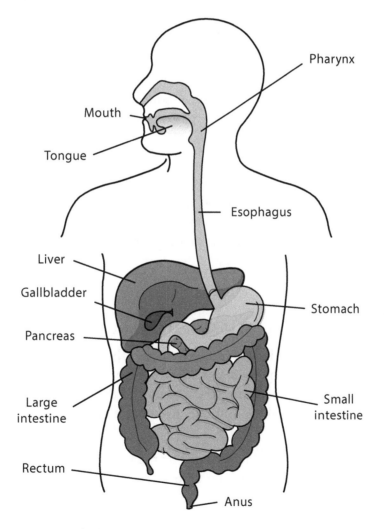

Figure 7.19. The Digestive System

The Esophagus

The ESOPHAGUS begins at the pharynx and continues to carry food all the way to the stomach. The esophagus is a muscular tube, and the muscles in its wall help to push food down. During vomiting, it pushes food up.

The esophagus has two rings of muscle, called SPHINCTERS. These sphincters close at the top and the bottom ends of the esophagus when food is not passing through it. Heartburn occurs when the bottom sphincter cannot close entirely and allows the contents of the stomach to enter the esophagus.

The Stomach

The stomach is a round organ located on the left side of the body just beneath the diaphragm. It is divided into four different regions. The CARDIA connects the stomach to the esophagus, transitioning from the tube-like shape of the esophagus into the sack shape of the rest of the stomach. The cardia is also where the lower sphincter of the esophagus is located.

The BODY of the stomach is its largest part, and the FUNDUS is located above the body. The last part of the stomach is the PYLORUS, a funnel-shaped region located beneath the body of the stomach. It controls the passage of partially digested food further down the GI tract through the PYLORIC SPHINCTER.

The stomach is made out of four layers of tissue. The innermost layer, the MUCOSA, contains a smooth muscle and the mucus membrane that secretes digestive enzymes and hydrochloric acid. The cells that secrete these products are located within the small pores called the GASTRIC PITS. The mucus membrane also secretes mucus to protect the stomach from its own digestive enzymes.

The SUBMUCOSA is located around the mucosa and is made of connective tissue; it contains nerves and blood vessels. The MUSCULARIS layer enables the movement of the stomach; it is made up of three layers of smooth muscle. The outermost layer of the stomach is the SEROSA. It secretes SEROUS FLUID that keeps the stomach wet and reduces friction between the stomach and the surrounding organs.

The Small Intestine

The SMALL INTESTINE continues from the stomach and takes up most of the space in the abdomen. Attached to the wall of the abdomen, it measures around twenty-two feet long.

The small intestine can be divided into three parts. The DUODENUM is the part of the small intestine that receives the food and chemicals from the stomach. The JEJUNUM, which continues from the duodenum, is where most of the nutrients are absorbed into the blood. Lastly, the ILEUM, which continues from the jejunum, is where the rest of the nutrients are absorbed.

Absorption in the small intestine is helped by the VILLI, which are small protrusions that increase the surface area available for absorption. The villi are made out of smaller microvilli.

The Liver and Gallbladder

The **LIVER** is not a part of the GI tract. However, it performs roles that are vital for digestion and life itself. It is involved in detoxification of the blood, storage of nutrients, and production of components of blood plasma. Its role in digestion is to produce **BILE**, a fluid that aids in the digestion of fats. After its production, bile is carried through the bile ducts to the **GALLBLADDER**, a small, muscular, pear-shaped organ that stores and releases bile.

The liver is located just beneath the diaphragm and is the largest organ in the body after the skin. Triangular in shape, it extends across the whole width of the abdomen. It is divided into four lobes: the left lobe, the right lobe, the caudate lobe (which wraps around the inferior vena cava), and the quadrate lobe (which wraps around the gallbladder).

The Pancreas

The **PANCREAS** is another organ that is not part of the GI tract but which plays a role in digestion. It is located below and to the left of the stomach. The pancreas secretes both the enzymes that digest food and the hormones *insulin* and *glucagon*, which control blood sugar levels.

The pancreas is known as a **HETEROCRINE GLAND**, which means it contains both endocrine tissue, which produces insulin and glucagon that move directly into the bloodstream, and exocrine tissue, which produces digestive enzymes that pass into the small intestine. These enzymes include:

- pancreatic amylase that breaks large polysaccharides into smaller sugars
- trypsin, chymotrypsin, and carboxypeptidase that break down proteins into amino acid subunits
- pancreatic lipase that breaks down large fat molecules into fatty acids and monoglycerides
- ribonuclease and deoxyribonuclease that digest nucleic acids

The Large Intestine

The **LARGE INTESTINE** continues from the small intestine and loops around it. No digestion actually takes place in the large intestine. Rather, it absorbs water and some leftover vitamins. The large intestine carries waste (*feces*) to the **RECTUM**, where it is stored until it is expelled through the **ANUS**.

Examples

1. Which of the following organs does food NOT pass through as part of digestion?

   A) stomach

   B) large intestine

   C) esophagus

   D) liver

   Answer:

   D) is correct. The liver is an accessory organ of the digestive system: it produces fluids that aid in digestion, but food does not pass through it.

2. Which layer of the stomach contains blood vessels and nerves?

  A) the mucosa

  B) the submucosa

  C) the serosa

  D) the cardia

Answer:

B) is correct. The submucosa, which surrounds the inner mucosa layer, contains the blood vessels and nerves that serve the stomach.

THE IMMUNE SYSTEM

The immune system is primarily responsible for acting as a line of defense against pathogens that enter the body. PATHOGENS are any foreign substances that cause disease or infection, including microbes such as viruses, bacteria, and fungi. Most microorganisms are harmless; however, there are still many that can cause disease by dissolving, blocking, or destroying human cells. The immune system works both by keeping pathogens out and by destroying pathogens that do enter the body.

The immune system is divided into the innate and adaptive systems. The innate system uses nonspecific defenses to prevent diseases while the adaptive system targets specific pathogens.

The Innate Immune System

The INNATE IMMUNE SYSTEM uses nonspecific defenses that target any microorganism or injured cell that could pose a pathogenic threat to the body. The body's first line of defense are physical barriers: the skin acts as a barrier to pathogens, and cilia, tears, mucus, and saliva trap pathogens that enter the body via the mouth, eyes, or nose.

INFLAMMATION is initiated by the innate immune system as a response to pathogens that enter the body. When body tissue is injured or damaged, the localized tissue surrounding the damage releases HISTAMINES that raise the temperature and increase blood flow into the area in order to stimulate more neutrophils, a type of white blood cell, to enter the tissue for repair. Other innate responses include ANTIMICROBIAL PEPTIDES, which destroy bacteria by interfering with the functions of their membranes or DNA, and INTERFERON, which causes nearby cells to increase their defenses.

Fever is another innate response to potential infection. This occurs when pathogens enter and affect the body in multiple locations, triggering the release of enough histamines to raise the overall body temperature in response. Low to moderate fevers are beneficial to the immune system, killing any pathogens that are negatively impacting the body.

The Adaptive Immune System

The body's ADAPTIVE IMMUNE SYSTEM specifically targets pathogens and attacks them based on their specific properties. These properties are expressed by ANTIGENS—substances that exist on the surface of pathogenic cells that the immune system does not recognize. When antigens are detected on a foreign substance, the immune system is triggered to attack the cell. The series of events that occurs next is collectively referred to as the IMMUNE RESPONSE.

Immune responses are performed by two distinct kinds of white blood cells called LYMPHOCYTES. T-CELLS are the first type of lymphocyte that detects antigens. After a phagocyte ingests a pathogen cell, T-cells are alerted to the presence of antigens that now exist in the phagocyte membrane. T-cells rapidly divide and form different kinds of T-cells that perform different functions. HELPER T-CELLS are activated to seek out and bind to the antigen. These helper T-cells are known as the coordinators of immune response due to their ability to stimulate one of two different kinds of immune responses.

Helper T-cells can stimulate CYTOTOXIC T-CELLS to actively destroy the infected cells in a CELL-MEDIATED RESPONSE. This response differs from a nonspecific response because the cytotoxic cells bind to the targeted cell's surface in order to kill it.

Helper T-cells can also stimulate the production of **B-cells** in order to trigger an ANTIBODY-MEDIATED RESPONSE. Two kinds of B-cells arise in this response: plasma cells and memory cells. Rather than respond by killing the cell, the PLASMA CELLS produce ANTIBODIES, proteins that bind to the antigen to neutralize it and stimulate phagocytes to ingest the entire structure. The MEMORY CELLS then store the information for producing the antibody and are quickly sprung into action if and when the same antigen appears in the body. This resistance to a now-known pathogen is called IMMUNITY.

> Memory B-cells are the underlying mechanisms behind vaccines, which introduce a harmless version of a pathogen into the body to activate the body's adaptive immune response.

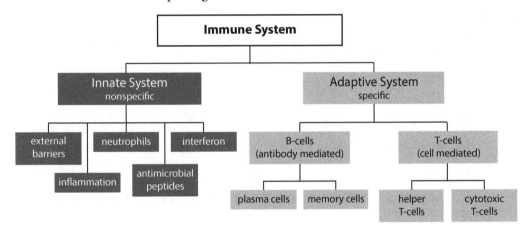

Figure 7.20. Divisions of the Immune System

White Blood Cells

WHITE BLOOD CELLS (WBCs), also called LEUKOCYTES, are an integral part of both the innate and adaptive immune systems. There are two classes of white blood cells: granular and agranular leukocytes. GRANULAR LEUKOCYTES are divided into three types: the neutrophils that digest bacteria, the eosinophils that digest viruses, and the basophils that release histamine. AGRANULAR LEUKOCYTES are divided into two classes: the lymphocytes, which fight off viral infections and produce antibodies for fighting pathogen-induced infection, and the monocytes, which play a role in removing pathogens and dead cells from wounds.

> In humans, white blood cells are produced by the endocrine system and are transported through the cardiovascular and lymphatic systems. In what other ways do organ systems work together to prevent disease?

Table 7.2. Types of White Blood Cells

TYPE OF CELL	NAME OF CELL	ROLE	INNATE OR ADAPTIVE?	PREVALENCE
Granulocyte	Neutrophil	first responders that quickly migrate to the site of infections to destroy bacterial invaders	innate	very common
	Eosinophil	attack multicellular parasites	innate	rare
	Basophil	large cell responsible for inflammatory reactions, including allergies	innate	very rare
Lymphocyte	B-cell	respond to antigens by releasing antibodies	adaptive	
	T-cell	respond to antigens by destroying invaders and infected cells	adaptive	common
	Natural killer cell	destroy virus-infected cells and tumor cells	innate and adaptive	
Monocyte	Macrophage	engulf and destroy microbes, foreign substances, and cancer cells	innate and adaptive	rare

Examples

1. Which of the following immune system processes is NOT considered a nonspecific defense of the innate immune system?

   A) fever

   B) inflammation

   C) phagocyte production

   D) antibody production

   Answer:

   D) is correct. Antibodies are produced by B-cells as part of an adaptive immunity response.

2. Which of the following types of cells coordinates both cell-mediated and antibody-mediated responses?

   A) helper T-cells

   B) memory cells

   C) B-cells

   D) phagocytes

   Answer:

   A) is correct. Helper T-cells are lymphocytes that attach to antigens and can trigger either cell-mediated or antibody-mediated responses.

THE ENDOCRINE SYSTEM

The **ENDOCRINE SYSTEM** consists of many **GLANDS** that produce and secrete hormones, which send signals to molecules that are traveling through the bloodstream. **HORMONES** allow cells, tissues, and organs to communicate with each other. Hormones play a role in almost all bodily functions, including growth, sleeping, digestion, response to stress, and sexual functioning. The glands of the endocrine system are scattered throughout the body, and each has a specific role to play.

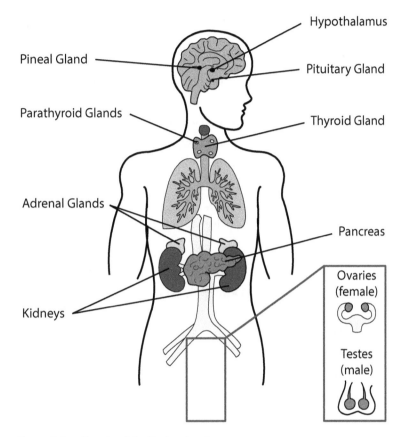

Figure 7.21. Glands of the Endocrine System

- The **PITUITARY GLAND** hangs from the base of your brain and produces the hormone which controls growth and some aspects of sexual functioning. (Hormones produced: growth hormone, thyroid-stimulating hormone, oxytocin, follicle-stimulating hormone)

- The **HYPOTHALAMUS** is also located in the brain. Its main function is to control the pituitary gland, and many of the hormones it releases stimulate the pituitary gland to in turn release hormones itself. (Hormones produced: dopamine, thyrotropin-releasing hormone, growth-hormone–releasing hormone)

- The **PINEAL GLAND**, located in the brain, releases melatonin, a hormone that induces drowsiness and lowers body temperature. (Hormone produced: melatonin)

- The **THYROID GLAND** is found in the neck just below the Adam's apple. It controls protein production and the body's use of energy. The thyroid is regulated by the thyroid-stimulating hormone, which is released by the pituitary gland. (Hormones produced: T3 and thyroxine)

- The four PARATHYROID GLANDS are located on the back of the thyroid. They produce parathyroid hormone, which regulates calcium and phosphate levels in the body. (Hormone produced: parathyroid hormone)

- The PANCREAS, discussed above, is located behind the stomach and releases hormones that regulate digestion and blood-sugar levels. (Hormones produced: insulin, glucagon, somatostatin)

- The ADRENAL GLANDS sit atop the kidneys. The adrenal glands have two regions that produce two sets of hormones: the adrenal cortex releases corticosteroids and androgens, while the adrenal medulla regulates the fight-or-flight response. (Hormones produced: cortisol, testosterone, adrenaline, noradrenaline, dopamine)

- The TESTES are glands found in males; they regulate maturation of sex organs and the development of secondary sex characteristics like muscle mass and growth of axillary hair. (Hormones produced: testosterone, estradiol)

- The OVARIES are glands found in females; they regulate the menstrual cycle, pregnancy, and secondary sex characteristics like enlargement of the breasts and the widening of the hips. (Hormones produced: progesterone, estrogen)

Examples

1. Which of the following glands indirectly controls growth by acting on the pituitary gland?

   A) hypothalamus

   B) thyroid gland

   C) adrenal glands

   D) parathyroid glands

   Answer:

   A) is correct. The hypothalamus releases hormones that in turn cause the pituitary gland to release growth-related hormones.

2. Which hormone is primarily responsible for the development of male secondary sexual characteristics?

   A) melatonin

   B) follicle-stimulating hormone

   C) estrogen

   D) testosterone

   Answer:

   D) is correct. Testosterone is produced by the testes, which are only found in males. It is responsible for the development of male secondary sexual characteristics.

3. A patient experiencing symptoms such as kidney stones and arthritis due to a calcium imbalance probably has a disorder of which of the following glands?

   A) hypothalamus

   B) thyroid gland

   C) parathyroid glands

   D) adrenal glands

   Answer:

   C) is correct. The parathyroid glands regulate levels of calcium and phosphate in the body.

THE REPRODUCTIVE SYSTEM

Reproductive systems are the groups of organs that enable the successful reproduction of a species. In humans, fertilization is internal, with sperm being transferred from the male to the female during copulation.

The Male Reproductive System

The male reproductive system consists of the organs that produce and ejaculate SPERM, the male gamete. Sperm are produced in the TESTES, specifically in bodies called SEMINIFEROUS TUBULES; mature sperm are stored in the EPIDIDYMIS. The testes are housed in the SCROTUM, located under the PENIS.

During sexual arousal, the VAS DEFERENS carry sperm to the URETHRA, the tube which runs through the penis and carries semen (and urine) out of the body. Along the way, the sperm is joined by fluids from three glands to form SEMEN. The SEMINAL VESICLES secrete the bulk of the fluid which makes up semen, which is

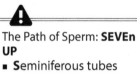

The Path of Sperm: **SEVEn UP**

- **S**eminiferous tubes
- **E**pididymis
- **V**as deferens
- **E**jaculatory duct
- **U**rethra
- **P**enis

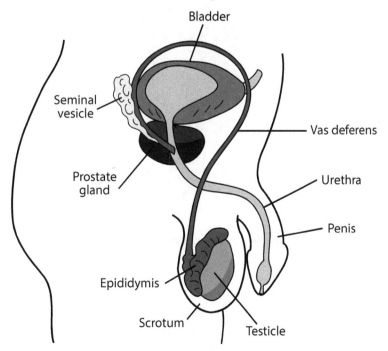

Figure 7.22. The Male Reproductive System

composed of various proteins, sugars, and enzymes. The **PROSTATE** contributes an alkaline fluid that counteracts the acidity of the vaginal tract. Finally, the **COWPER'S GLANDS** secrete a protein-rich fluid that acts as a lubricant.

The main hormone associated with the male reproductive system is **TESTOSTERONE**, which is released by the testes (and in the adrenal glands in much smaller amounts). Testosterone is responsible for the development of the male reproductive system and male secondary sexual characteristics, including muscle development and facial hair growth.

The Female Reproductive System

Sexual reproduction in animals occurs in cycles that depend on the production of an **OVULE**, or egg, by the female of the species. In humans, the reproductive cycle occurs approximately once a month, when an egg is released from the female's ovaries.

The female reproductive organs, or gonads, are called **OVARIES**. Each ovary has a follicle that contains **OOCYTES**, or undeveloped eggs. The surrounding cells in the ovary help to protect and nourish the oocyte until it is needed. During the menstrual cycle, one or more oocytes will mature into an egg with help from the **CORPUS LUTEUM**, a mass of follicular tissue that provides nutrients to the egg and secretes estradiol and progesterone.

> ✔
> What type of muscle is most likely found in the uterus?

Once it has matured, the egg will be released into the **FALLOPIAN TUBE**, where fertilization will take place if sperm are present. The egg will then travel into the **UTERUS**. Unfertilized eggs are shed along with the uterine lining during **MENSTRUATION**. Fertilized eggs, known as **ZYGOTES**, implant in the lining of the uterus where they continue to develop.

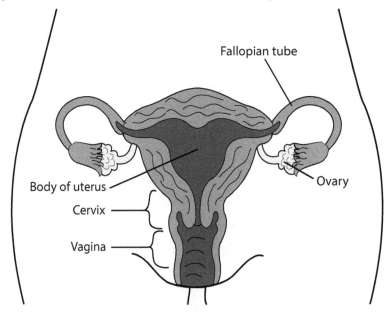

Figure 7.23. The Female Reproductive System

Embryo Fertilization and Development

After fertilization, the cell will start to divide and, after four to five days, become a ball of cells known as a **BLASTOCYST**. The blastocyst is then implanted into the **ENDOMETRIUM** of the uterus. After the blastocyst has been implanted into the endometrium, the placenta develops. The PLACENTA is a temporary organ that attaches the embryo to the mother; it provides nutrients to the fetus, carries waste away from the fetus, protects the fetus from infection, and produces hormones that support pregnancy. The placenta develops from cells called the TROPHOBLAST, which come from the outer layer of the blastocyst.

In humans, the gestation period of the EMBRYO (also called the FETUS), is 266 days or roughly 8.8 months. The human development cycle in the womb is divided into three trimesters. In the first trimester, the organs responsible for the embryo's growth develop. These include the placenta and umbilical cord. During this time, ORGANOGENESIS occurs, and the various stem cells from the blastocyst differentiate into the organs of the body. The organs are not fully developed at this point, but they do exist.

In the second trimester, the fetus experiences rapid growth, up to about twenty-five to thirty centimeters in length. At this point, it is usually apparent that the woman is pregnant, as the uterus grows and extends, and the woman's belly becomes slightly distended. In the third trimester, the fetus finishes developing. The baby exits the uterus through the CERVIX and leaves the body through the VAGINA.

Examples

1. Which of the following organs does NOT contribute material to semen?

    A) the prostate

    B) the Cowper's glands

    C) the penis

    D) the testes

    Answer:

    C) is correct. Semen travels through the penis to exit the body, but the penis does not itself produce any material to contribute to semen.

2. Fertilization typically takes place in the:

    A) fallopian tube

    B) ovaries

    C) uterus

    D) cervix

    Answer:

    A) is correct. Fertilization take place when a sperm enters an egg in the fallopian tube.

THE GENITOURINARY SYSTEM

The URINARY SYSTEM excretes water and waste from the body and is crucial for maintaining the body's electrolyte balance (the balance of water and salt in the blood). Because many organs function as part of both the reproductive and urinary systems, the two are sometimes referred to collectively as the GENITOURINARY SYSTEM.

The main organs of the urinary system are the KIDNEYS, which filter waste from the blood; maintain the electrolyte balance in the blood; and regulate blood volume, pressure, and pH. The kidneys also function as an endocrine organ and release several important hormones. These include RENIN, which regulates blood pressure, and CALCITRIOL, the active form of vitamin D. The kidney is divided into two regions: the RENAL CORTEX, which is the outermost layer, and the RENAL MEDULLA, which is the inner layer.

The functional unit of the kidney is the NEPHRON, which is a series of looping tubes that filter electrolytes, metabolic waste, and other water-soluble waste molecules from the blood. These wastes include UREA, which is a nitrogenous byproduct of protein catabolism, and URIC ACID, a byproduct of nucleic acid metabolism. Together, these waste products are excreted from the body in URINE.

Filtration begins in a network of capillaries called a GLOMERULUS which is located in the renal cortex of each kidney. This waste is then funneled into COLLECTING DUCTS in the renal medulla. From the collecting ducts, urine passes through the RENAL PELVIS and then through two long tubes called URETERS.

The two ureters drain into the urinary bladder, which holds up to 1,000 milliliters of liquid. The bladder exit is controlled by two sphincters, both of which must open for urine to pass. The internal sphincter is made of smooth involuntary muscle, while the external sphincter can be voluntarily controlled. In males, the external sphincter also closes to prevent movement of seminal fluid into the bladder during sexual activity.

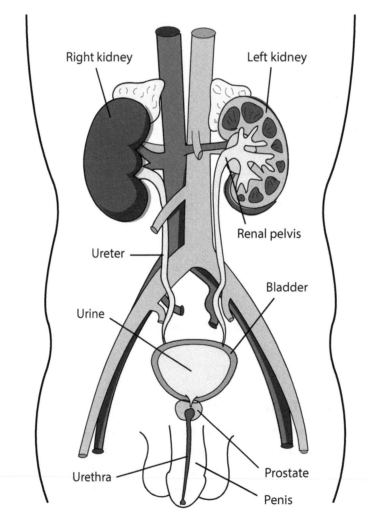

Figure 7.24. The Male Genitourinary System

Urine exits the bladder through the URETHRA. In males, the urethra goes through the penis and also carries semen. In females, the much shorter urethra ends just above the vaginal opening.

Examples

1. Which of the following is the outermost layer of the kidney?

   A) renal cortex

   B) renal medulla

   C) renal pelvis

   D) nephron

   Answer:

   A) is correct. The outermost layer of the kidney is the renal cortex.

2. Which of the following organs holds urine before it passes into the urethra?

   A) prostate

   B) kidney

   C) ureter

   D) urinary bladder

   Answer:

   D) is correct. The urinary bladder holds urine before it passes to the urethra to be excreted.

THE INTEGUMENTARY SYSTEM

The INTEGUMENTARY SYSTEM refers to the skin (the largest organ in the body) and related structures, including the hair and nails. Skin is composed of three layers. The EPIDERMIS is the outermost layer of the skin. This waterproof layer contains no blood vessels and acts mainly to protect the body. Under the epidermis lies the DERMIS, which consists of dense connective tissue that allows skin to stretch and flex. The dermis is home to blood vessels, glands, and HAIR FOLLICLES. The HYPODERMIS is a layer of fat below the dermis that stores energy (in the form of fat) and acts as a cushion for the body. The hypodermis is sometimes called the SUBCUTANEOUS LAYER.

The skin has several important roles. It acts as a barrier to protect the body from injury, the intrusion of foreign particles, and the loss of water and nutrients. It is also important for THERMOREGULATION. Blood vessels near the surface of the skin can dilate, allowing for higher blood flow and the release of heat. They can also constrict to reduce the amount of blood that travels near the surface of the skin, which helps conserve heat. Finally, the skin produces vitamin D when exposed to sunlight.

Because the skin covers the whole body, it plays a vital role in allowing organisms to interact with the environment. It is home to nerve endings that sense temperature, pressure, and pain; it also houses glands that help maintain homeostasis. ECCRINE glands, which are located primarily in the palms of the hands and soles of the feet (and to a lesser degree in other areas of the body), release

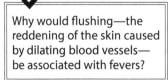

Why would flushing—the reddening of the skin caused by dilating blood vessels—be associated with fevers?

the water and salt (NaCl) mixture called SWEAT. These glands help the body maintain the appropriate salt/water balance. Sweat can also contain small amounts of other substances the body needs to expel, including alcohol, lactic acid, and urea.

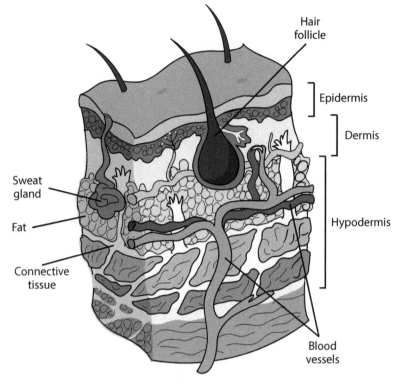

Figure 7.25. The Skin

APOCRINE glands, which are located primarily in the armpit and groin, release an oily substance that contains pheromones. They are also sensitive to adrenaline, and are responsible for most of the sweating that occurs due to stress, fear, anxiety, or pain. Apocrine glands are largely inactive until puberty.

Examples

1. Which of the following is NOT a function of the skin?
   A) regulating body temperature
   B) protecting against injury
   C) producing adrenaline
   D) maintaining water/salt balance

   Answer:

   C) is correct. The skin does not produce adrenaline. (Adrenaline is produced and released by the adrenal glands.)

2. Which of the following is the outermost layer of the skin?

A) hypodermis

B) dermis

C) epidermis

D) apocrine

Answer:

C) is correct. The epidermis is the outermost layer of the skin. It is waterproof and does not contain any blood vessels.

8

PHYSICS

Physics is the science of matter and energy and the interaction between the two. Physics is grouped into fields such as acoustics (the study of sound), optics (the study of light), mechanics (the study of motion), and electromagnetism (the study of electric and magnetic fields).

MECHANICS

Motion

$d = \frac{1}{2}at^2 + v_it$ ($d = vt$ when $a = 0$)

$v_f = v_i + at$

$v_f^2 = v_i^2 + 2ad$

Newtonian mechanics is the study of masses in motion using five main variables. **MASS** (m) is the amount of matter in an object; it is measured in kilograms (kg). **DISPLACEMENT** (d) is a measure of how far an object has moved from its starting point, usually given in meters (m). **VELOCITY** is the distance covered by an object over a given period of **TIME**, usually given in meters per second (m/s). Finally, the change in velocity over time is called **ACCELERATION** (a) and is measured in meters per second squared (m/s²).

m = mass (kg)
d = displacement (m)
v = velocity (m/s)
a = acceleration (m/s²)
t = time (s)

Velocity and displacement are both **VECTORS**, meaning they have a magnitude (e.g., 4 m/s) and a direction (e.g., 45°). **SCALARS**, on the other hand, have only a magnitude. **DISTANCE** is a scalar: it describes how far something has traveled. So, if you run 1000 meters around a track and end up back where you started, your displacement is 0 meters, but the distance you covered was 1000 meters. **SPEED** is also a scalar; it is the distance traveled over the time the trip took.

The motion of objects with uniform acceleration is described by a set of equations that define the relationships between distance, velocity, time, and acceleration. These equations can be used to solve for any of these four variables. When the object is moving in a single dimension, problems can be solved using the following steps:

1. Identify the variables given in the problem and the variable to be solved for.
2. Choose the equation that includes the variables from Step 1.
3. Plug the values from the problem into the equation and solve.

When the object is moving in two dimensions, it's necessary to separate the variables into their horizontal and vertical components because only variables in a single dimension can be used within the same equation. Often, it's necessary to solve for a variable in one dimension and use that value to solve for a variable in the second dimension.

Examples

1. How far will a car moving with a constant velocity of 40 miles per hour travel in 15 minutes?

    A) 2.7 miles

    B) 10 miles

    C) 40 miles

    D) 600 miles

    Answer:

    B) is correct.

    Convert hours to minutes: $\frac{40 \text{ mi.}}{\text{hr}} \times \frac{1 \text{ hr}}{60 \text{ min}} = \frac{2}{3}$ miles per minute

    Use the formula for distance: $d = vt = \left(\frac{2}{3} \text{ mi/min}\right)(15 \text{ min}) = \mathbf{10 \text{ miles}}$

2. A ball is dropped from a building with a height of 20 meters. If there is no air resistance, how long will it take the ball to reach the ground ($g = 9.8$ m/s²)?

    A) 2 seconds

    B) 4 seconds

    C) 5 seconds

    D) 10 seconds

    Answer:

    A) is correct.

    Identify the given variables:

    $d = 20$ m

    $v_i = 0$ m/s

    $a = g = 9.8$ m/s²

    $t = ?$

    Plug the variables into the appropriate formula and solve for time:

    $d = v_i(t) + \frac{1}{2}at^2$

    $20 = 0(t) + \frac{1}{2}(9.8)t^2$

    $t = \sqrt{\frac{20(2)}{9.8}} \approx \mathbf{2 \text{ seconds}}$

Momentum

$p = mv$

$J = \Delta P$

$m_1 v_{1i} + m_2 v_{2i} = m_1 v_{1f} + m_2 v_{2f}$ (elastic collision)

$m_1 v_1 + m_2 v_2 = (m_1 + m_2) v_f$ (inelastic collision)

Multiplying an object's mass by its velocity gives a quantity called **MOMENTUM** (p), which is measured in kilogram meters per second ((kg·m)/s). Momentum is always conserved, meaning when objects collide, the sum of their momentums before the collision will be the same as the sum after (although their kinetic energy may not remain the same). Because momentum is derived from velocity, it is a vector.

$p = $ momentum (kg · m/s)

Examples

1. What is the momentum of an object with a mass of 1.5 kilograms moving with a velocity of 10 meters per second?

   A) 1.5 (kg · m)/s

   B) 15 (kg · m)/s

   C) 150 (kg · m)/s

   D) 1500 (kg · m)/s

   Answer:

   B) is correct.

   Use the formula for momentum: $p = mv = (1.5 \text{ kg})(10 \text{ m/s}) = $ **15(kg · m)/s**

2. Two objects are traveling in the same direction at different speeds. Object 1 moves at 5 meters per second and has a mass of 1 kilogram. Object 2 moves at 2 meters per second and has a mass of 0.5 kilograms. If object 1 collides with object 2 and they stick together, what will be the final velocity of the two objects?

   A) 2.5 m/s

   B) 3 m/s

   C) 4 m/s

   D) 7 m/s

   Answer:

   C) is correct.

   The objects stick together, so the collision is inelastic. Use the formula for conservation of momentum and solve for final velocity.

   $m_1 = 1$ kg

   $v_1 = 5$ m/s

   $m_2 = 0.5$ kg

   $v_2 = 2$ m/s

   $v_f = ?$

   $m_1 v_1 + m_2 v_2 = (m_1 + m_2) v_f$

   $v_f = \dfrac{m_1 v_1 + m_2 v_2}{m_1 v_1} = \dfrac{(1 \text{ kg})(5 \text{ m/s}) + (0.5 \text{ kg})(2 \text{ m/s})}{1 \text{ kg} + 0.5 \text{ kg}} = $ **4 m/s**

FORCES

$G = 6.67408 \times 10^{-11}$ m^3 kg^{-1} s^{-2} (gravitational constant)

$g = 9.8$ m/s^2

$F_g = mg$ (for falling objects)

$F_g = \dfrac{Gm_1 m_2}{r_2}$ (for the gravitational force between two masses)

$F = ma$

$F_f = \mu_k F_N$

> ⚠
>
> F = force (N)

Obviously, objects need a reason to get moving: they don't just start accelerating on their own. The "push" that starts or stops an object's motion is called a **FORCE** (F) and is measured in Newtons (N). Examples of forces include **GRAVITY** (created by mass of objects), **FRICTION** (created by the movement of two surfaces in contact with each other), **TENSION** (created by hanging a mass from a string or chain), and **ELECTRICAL FORCE** (created by charged particles). A force that creates circular motion is called a **CENTRIPETAL FORCE**.

> ⚠
>
> Gravitational force is proportional to the masses of two objects and the distance between the center of mass of the two objects, not the distance between the surfaces.

Note that all of these forces are vectors with a magnitude and direction. Gravity, for example, always points down toward the earth, and friction always points in the opposite direction of the object's motion. On a **FREE BODY DIAGRAM**, forces are drawn as vectors, and vectors in the horizontal and vertical directions can be added to find the total force.

Newton's three laws of motion describe how these forces work to create motion:

LAW #1: An object at rest will remain at rest, and an object in motion will continue with the same speed and direction unless acted on by a force. This law is often called "the law of inertia."

LAW #2: Acceleration is produced when a force acts on a mass. The greater the mass of the object being accelerated, the greater the amount of force needed to accelerate the object.

LAW #3: Every action requires an equal and opposite reaction. This means that for every force, there is a reacting force both equal in size and opposite in direction. In other words, whenever an object pushes another object, it gets pushed back in the opposite direction with equal force.

Examples

1. An object is being acted on by only 2 forces as shown below. If the magnitudes of F_1 and F_2 are equal, which of the following statements must be true?

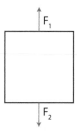

A) The velocity of the object must be zero.

B) The velocity of the object must be constant.

C) The velocity of the object must be increasing.

D) The velocity of the object must be decreasing.

Answer:

B) is correct.

The net force on the object ($F_1 + F_2$) is zero, so the acceleration of the object is zero. Since there is no acceleration, **the velocity must be constant**.

2. An object is pulled across a rough surface with a force of 20 Newtons. If the object moves with a constant velocity and the surface has a coefficient of kinetic friction equal to 0.2, what is the magnitude of the normal force acting on the object?

A) 4 Newtons

B) 10 Newtons

C) 20 Newtons

D) 100 Newtons

Answer:

D) is correct.

Use the formula for frictional force and solve for the normal force.

$F_n = 20$ N

$\mu = 0.2$

$F_f = \mu \cdot F_n$

$F_n = \dfrac{F_f}{\mu} = \dfrac{20}{0.2} = \textbf{100 N}$

CIRCULAR AND ROTATIONAL MOTION

Rotational Motion

$\theta = \frac{1}{2}\alpha t^2 + \omega_i t$

$\omega_f = \omega_i + \alpha t$

$\omega_f^2 = \omega_i^2 + 2\alpha\theta$

In addition to moving in a straight line, objects can also rotate. This **ROTATIONAL MOTION** is described using a similar set of variables and equations to those used for linear motion. However, the variables have been converted to represent rotational motion, as shown in the table below.

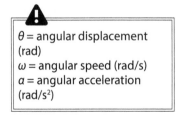

θ = angular displacement (rad)
ω = angular speed (rad/s)
α = angular acceleration (rad/s²)

Table 8.1. Rotational Motion

LINEAR VARIABLE	ROTATIONAL VARIABLE
displacement (d)	angular displacement (θ)
velocity (v)	angular speed (ω)
acceleration (a)	angular acceleration (α)

Example

The motor of an engine is rotating about its axis with an angular velocity of 100 revolutions per minute. After being switched off, it decelerates at a constant rate of 200 rad/s². How long will it take for the motor to stop rotating?

A) 2 seconds

B) 3 seconds

C) 5 seconds

D) 6 seconds

Answer:

B) is correct.

Convert the angular velocity to radians per second:

$$\omega = \frac{100 \text{ rev}}{\text{min}} \times \frac{1 \text{ min}}{60 \text{ s}} \times \frac{360 \text{ rad}}{1 \text{ rev}} = 600 \text{ rad/s}$$

Identify the variables:

$\omega_i = 600$ rad/s

$\omega_f = 0$ rad/s

$a = -200$ rad/s

$t = ?$

Use the appropriate formula to solve for time:

$\omega_f = \omega_i + at$

0 rad/s = 600 rad/s + (−200 rad/s)(t)

t = 3 seconds

Torque

$\tau = rF\sin(\theta)$

τ = torque (N · m)

TORQUE is a form of work that is applied in a circular motion; it is measured in newton meters (N·m). A wrench, for example, employs torque to apply force to turning a bolt. The specific definition of torque is a force that is applied over a distance and an angle to generate circular motion (as seen below). The amount of torque depends on the radius of the arm (*r*), the force applied (*F*), and the angle of the force (*θ*). Maximum torque is applied when the force is perpendicular to the arm (*θ* = 90°).

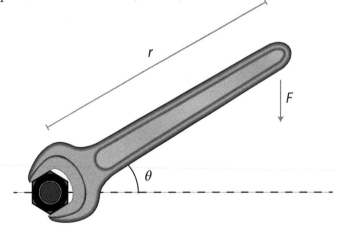

Figure 8.1. Torque

Example

A force of magnitude 10 Newtons is applied at point A, causing the bar to rotate around point B. What is the torque produced by the force?

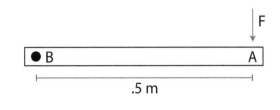

A) 5 N · m clockwise

B) 20 N · m clockwise

C) 5 N · m counterclockwise

D) 20 N · m counterclockwise

Answer:

A) is correct.

A downward force at point A will make the rod rotate clockwise. Use the formula for torque to find the magnitude:

$\tau = rF \sin\theta = 10(0.5)(1) = $ **5 N · m clockwise**

Circular Motion

$a = \frac{v^2}{r}$

$F = ma_c = m \times \frac{v^2}{r}$

CIRCULAR MOTION is the movement of an object around a central point. **CENTRIPETAL ACCELERATION**, which points toward the center of the circle, changes the direction of the object's velocity and keeps the object on a circular path. The force that creates centripetal acceleration can be tension (e.g., swing a weight on a string), friction(e.g., car tires on a turn), or other forces.

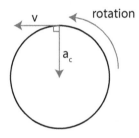

Figure 8.2. Circular Motion

Example

A weight is attached to a strength with a length of 2 meters. If the weight is swung in a circle with a velocity of 6 meters per second, what is the weight's centripetal acceleration?

A) 3 m/s²

B) 6 m/s²

C) 12 m/s²

D) 18 m/s²

Answer:

D) is correct.

Identify the variables:

$r = 2$ m

$v = 6$ m/s

$ac = ?$

Use the formula for circular motion to find the centripetal acceleration:

$$a = \frac{v^2}{r} = \frac{(6 \text{ m/s})^2}{2 \text{ m}} = \textbf{18 m/s}^2$$

ENERGY, WORK, AND POWER

Energy

$$KE = \frac{1}{2}mv^2$$

$$PE_g = mgh$$

In simple terms, energy is the capacity to do work; in other words, it's a measurement of how much force a system could apply. Energy is measured in Joules (J), which are J = kg · m²/s². There are two main categories of energy. The energy stored within an object due to its relative position is its **POTENTIAL ENERGY**: that object has the potential to do work. Potential energy can be created in a number of ways, including raising an object off the ground or compressing a spring. **KINETIC ENERGY** is present when an object is in motion. The sum of an object's kinetic and potential energies is called its **MECHANICAL ENERGY**.

Generally, kinetic energy is the energy of an object in motion, and potential energy is the energy of an object at rest.

Energy can be neither created nor destroyed; it can only be converted from one form to another. For example, when a rock is lifted some distance from the ground it has **GRAVITATIONAL POTENTIAL ENERGY**; when it's released, it begins to move toward the earth and that potential energy becomes kinetic energy. A pendulum is another example: at the height of its swing, the pendulum will have potential energy but no kinetic energy; at the bottom of its swing, it has kinetic energy but no more potential energy.

Examples

1. The mass of a rider and his cycle combined is 90 kilograms. What is the increase in kinetic energy if the rider increases his speed from 6 kilometers per hour to 12 kilometers per hour?

   A) 300 Joules

   B) 350 Joules

   C) 375 Joules

   D) 400 Joules

   Answer:

   C) is correct.

   Convert both velocities to meters per second:

   $$\frac{6 \text{ km}}{\text{hr}} \times \frac{1 \text{ hr}}{3600 \text{ s}} \times \frac{1000 \text{ m}}{1 \text{ km}} = 1.67 \text{ m/s}$$

   $$\frac{12 \text{ km}}{\text{hr}} \times \frac{1 \text{ hr}}{3600 \text{ s}} \times \frac{1000 \text{ m}}{1 \text{ km}} = 3.33 \text{ m/s}$$

   Use the kinetic energy formula to find the rider's initial and final kinetic energy:

   $$KE_i = \frac{1}{2}mv_i^2 = \frac{1}{2}(90 \text{ kg})(1.67 \text{ m/s})^2 = 125 \text{ J}$$

   $$KE_f = \frac{1}{2}mv_f^2 = \frac{1}{2}(90 \text{ kg})(3.33 \text{ m/s})^2 = 500 \text{ J}$$

   Subtract the initial kinetic energy from final kinetic energy to find the change:

   500 J – 125 J = **375 Joules**

2. A skier starts from rest at the top of a hill. If the height of the hill is 20 m, what is the speed of the skier at the bottom of the hill? (Assume no air resistance or friction.)

A) 4 m/s

B) 20 m/s

C) 200 m/s

D) 400 m/s

Answer:

B) is correct.

Without air resistance or friction, total mechanical energy is conserved. The skier's potential energy at the top of the hill will be completely transformed into kinetic energy at the bottom of the hill:

$PE_i = KE_f$

$\frac{1}{2}mv^2 = mgh$

Solve for velocity (mass cancels out of both sides of the equation):

$v = \sqrt{2gh} = \sqrt{2(9.8 \text{ m/s}^2)(20 \text{ m})} \approx$ **20 m/s**

Work

$W = Fd$

$P = \frac{W}{t}$

WORK is defined in physics as a force exerted over a distance; work is also measured in Joules (J). Work has to take place over a distance: if an object is acted upon by a force, but does not move, then no work has been performed. For example, if someone pushes against a wall with 50 N of force, she has not performed any work. However, if she lifted a baseball off the ground, then she performed work.

P = power (W)

Work is a scalar quantity, and cannot be expressed in terms of a vector. However, the force applied to do work is a vector quantity, and thus the net force used to perform work can change depending on the angle at which it is applied.

POWER is force applied over time; it is measured in Watts.

Examples

1. A child pushes a truck for 5 seconds across the floor using 1 Newton of force. The truck moves 5 meters. How much work did the child do?

A) 0.25 Joules

B) 5 Joules

C) 2.5 Joules

D) 25 Joules

Answer:

B) is correct.

Use the formula for work: $W = Fd = (1 \text{ m/s})(5 \text{ m}) =$ **5 J**

2. How much power did the child deliver to the truck?

A) 0.05 Watts

B) 0.25 Watts

C) 0.5 Watts

D) 1 Watt

Answer:

D) is correct.

Use the formula for power and solve: $P = \dfrac{W}{t} = \dfrac{5\,J}{5\,s} = $ **1 W**

WAVES

Types of Waves

A **WAVE** is a periodic motion that carries energy through space or matter. There are two main types of waves: mechanical and electromagnetic. **MECHANICAL WAVES** travel through a physical medium; ripples in a pond and sound waves traveling through the air are both examples of mechanical waves. **ELECTROMAGNETIC WAVES** do not require a medium to travel because they consist of oscillating magnetic and electric fields. These waves are classified on the **ELECTROMAGNETIC SPECTRUM** and include visible light, x-rays, and radio waves.

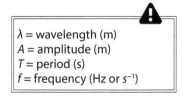

λ = wavelength (m)
A = amplitude (m)
T = period (s)
f = frequency (Hz or s^{-1})

Waves can also be classified by how the particles in the wave vibrate. **LONGITUDINAL WAVES** cause particles to vibrate parallel to the movement of the wave; **TRANSVERSE WAVES** cause particles to vibrate perpendicular to the movement of the wave.

longitudinal wave

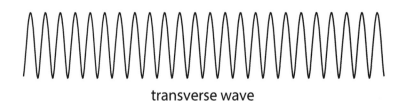

transverse wave

Figure 8.3. Types of Waves

Example

Which of the following requires a medium to travel?

A) visible light

B) microwaves

C) radio waves

D) sound waves

Answer:

D) is correct.

Sound waves are mechanical, so they need a medium to travel. The other waves are part of the electromagnetic spectrum, and so do not travel through a medium.

Characteristics of Waves

$$v = \lambda f = \frac{\lambda}{T}$$

$$T = \frac{1}{f}$$

The four major characteristics of waves are wavelength, amplitude, period, and frequency. The **WAVELENGTH** (λ) is the distance from the peak of one wave to the next (or from the trough of one wave to the next). The **AMPLITUDE** (A) of a wave is the distance from the top of the wave to the bottom. Both wavelength and amplitude are measured in meters (the SI unit for distance).

The **PERIOD** (T) of a wave is the time it takes the wave to complete one oscillation; it is usually measured in seconds. The **FREQUENCY** (f) of a wave is the number of oscillations that occur per second; it is measured in Hertz (Hz). The period and frequency of a wave are inverses of each other: the shorter the period of a wave, the higher its frequency.

Example

A wave with a speed of 10 meters per second is traveling on a string at a frequency of 20 oscillations per second. What is the wave's wavelength?

A) 0.2 meters

B) 0.5 meters

C) 2 meters

D) 200 meters

Answer:

B) is correct.

Identify the variables:

$v = 10$ m/s

$f = 20$ s^{-1}

Use the formula for velocity of a wave to solve for wavelength: $v = \lambda f$

$\lambda = \frac{v}{f} = \frac{10 \text{ m/s}}{20 \text{ s}^{-1}} = \textbf{0.5 m}$

Properties of Waves

Waves of all kinds exhibit particular behaviors. Waves can interact either to create CONSTRUCTIVE INTERFERENCE, where the resulting wave is bigger than either original wave, or DESTRUCTIVE INTERFERENCE, which creates a wave that is smaller than either original wave. Waves will also bend when passing through a slit, a process called DIFFRACTION. Waves will also REFRACT, or bend, when they pass from one medium into another.

Example

What is the maximum possible amplitude of the wave created by the interference of a wave with an amplitude of 0.5 meters and a wave with an amplitude of 2 meters?

A) 0 meters

B) 0.5 meters

C) 2.5 meters

D) 5 meters

Answer:

C) is correct.

The range of amplitudes for the interference is from the difference between the amplitudes to the sum of the amplitudes. The maximum amplitude will be the sum of the amplitudes:

0.5 m + 2 m = **2.5 m**

Sound

SOUND is comprised of waves that are usually produced by the vibration of an object, such as the strings of an instrument or the human vocal cords. The vibrations cause the air to vibrate as well, which creates a pressure variation in the air, creating a longitudinal wave.

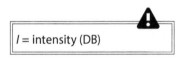
I = intensity (DB)

When humans hear a sound, it is the detection of the pressure variation by our ear drums. The speed of a sound wave depends on the medium that it is moving through. In air, sound has a speed of about 340 meters per second or 761 miles per hour.

Humans can typically detect sound waves between 20 Hz to 20,000 Hz. Sound waves with a lower frequency have a "lower" pitch to human ears and sound waves with a high frequency have a "high" pitch to human ears.

Sound waves travel much faster in water than in air.

Sound INTENSITY (I) is the sound power over a specific area; it's measured in W/m^2 or decibels (DB). Intensity represents the amount of energy carried by the sound wave; the louder the sound (and larger the amplitude), the greater the intensity. However, sound wave energy is inversely proportional to the distance from which it is heard. Thus, as you move away from a sound source, the intensity of the sound decreases exponentially.

Example

Sound waves will move fastest through which medium?

A) water

B) air

C) a vacuum

D) wood

LIGHT

LIGHT is a form of electromagnetic radiation that makes up a small spectrum of all the electromagnetic waves. Visible light is the wavelength range of 400 to 800 nanometers, and is one of the few types of radiation that is able to penetrate the Earth's atmosphere.

n = index of refraction (no unit)

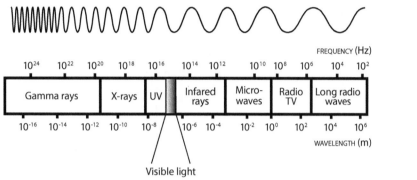

Figure 8.4. Electromagnetic Spectrum

Properties of Light

$$n_1 \sin\theta_1 = n_2 \sin\theta_2$$

$$n = \frac{c}{v_s}$$

Light, which is an electromagnetic wave, has a number of special properties because it acts as both a particle and a wave—a phenomenon called the **WAVE-PARTICLE DUALITY OF LIGHT**. Light will reflect off some materials: the **INCIDENT RAY** will bounce off a surface,

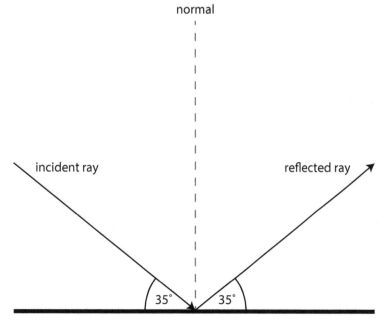

Figure 8.5. Reflection

and the incident angle will be equal to the angle of reflection. Light will also bend when it passes from one media to another in a process called REFRACTION. The angle of refraction can be found using Snell's law and the material's index of refraction (*n*).

Light waves can experience both interference and diffraction like any other wave. Because light is made up of discrete packets of energy (called quanta), light also sometimes acts as a particle. For example, when light strikes a metal surface, the packets of energy can eject electrons from atoms in a process called the PHOTOELECTRIC EFFECT.

Example

A ray of light is directed at a reflective surface as shown below.

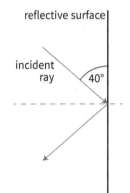

What angle does the reflected ray make with respect to the normal?

A) 0°

B) 40°

C) 50°

D) 90°

Answer:

C) is correct.

The law of reflection states that the reflected ray angle will be the same as the incident ray angle. Thus, the reflected ray will be at **angle of 50°** to the normal, just like the incident ray.

ELECTRICITY

Electric Charge

$k = 9 \times 10^9 \text{ N·m}^2/\text{C}^2$

$F = k\dfrac{q_1 q_2}{r^2}$

⚠️

q = charge (C)

An electric charge is generated due to the difference in CHARGE (*q*) potential between protons, which have a +1 charge, and electrons, which have a –1 charge. The charges on a proton or electron are elementary, meaning that they cannot be further subdivided into smaller units. The charge is measured in coulombs (C). A single electron has a charge of –1.6 × 10^{-19} C. One proton has the exact same amount of charge, but of the opposite sign. Electricity is generated by the flow of electrons through a conducting coil, such as copper or steel.

Charged particles are naturally attracted to or repulsed from each other based on their charge. An electron will repel another electron, and a proton will repel another proton. An electron and proton will be attracted to one another. COULOMB'S LAW is used to predict the strength of the attractive or repulsive force between two particles. A positive value of force indicates that the particles are being repelled from one another.

Example

Two particles are separated by a distance of 0.5 m. If one particle has a charge of 1 μC and the other particle has a charge of −2 μC, what is the magnitude of the force between the particles ($k = 9 \times 10^9$ Nm²/C²)?

A) 9×10^{-3} N

B) 7.2×10^{-2} N

C) 7.2×10^{10} N

D) 9×10^9 N

Answer:

B) is correct.

Use Coulomb's law to solve for the force:

$$F_e = \frac{kq_1q_2}{r^2} = \frac{(9 \times 10^9 \text{ Nm}^2/\text{C}^2)(1 \times 10^{-6} \text{ μC})(2 \times 10^{-6} \text{ μC})}{(0.5 \text{ m})^2} = \textbf{7.2×10}^{-2} \textbf{ N}$$

Electric Fields

$\Delta V = Ed$

Charged particles create an ELECTRIC FIELD (E) in which they will exert an electric force on other charged particles. The strength of an electric field is measured in newtons per coulomb and is proportional to the charge of the particle experiencing the force (i.e., a particle with a higher charge will experience a larger force, and vice versa).

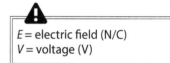
E = electric field (N/C)
V = voltage (V)

Moving a particle through an electric field will change the potential electrical energy of that particle in an amount proportional to the displacement and force of the electric field. The difference in potential electrical energy between two points is known as VOLTAGE (V), which is measured in volts.

Example

A particle is placed in a uniform electric field of magnitude 1×10^4 N per coulomb. If the particle experiences a force of 0.1 N, what is the magnitude of the charge on the particle?

A) 0.1 μC

B) 1 μC

C) 10 μC

D) 100 μC

Answer:

C) is correct.

Use the formula for electric field strength and solve for the charge of the particle:

$$E = \frac{F}{q}$$

$$q = \frac{F}{E} = \frac{0.1\ \text{N}}{1 \times 10^4\ \text{N/C}} = 1 \times 10^{-5}\ \text{C} = \textbf{10 μC}$$

Circuits

$$V = IR$$

I = current (A)
R = resistance (Ω)

In an electric **CIRCUIT**, a closed loop is formed that is connected to the positive and negative ends of a voltage source. The voltage source provides the charge potential that drives electrons through the circuit to create electricity. The movement of electrons is called **CURRENT**, which is measured in Amps (A).

Current in a circuit can be thought of as analogous to water in a pipe.

A **RESISTOR** is an electrical component that provides resistance to the flow of current through an electric circuit. A resistor is usually composed of a series of materials that are not conducive to electron flow. The units of resistance are Ω. According to Ohm's law, current and resistance are inversely related, and both are proportional to voltage.

Resistors in a circuit can be wired in series or in parallel. In a **SERIES** circuit, the current can only follow one path, while in a **PARALLEL** circuit the current can follow multiple pathways.

Table 8.2. Series and Parallel Circuits

	SERIES	PARALLEL
Current	$I_1 = I_2 = I_3 = \dots = I_n$	$I_t = I_1 + I_2 + \dots + I_n$
Voltage	$V_t = V_1 + V_2 + \dots + V_n$	$V_1 = V_2 = V_3 = \dots = V_n$
Resistance	$R_t = R_1 + R_2 + \dots + R_n$	$\frac{1}{R_t} = \frac{1}{R_1} + \frac{1}{R_2} + \dots + \frac{1}{R_n}$

Examples

1. What is the current running through a 2 Ω resistor in a circuit with a 10 V battery?

A) 2 Amps

B) 5 Amps

C) 20 Amps

D) 50 Amps

Answer:

B) is correct.

Use Ohm's law and solve for the current:

$$V = IR$$

$$I = \frac{V}{R} = \frac{10\ \text{V}}{2\ \Omega} = \textbf{5A}$$

2. If a circuit wired in series includes five 10 Ω resistors, what is the total resistance of the circuit?

A) 2 Ω

B) 10 Ω

C) 50 Ω

D) 500 Ω

Answer:

C) is correct.

The total equivalent resistance for a series circuit is found by finding the sum of the resistors:

$R_{eq} = R_1 + R_2 + R_3 + R_4 + R_5 = 10 + 10 + 10 + 10 + 10 = \textbf{50 Ω}$

MAGNETISM

MAGNETIC FIELDS can be produced by moving electric charges or can be the result of the alignment of subatomic particles in a substance. The SI unit for magnetism is the Tesla, named after the Russian inventor Nikola Tesla. Electricity and magnetism are closely related: moving particles (like electricity) will create magnetic fields. Similarly, magnetic fields will exert a force on moving charged particles, and a moving magnetic field will create an electric current.

All magnets have a north and a south pole. As with charges, like poles repel each other and opposite poles attract each other; the magnitude of this force is directly proportional to the strength of the magnets and inversely proportional to their distance. Magnetic field lines always flow from north to south.

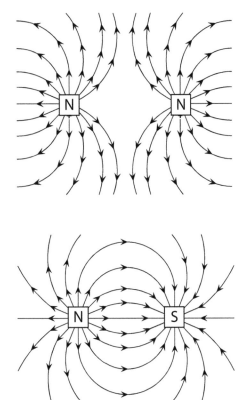

Figure 8.6. Magnetic Field Lines

Example

The north poles of two magnets are held near each other. At which distance will the magnets experience the most force?

A) 0.1 meters

B) 1 meters

C) 10 meters

D) 100 meters

Answer:

A) is correct.

Magnetic force is inversely proportional to the distance between two objects, so the smallest distance will create the largest force.

9

PRACTICE TEST

MATHEMATICS

1. Which of the following has the greatest value?

   A) −4(3)(−2)
   B) −16 − 17 + 31
   C) 18 − 15 + 27
   D) −20 + 10 + 10

2. In a theater, there are 4,500 lower-level seats and 2,000 upper-level seats. What is the ratio of lower-level seats to total seats?

   A) $\frac{4}{9}$
   B) $\frac{4}{13}$
   C) $\frac{9}{13}$
   D) $\frac{9}{4}$

3. The formula for distance is $d = v \times t$, where v is the object's velocity and t is the time. How long will it take a plane to fly 4000 miles from Chicago to London if the plane flies at a constant rate of 500 mph?

   A) 3.5 hours
   B) 8 hours
   C) 20 hours
   D) 45 hours

4. If a person reads 40 pages in 45 minutes, approximately how many minutes will it take her to read 265 pages?

   A) 202
   B) 236
   C) 265
   D) 298

5. If a student answers 42 out of 48 questions correctly on a quiz, what percentage of questions did she answer correctly?

   A) 82.5%
   B) 85%
   C) 87.5%
   D) 90%

6. Justin has a summer lawn care business and earns $40 for each lawn he mows. He also pays $35 per week in business expenses. Which of the following expressions represents Justin's profit after x weeks if he mows m number of lawns?

   A) $40m − 35x$
   B) $40m + 35x$
   C) $35x(40 + m)$
   D) $35(40m + x)$

7. Which of the following is listed in order from least to greatest?

   A) $-0.95, 0, \frac{2}{5}, 0.35, \frac{3}{4}$

   B) $-1, -\frac{1}{10}, -0.11, \frac{5}{6}, 0.75$

   C) $-\frac{3}{4}, -0.2, 0, \frac{2}{3}, 0.55$

   D) $-1.1, -\frac{4}{5}, -0.13, 0.7, \frac{9}{11}$

8. A teacher has 50 notebooks to hand out to students. If she has 16 students in her class, and each student receives 2 notebooks, how many notebooks will she have left over?

   A) 2
   B) 16
   C) 18
   D) 32

9. 40% of what number is equal to 17?

   A) 2.35
   B) 6.8
   C) 42.5
   D) 680

10. Allison used $2\frac{1}{2}$ cups of flour to make a cake, and $\frac{3}{4}$ of a cup of flour to make a pie. If she started with 4 cups of flour, how many cups of flour does she have left?

    A) $\frac{3}{4}$
    B) 1
    C) $\frac{5}{2}$
    D) $\frac{13}{4}$

11. Michael is making cupcakes. He plans to give $\frac{1}{2}$ of the cupcakes to a friend and $\frac{1}{3}$ of the cupcakes to his coworkers. If he makes 48 cupcakes, how many will he have left over?

    A) 8
    B) 10
    C) 16
    D) 24

12. Which of the following is closest in value to 129,113 + 34,602?

    A) 162,000
    B) 163,000
    C) 164,000
    D) 165,000

13. If $j = 4$, what is the value of $2(j - 4)^4 - j + \frac{1}{2}j$?

    A. 0
    B. -2
    C. 2
    D. 4

14. Students board a bus at 7:45 a.m. and arrive at school at 8:20 a.m. How long are the students on the bus?

    A) 30 minutes
    B) 35 minutes
    C) 45 minutes
    D) 60 minutes

15. In an algebraic equation m represents a car's average mileage in miles per gallon, p represents the price of gas in dollars per gallon, and d represents a distance in miles. Which algebraic equation represents the cost (c) of gas per mile?

    A) $c = \frac{dp}{m}$

    B) $c = \frac{p}{m}$

    C) $c = \frac{mp}{d}$

    D) $c = \frac{m}{p}$

16. Micah has invited 23 friends to his house and is having pizza for dinner. If each pizza feeds 4 people, how many pizzas should he order?

    A) 4
    B) 5
    C) 6
    D) 7

17. An ice chest contains 24 sodas, some regular and some diet. The ratio of diet soda to regular soda is 1:3. How many regular sodas are there in the ice chest?

A)   1
B)   4
C)   18
D)   24

18. A table is 150 centimeters long. How many millimeters long is the table?

A)   1.5 mm
B)   15 mm
C)   150 mm
D)   1500 mm

19. Noah and Jennifer have a total of $10.00 to spend on lunch. If each buys his or her own order of french fries and a soda, how many orders of chicken strips can they share?

Menu	
ITEM	PRICE
Hamburger	$4.00
Chicken Strips	$4.00
Onion Rings	$3.00
French Fries	$2.00
Soda	$1.00
Shake	$1.00

A)   0
B)   1
C)   2
D)   3

20. Which expression is equivalent to dividing 300 by 12?

A) $2(150 - 6)$
B) $(300 \div 4) \div 6$
C) $(120 \div 6) + (180 \div 6)$
D) $(120 \div 12) + (180 \div 12)$

21. A fruit stand sells apples, bananas, and oranges at a ratio of 3:2:1. If the fruit stand sells 20 bananas, how many total pieces of fruit does the fruit stand sell?

A)   10
B)   30
C)   40
D)   60

22. Out of 1560 students at Ward Middle School, 15% want to take French. Which expression represents how many students want to take French?

A) $1560 \div 15$
B) 1560×15
C) 1560×0.15
D) $1560 \div 0.15$

23. Erica is at work for $8\frac{1}{2}$ hours a day. If she takes one 30-minute lunch break and two 15-minute breaks during the day, how many hours does she work?

A)   6 hours, 30 minutes
B)   6 hours, 45 minutes
C)   7 hours, 15 minutes
D)   7 hours, 30 minutes

24. At the grocery store, apples cost $1.89 per pound and oranges cost $2.19 per pound. How much would it cost to purchase 2 pounds of apples and 1.5 pounds of oranges?

A) $6.62
B) $7.07
C) $7.14
D) $7.22

25. Which of the following is a solution of the given equation?

$$4(m + 4)^2 - 4m^2 + 20 = 276$$

A)   3
B)   6
C)   12
D)   24

26. Kendrick has $2,386.52 in his checking account. If he pays $792.00 for rent, $84.63 for groceries, and $112.15 for his car insurance, how much money will he have left in his account?

A) $1,397.74

B) $1,482.37

C) $1,509.89

D) $2,189.22

27. If a car uses 8 gallons of gas to travel 650 miles, how many miles can it travel using 12 gallons of gas?

A) 870 miles

B) 895 miles

C) 915 miles

D) 975 miles

28. Jane earns $15 per hour babysitting. If she starts with $275 in her bank account, which equation represents how many hours (h) she will have to babysit for her account to reach $400?

A. $400 = 275 + 15h$

B. $400 = 15h$

C. $400 = \frac{15}{h} + 275$

D. $400 = -275 - 15h$

29. A car traveled at 65 miles per hour for $1\frac{1}{2}$ hours and then traveled at 50 miles per hour for $2\frac{1}{2}$ hours. How many miles did the car travel?

A) 190.5 miles

B) 215.0 miles

C) 222.5 miles

D) 237.5 miles

30. Which digit is in the hundredths place when 1.3208 is divided by 5.2?

A) 0

B) 4

C) 5

D) 8

31. A grocery store sold 30% of its pears and had 455 pears remaining. How many pears did the grocery store start with?

A) 602

B) 650

C) 692

D) 700

32. Which of the following is closest to 15,886 × 210?

A) 33,000

B) 330,000

C) 3,300,000

D) 33,000,000

33. $\frac{15}{25} =$

A) 0.06

B) 0.15

C) 0.375

D) 0.6

34. 15 is 8% of what number?

A) 1.2

B) 53.3

C) 120

D) 187.5

35. A woman's dinner bill is $48.30. If she adds a 20% tip, what will she pay in total?

A) $9.66

B) $38.64

C) $57.96

D) $68.30

36. In a neighborhood, $\frac{2}{5}$ of the houses are painted yellow. If there are 24 houses that are NOT painted yellow, how many yellow houses are in the neighborhood?

A) 16

B) 9.6

C) 24

D) 40

37. $\frac{8}{15} \div \frac{1}{6} =$

A) $\frac{4}{45}$

B) $\frac{15}{48}$

C) $\frac{16}{5}$

D) $\frac{46}{15}$

38. What percent of 14 is 35?

A) 4.9%

B) 2.5%

C) 40%

D) 250%

39. Megan has $\frac{13}{16}$ of a cake left. If her dad eats $\frac{1}{3}$ of the remaining cake, what proportion of the total cake is left?

A) $\frac{1}{4}$

B) $\frac{23}{48}$

C) $\frac{13}{24}$

D) $\frac{3}{4}$

40. A restaurant employs servers, hosts, and managers in a ratio of 9:2:1. If there are 36 total employees, how many hosts work at the restaurant?

A) 3

B) 4

C) 6

D) 8

41. $1\frac{3}{4} + 2\frac{3}{8} =$

A) $3\frac{3}{4}$

B) $3\frac{7}{8}$

C) 4

D) $4\frac{1}{8}$

42. Solve for x: $5x - 4 = 3(8 + 3x)$

A) -7

B) $-\frac{3}{4}$

C) $\frac{3}{4}$

D) 7

43. Which list of numbers is in order from least to greatest?

A) $0.125, \frac{1}{7}, \frac{6}{9}, 0.60$

B) $\frac{1}{7}, 0.125, 0.60, \frac{6}{9}$

C) $0.125, \frac{1}{7}, 0.60, \frac{6}{9}$

D) $\frac{1}{7}, 0.125, \frac{6}{9}, 0.60$

44. If the value of y is between 0.0047 and 0.0162, which of the following could be the value of y?

A) 0.0035

B) 0.0055

C) 0.0185

D) 0.0238

45. $4\frac{1}{2} - 1\frac{2}{3} =$

A) $2\frac{1}{3}$

B) $2\frac{5}{6}$

C) $3\frac{1}{6}$

D) $3\frac{5}{6}$

46. 7 is what percent of 60?

A) 4.20

B) 8.57

C) 10.11

D) 11.67

47. If $3a + 4 = 2a$, then $a = ?$

A) -4

B) $-\frac{4}{5}$

C) $\frac{4}{5}$

D) 4

48. $10\frac{3}{8} \div \frac{1}{3} =$

A) $3\frac{13}{24}$

B) $6\frac{3}{4}$

C) $15\frac{3}{4}$

D) $31\frac{1}{8}$

49. A car dealership has sedans, SUVs, and minivans in a ratio of 6:3:1, respectively. What proportion of the vehicles at the dealership are sedans?

A) $\frac{1}{6}$

B) $\frac{3}{10}$

C) $\frac{1}{2}$

D) $\frac{3}{5}$

50. There are 380 female students in a class. Male students make up 60% of the class. What is the total number of students in the class?

A) 570

B) 633

C) 950

D) 2,280

51. A marinade recipe includes 2 tablespoons of lemon juice for $\frac{1}{4}$ cup of olive oil. How many tablespoons of lemon juice would be used with $\frac{2}{3}$ cup olive oil?

A) $\frac{3}{4}$

B) $2\frac{1}{3}$

C) 4

D) $5\frac{1}{3}$

52. How many digits are in the sum 951.4 + 98.908 + 1.053?

A) 4

B) 5

C) 6

D) 7

53. Which value is the least?

A) 1.068

B) 1.680

C) 1.608

D) 1.086

54. Which list of numbers is in order from least to greatest?

A) $\frac{1}{24} < \frac{3}{32} < \frac{5}{48} < \frac{2}{16} < \frac{3}{16}$

B) $\frac{1}{24} < \frac{5}{48} < \frac{3}{32} < \frac{2}{16} < \frac{3}{16}$

C) $\frac{1}{24} < \frac{3}{32} < \frac{2}{16} < \frac{3}{16} < \frac{5}{48}$

D) $\frac{1}{24} < \frac{2}{16} < \frac{3}{32} < \frac{3}{16} < \frac{5}{48}$

55. A chemical experiment requires that a solute be diluted with 4 parts (by mass) water for every 1 part (by mass) solute. If the desired mass for the solution is 90 grams, how many grams of solute should be used?

A) 15 grams

B) 16.5 grams

C) 18 grams

D) 22.5 grams

READING COMPREHENSION

Taking a person's temperature is one of the most basic and common health care tasks. Everyone from nurses to emergency medical technicians to concerned parents should be able to grab a thermometer to take a patient or loved one's temperature. But what's the best way to get an accurate reading? The answer depends on the situation.

The most common way people measure body temperature is orally. A simple digital or disposable thermometer is placed under the tongue for a few minutes, and the task is done. There are many situations, however, when measuring temperature orally isn't an option. For example, when a person can't breathe through his nose, he won't be able to keep his mouth closed long enough to get an accurate reading. In these situations, it's often preferable to place the thermometer in the rectum or armpit. Using the rectum also has the added benefit of providing a much more accurate reading than other locations can provide.

It's also often the case that certain people, like agitated patients or fussy babies, won't be able to sit still long enough for an accurate reading. In these situations, it's best to use a thermometer that works much more quickly, such as one that measures temperature in the ear or at the temporal artery. No matter which method is chosen, however, it's important to check the average temperature for each region, as it can vary by several degrees.

1. According to the passage, why is it sometimes preferable to take a person's temperature rectally?

   A) Rectal readings are more accurate than oral readings.

   B) Many people cannot sit still long enough to have their temperatures taken orally.

   C) Temperature readings can vary widely between regions of the body.

   D) Many people do not have access to quick-acting thermometers.

2. Which statement is NOT a detail from the passage?

   A) Taking a temperature in the ear or at the temporal artery is more accurate than taking it orally.

   B) If an individual cannot breathe through the nose, taking his or her temperature orally will likely give an inaccurate reading.

   C) The standard human body temperature varies depending on whether it's measured in the mouth, rectum, armpit, ear, or temporal artery.

   D) The most common way to measure temperature is by placing a thermometer in the mouth.

3. What is the author's primary purpose in writing this essay?

   A) to advocate for the use of thermometers that measure temperature in the ear or at the temporal artery

   B) to explain the methods available to measure a person's temperature and the situation where each method is appropriate

   C) to warn readers that the average temperature of the human body varies by region

   D) to discuss how nurses use different types of thermometers depending on the type of patient they are examining

4. What is the meaning of the word *agitated* in the last paragraph?

   A) obviously upset

   B) quickly moving

   C) violently ill

   D) slightly dirty

5. What is the best summary of this passage?

   A) It's important that everyone know the best way to take a person's temperature in any given situation.

   B) The most common method of taking a person's temperature—orally—isn't appropriate in some situations.

   C) The most accurate way to take a temperature is placing a digital thermometer in the rectum.

   D) There are many different ways to take a person's temperature, and which is appropriate will depend on the situation.

The greatest changes in sensory, motor, and perceptual development happen in the first two years of life. When babies are first born, most of their senses operate in a similar way to those of adults. For example, babies are able to hear before they are born; studies show that babies turn toward the sound of their mothers' voices just minutes after being born, indicating they recognize the mother's voice from their time in the womb.

The exception to this rule is vision. A baby's vision changes significantly in its first year of life; initially it has a range of vision of only 8 – 12 inches and no depth perception. As a result, infants rely primarily on hearing; vision does not become the dominant sense until around the age of 12 months. Babies also prefer faces to other objects. This preference, along with their limited vision range, means that their sight is initially focused on their caregiver.

6. What is the best summary of this passage?

   A) Babies have no depth perception until 12 months, which is why they focus only on their caregivers' faces.

   B) Babies can recognize their mothers' voices when born, so they initially rely primarily on their sense of hearing.

   C) Babies have senses similar to those of adults except for their sense of sight, which doesn't fully develop until 12 months.

   D) Babies' senses go through many changes in the first year of their lives.

7. Which sense do babies primarily rely on?

   A) vision
   B) hearing
   C) touch
   D) smell

8. Which of the following best describes the mode of the passage?

   A) expository
   B) narrative
   C) persuasive
   D) descriptive

Hand washing is one of our simplest and most powerful weapons against infection. The idea behind hand washing is deceptively simple. Many illnesses are spread when people touch infected surfaces, such as door handles or other people's hands, and then touch their own eyes, mouths, or noses. So, if pathogens can be removed from the hands before they spread, infections can be prevented. When done correctly, hand washing can prevent the spread of many dangerous bacteria and viruses, including those that cause the flu, the common cold, diarrhea, and many acute respiratory illnesses.

The most basic method of hand washing involves only soap and water. Just twenty seconds of scrubbing with soap and a complete rinsing with water is enough to kill and/or wash away many pathogens. The process doesn't even require warm water—studies have shown that cold water is just as effective at reducing the number of microbes on the hands. Antibacterial soaps are also available, although several studies have shown that simple soap and cold water is just as effective.

In recent years, hand sanitizers have become popular as an alternative to hand washing. These gels, liquids, and foams contain a high concentration of alcohol (usually at least 60 percent) that kills most bacteria and fungi; they can also be effective against some, but not all, viruses. There is a downside to hand sanitizer, however. Because the sanitizer isn't rinsed from hands, it only kills pathogens and does nothing to remove organic matter. So, hands "cleaned" with hand sanitizer may still harbor pathogens. Thus, while hand sanitizer can be helpful in situations where soap and clean water isn't available, a simple hand washing is still the best option.

9. What is the meaning of the word *harbor* in the last paragraph?

   A) to disguise

   B) to hide

   C) to wash away

   D) to give a home

10. Which of the following is NOT a fact stated in the passage?

    A) Many infections occur because people get pathogens on their hands and then touch their own eyes, mouths, or noses.

    B) Antibacterial soaps and warm water are the best way to remove pathogens from hands.

    C) Most hand sanitizers have a concentration of at least 60 percent alcohol.

    D) Hand sanitizer can be an acceptable alternative to hand washing when soap and water aren't available.

11. Knowing that the temperature of the water does not affect the efficacy of hand washing, one can conclude that water plays an important role in hand washing because it _____.

    A) has antibacterial properties

    B) physically removes pathogens from hands

    C) cools hands to make them inhospitable to dangerous bacteria

    D) is hot enough to kill bacteria

12. What is the best summary of this passage?

    A) Many diseases are spread by pathogens that can live on the hands. Hand washing is the best way to remove these pathogens and prevent disease.

    B) Simple hand washing can prevent the spread of many common illnesses, including the flu, the common cold, diarrhea, and many acute respiratory illnesses. Hand sanitizer can also kill the pathogens that cause these diseases.

    C) Simple hand washing with soap and cold water is an effective way to reduce the spread of disease. Antibacterial soaps and hand sanitizers may also be used but are not significantly more effective.

    D) Using hand sanitizer will kill many pathogens but will not remove organic matter. Hand washing with soap and water is a better option when available.

13. What is the author's primary purpose in writing this essay?

    A) to persuade readers of the importance and effectiveness of hand washing with soap and cold water

    B) to dissuade readers from using hand sanitizer

    C) to explain how many common diseases are spread through daily interaction

    D) to describe the many ways hand washing and hand sanitizer provide health benefits

14. What can the reader conclude from the passage about hand washing and hand sanitizer?

    A) Hand washing would do little to limit infections that spread through particles in the air.

    B) Hand washing is not necessary for people who do not touch their eyes, mouths, or noses with their hands.

    C) Hand sanitizer serves no purpose and should not be used as an alternative to hand washing.

    D) Hand sanitizer will likely soon replace hand washing as the preferred method of removing pathogens from hands.

In its most basic form, geography is the study of space; more specifically, it studies the physical space of the earth and the ways in which it interacts with, shapes, and is shaped by its habitants. Geographers look at the world from a spatial perspective. This means that at the center of all geographic study is the question, *where?* For geographers, the *where* of any interaction, event, or development is a crucial element to understanding it.

This question of *where* can be asked in a variety of fields of study, so there are many sub-disciplines of geography. These can be organized into four main categories: 1) regional studies, which examine the characteristics of a particular place; 2) topical studies, which look at a single physical or human feature that impacts the whole world; 3) physical studies, which focus on the physical features of Earth; and 4) human studies, which examine the relationship between human activity and the environment.

15. A researcher studying the relationship between farming and river systems would be engaged in which geographical sub-discipline?

    A) regional studies

    B) topical studies

    C) physical studies

    D) human studies

16. Which of the following best describes the mode of the passage?

    A) expository

    B) narrative

    C) persuasive

    D) descriptive

17. What is the best summary of this passage?

    A) The most important question in geography is where an event or development took place.

    B) Geography, which is the study of the physical space on Earth, can be broken down into four sub-disciplines.

    C) Regional studies is the study of a single region or area.

    D) Geography can be broken down into four sub-disciplines: regional studies, topical studies, physical studies, and human studies.

Providing adequate nutrition is one of the most important responsibilities of acute and long-term care facilities. Patients enter these facilities with a wide range of health issues from fractures and infections to dementia or cancer. Because the needs of every patient will be different, it's the task of every health care facility to ensure that patients receive the proper nutrition.

Patients, like all people, have two basic nutritional needs: they require macronutrients, the carbohydrates, fats, and proteins that provide energy; and micronutrients, which are the vitamins and elements the body needs to function properly. A good diet will provide the appropriate amount of macronutrients, or calories, to keep the patients energized and satiated without leading to weight gain while also providing necessary amounts of micronutrients. Such a diet will help patients remain comfortable and heal properly. A poor diet, on the other hand, can make recovery significantly more difficult.

The energy needs of patients can vary widely. Generally, energy needs are directly related to a person's weight and inversely related to age; it's also generally true that men require more calories than women. Thus, a thirty-five-year-old woman who weighs 135 pounds will require around 1800 calories a day, while an older woman would require fewer, and a heavier woman would require more. A man of the same age and weight would require 2000 calories a day.

Activity level also has a significant impact on a patient's energy needs. A bedridden patient will obviously expend fewer calories and thus will need to eat fewer. An elderly, bedridden women can need as little as 8.5 calories per pound of body weight: if such a patient weighed 135 pounds, she would need only 1150 calories a day. However, many patients, bedridden or otherwise, have hidden energy needs. The process of healing can be extremely energy intensive—even an immobile patient can use up vast reserves of calories as her body fights infection, knits a fracture, or heals bed sores. Patients on a low-energy diet may also develop deficiencies in micronutrients if the quality of their meals is not monitored closely.

18. What is the main idea of the passage?

A) Patients' diets should include a balance of macro- and micronutrients.

B) Health care workers can determine how many calories patients need by looking at their weight, age, and activity level.

C) Meeting the nutritional needs of patients is a complicated but vital responsibility of health care workers.

D) Activity level of patients should be monitored closely to ensure that each patient receives the amount of macronutrients he or she requires to heal properly.

19. What is the meaning of the word *hidden* in the last paragraph?

A) intentionally kept out of sight

B) not obvious to the casual observer

C) easily forgotten

D) masked by outside complications

20. According to the passage, which of the patients described below would likely need to consume the most calories per day?

A) an elderly man on bed rest

B) a young, overweight man undergoing physical therapy for a broken leg

C) an elderly man with chronic bed sores

D) a young, underweight man recovering from a respiratory infection

21. Which of the following is NOT a detail stated in the passage?

A) A thirty-five-year-old woman who weighs 135 pounds would require at least 2000 calories a day.

B) Patients' energy needs vary directly with weight and inversely with age.

C) Carbohydrates, fats, and proteins are macronutrients.

D) An elderly, bedridden female patient can require as little as 8.5 calories per pound of body weight.

22. Which of the following is NOT a fact stated in the passage?

A) Patients require energy from carbohydrates, fats, and proteins as well as essential vitamins and elements to heal properly.

B) A bedridden patient may require extra calories to provide the body with energy to fuel the healing process.

C) A poor diet can delay healing in patients.

D) Female patients should receive fewer calories than male patients so they don't gain weight.

It could be said that the great battle between the North and South we call the Civil War was a battle for individual identity. The states of the South had their own culture, one based on farming, independence, and the rights of both man and state to determine their own paths. Similarly, the North had forged its own identity as a center of centralized commerce and manufacturing. This clash of lifestyles was bound to create tension, and this tension was bound to lead to war. But people who try to sell you this narrative are wrong. The Civil War was not a battle of cultural identities—it was a battle about slavery. All other explanations for the war are either a direct consequence of the South's desire for wealth at the expense of her fellow man or a fanciful invention to cover up this sad portion of our nation's history. And it cannot be denied that this time in our past was very sad indeed.

23. What is the meaning of the word *fanciful* in the passage?

A) complicated

B) imaginative

C) successful

D) unfortunate

24. What is the author's primary purpose in writing this essay?

A) to convince readers that slavery was the main cause of the Civil War

B) to illustrate the cultural differences between the North and the South before the Civil War

C) to persuade readers that the North deserved to win the Civil War

D) to demonstrate that the history of the Civil War is too complicated to be understood clearly

25. What is the main idea of the passage?

A) The Civil War was the result of cultural differences between the North and South.

B) The Civil War was caused by the South's reliance on slave labor.

C) The North's use of commerce and manufacturing allowed it to win the war.

D) The South's belief in the rights of man and state cost them the war.

Influenza (also called the flu) has historically been one of the most common, and deadliest, human infections. While many people who contract the virus will recover, many others will not. Over the past 150 years, tens of millions of people have died from the flu, and millions more have been left with lingering complications such as secondary infections.

Although it's a common disease, the flu is not actually highly infectious, meaning it's relatively difficult to contract. The flu can only be transmitted when individuals come into direct contact with bodily fluids of people infected with the flu or when they are exposed to expelled aerosol particles (which result from coughing and sneezing). Because the viruses can only travel short distances as aerosol particles and will die within a few hours on hard surfaces, the virus can be contained with fairly simple health measures like hand washing and face masks.

However, the spread of the flu can only be contained when people are aware such measures need to be taken. One of the reasons the flu has historically been so deadly is the amount of time between when people become infectious and when they develop symptoms. Viral shedding—the process by which the body releases viruses that have been successfully reproducing during the infection—takes place two days after infection, while symptoms do not usually develop until the third day of infection. Thus, infected individuals have at least twenty-four hours in which they may unknowingly infect others.

26. What is the main idea of the passage?

   A) The flu is a deadly disease that's difficult to control because people become infectious before they show symptoms.

   B) For the flu to be transmitted, individuals must come in contact with bodily fluids from infected individuals.

   C) The spread of the flu is easy to contain because the viruses do not live long either as aerosol particles or on hard surfaces.

   D) The flu has killed tens of millions of people and can often cause deadly secondary infections.

27. Which of the following correctly describes the flu?

   A) The flu is easy to contract and always fatal.

   B) The flu is difficult to contract and always fatal.

   C) The flu is easy to contract and sometimes fatal.

   D) The flu is difficult to contract and sometimes fatal.

28. Why is the flu considered to not be highly infectious?

   A) Many people who get the flu will recover and have no lasting complications, so only a small number of people who become infected will die.

   B) The process of viral shedding takes two days, so infected individuals have enough time to implement simple health measures that stop the spread of the disease.

   C) The flu virus cannot travel far or live for long periods of time outside the human body, so its spread can easily be contained.

   D) Twenty-four hours is a relatively short period of time for the virus to spread among a population.

29. What is the meaning of the word *measures* in the last paragraph?

   A) a plan of action

   B) a standard unit

   C) an adequate amount

   D) a rhythmic movement

30. Which statement is NOT a detail from the passage?

- **A)** Tens of millions of people have been killed by the flu virus.
- **B)** There is typically a twenty-four hour window during which individuals are infectious but not showing flu symptoms.
- **C)** Viral shedding is the process by which people recover from the flu.
- **D)** The flu can be transmitted by direct contact with bodily fluids from infected individuals or by exposure to aerosol particles.

31. What can the reader conclude from the previous passage about the flu?

- **A)** Preemptively implementing health measures like hand washing and face masks could help stop the spread of the flu virus.
- **B)** Doctors are not sure how the flu virus is transmitted, so they are unsure how to stop it from spreading.
- **C)** The flu is dangerous because it is both deadly and highly infectious.
- **D)** Individuals stop being infectious three days after they are infected.

Skin coloration and markings have an important role to play in the world of snakes. Those intricate diamonds, stripes, and swirls help the animals hide from predators, but perhaps most importantly (for us humans, anyway), the markings can also indicate whether the snake is venomous. While it might seem counterintuitive for a venomous snake to stand out in bright red or blue, that fancy costume tells any nearby predator that approaching him would be a bad idea.

If you see a flashy-looking snake in the woods, though, those markings don't necessarily mean it's venomous: some snakes have found a way to ward off predators without the actual venom. The scarlet kingsnake, for example, has very similar markings to the venomous coral snake with whom it frequently shares a habitat. However, the kingsnake is actually nonvenomous; it's merely pretending to be dangerous to eat. A predatory hawk or eagle, usually hunting from high in the sky, can't tell the difference between the two species, and so the kingsnake gets passed over and lives another day.

32. What is the author's primary purpose in writing this essay?

- **A)** To explain how the markings on a snake are related to whether it's venomous.
- **B)** To teach readers the difference between coral snakes and kingsnakes.
- **C)** To illustrate why snakes are dangerous.
- **D)** To demonstrate how animals survive in difficult environments.

33. What is the meaning of the word *intricate* in the first paragraph?

- **A)** complex
- **B)** colorful
- **C)** purposeful
- **D)** changeable

34. What can the reader conclude from the passage about snakes?

- **A)** The kingsnake is dangerous to humans.
- **B)** The coral snake and the kingsnake are both hunted by the same predators.
- **C)** It's safe to handle snakes in the woods because you can easily tell whether they're poisonous.
- **D)** The kingsnake changes its markings when hawks or eagles are close by.

35. Which statement is NOT a detail from the passage?

- **A)** Predators will avoid eating kingsnakes because their markings are similar to those on coral snakes.
- **B)** Kingsnakes and coral snakes live in the same habitats.
- **C)** The coral snake uses its coloration to hide from predators.
- **D)** The kingsnake is not venomous.

36. What is the best summary of this passage?

A) Humans can use coloration and markings on snakes to determine whether they're venomous.

B) Animals often use coloration to hide from predators.

C) The scarlet kingsnake and the coral snake have nearly identical markings.

D) Venomous snakes often have bright markings, although nonvenomous snakes can also mimic those colors.

37. What is the difference between kingsnakes and coral snakes according to the passage?

A) Both kingsnakes and coral snakes are nonvenomous, but coral snakes have colorful markings.

B) Both kingsnakes and coral snakes are venomous, but kingsnakes have colorful markings.

C) Kingsnakes are nonvenomous while coral snakes are venomous.

D) Coral snakes are nonvenomous while kingsnakes are venomous.

We've been told for years that the recipe for weight loss is fewer calories in than calories out. In other words, eat less and exercise more, and your body will take care of the rest. As many of those who've tried to diet can attest, this edict doesn't always produce results. If you're one of those folks, you might have felt that you just weren't doing it right—that the failure was all your fault.

However, several new studies released this year have suggested that it might not be your fault at all. For example, a study of people who'd lost a high percentage of their body weight (>17%) in a short period of time found that they could not physically maintain their new weight. Scientists measured their resting metabolic rate and found that they'd need to consume only a few hundred calories a day to meet their metabolic needs. Basically, their bodies were in starvation mode and seemed to desperately hang on to each and every calorie. Eating even a single healthy, well-balanced meal a day would cause these subjects to start packing back on the pounds.

Other studies have shown that factors like intestinal bacteria, distribution of body fat, and hormone levels can affect the manner in which our bodies process calories. There's also the fact that it's actually quite difficult to measure the number of calories consumed during a particular meal and the number used while exercising.

38. Which of the following would be the best summary statement to conclude the passage?

A) It turns out that conventional dieting wisdom doesn't capture the whole picture of how our bodies function.

B) Still, counting calories and tracking exercise is a good idea if you want to lose weight.

C) In conclusion, it's important to lose weight responsibly: losing too much weight at once can negatively impact the body.

D) It's easy to see that diets don't work, so we should focus less on weight loss and more on overall health.

39. Which of the following would weaken the author's argument?

A) a new diet pill from a pharmaceutical company that promises to help patients lose weight by changing intestinal bacteria

B) the personal experience of a man who was able to lose a significant amount of weight by taking in fewer calories than he used

C) a study showing that people in different geographic locations lose different amounts of weight when on the same diet

D) a study showing that people often misreport their food intake when part of a scientific study on weight loss

In recent decades, jazz has been associated with New Orleans and festivals like Mardi Gras, but in the 1920s, jazz was a booming trend whose influence reached into many aspects of American culture. In fact, the years between World War I and the Great Depression were known as the Jazz Age, a term coined by F. Scott Fitzgerald in his famous novel *The Great Gatsby*. Sometimes also called the Roaring Twenties, this time period saw major urban centers experiencing new economic, cultural, and artistic vitality. In the United States, musicians flocked to cities like New York and Chicago, which would become famous hubs for jazz musicians. Ella Fitzgerald, for example, moved from Virginia to New York City to begin her much-lauded singing career, and jazz pioneer Louis Armstrong got his big break in Chicago.

Jazz music was played by and for a more expressive and freed populace than the United States had previously seen. Women gained the right to vote and were openly seen drinking and dancing to jazz music. This period marked the emergence of the flapper, a woman determined to make a statement about her new role in society. Jazz music also provided the soundtrack for the explosion of African American art and culture now known as the Harlem Renaissance. In addition to Fitzgerald and Armstrong, numerous musicians, including Duke Ellington, Fats Waller, and Bessie Smith, promoted their distinctive and complex music as an integral part of the emerging African American culture.

40. What is the main idea of the passage?

A) People should associate jazz music with the 1920s, not modern New Orleans.

B) Jazz music played an important role in many cultural movements of the 1920s.

C) Many famous jazz musicians began their careers in New York City and Chicago.

D) African Americans were instrumental in launching jazz into mainstream culture.

41. What can the reader conclude from the passage about jazz?

A) Jazz music was important to minority groups struggling for social equality in the 1920s.

B) Duke Ellington, Fats Waller, and Bessie Smith were the most important jazz musicians of the Harlem Renaissance.

C) Women gained the right to vote with the help of jazz musicians.

D) Duke Ellington, Fats Waller, and Bessie Smith all supported women's right to vote.

42. What is the author's primary purpose in writing this essay?

A) to explain the role jazz musicians played in the Harlem Renaissance

B) to inform the reader about the many important musicians playing jazz in the 1920s

C) to discuss how jazz influenced important cultural movements in the 1920s

D) to provide a history of jazz music in the 20th century

43. Which of the following is NOT a fact stated in the passage?

A) The years between World War I and the Great Depression were known as the Jazz Age.

B) Ella Fitzgerald and Louis Armstrong both moved to New York City to start their music careers.

C) Women danced to jazz music during the 1920s to make a statement about their role in society.

D) Jazz music was an integral part of the emerging African American culture of the 1920s.

The bacteria, fungi, insects, plants, and animals that live together in a habitat have evolved to share a pool of limited resources. They've competed for water, minerals, nutrients, sunlight, and space—sometimes for thousands or even millions of years. As these communities have evolved, the species in them have developed complex, long-term interspecies interactions known as symbiotic relationships.

Ecologists characterize these interactions based on whether each party benefits. In mutualism, both individuals benefit, while in synnecrosis, both organisms are harmed. A relationship where one individual benefits and the other is harmed is known as parasitism. Examples of these relationships can easily be seen in any ecosystem. Pollination, for example, is mutualistic—pollinators get nutrients from the flower, and the plant is able to reproduce—while tapeworms, which steal nutrients from their host, are parasitic.

There's yet another class of symbiosis that is controversial among scientists. As it's long been defined, commensalism is a relationship where one species benefits and the other is unaffected. But is it possible for two species to interact and for one to remain completely unaffected? Often, relationships described as commensal include one species that feeds on another species' leftovers; remoras, for instance, will attach themselves to sharks and eat the food particles they leave behind. It might seem like the shark gets nothing from the relationship, but a closer look will show that sharks in fact benefit from remoras, which clean the sharks' skin and remove parasites. In fact, many scientists claim that relationships currently described as commensal are just mutualistic or parasitic in ways that haven't been discovered yet.

44. What is the author's primary purpose in writing this essay?

A) to argue that commensalism isn't actually found in nature

B) to describe the many types of symbiotic relationships

C) to explain how competition for resources results in long-term interspecies relationships

D) to provide examples of the many different ways individual organisms interact

45. Which of the following is NOT a fact stated in the passage?

A) Mutualism is an interspecies relationship where both species benefit.

B) Synnecrosis is an interspecies relationship where both species are harmed.

C) The relationship between plants and pollinators is mutualistic.

D) The relationship between remoras and sharks is parasitic.

46. Epiphytes are plants that attach themselves to trees and derive nutrients from the air and surrounding debris. Sometimes, the weight of epiphytes can damage the trees on which they're growing. The relationship between epiphytes and their hosts would be described as _____.

A) mutualism

B) commensalism

C) parasitism

D) synnecrosis

47. Why is commensalism controversial among scientists?

A) Many scientists believe that an interspecies interaction where one species is unaffected does not exist.

B) Some scientists believe that relationships where one species feeds on the leftovers of another should be classified as parasitism.

C) Because remoras and sharks have a mutualistic relationship, no interaction should be classified as commensalism.

D) Only relationships among animal species should be classified as commensalism.

48. What can the reader conclude from this passage about symbiotic relationships?

- **A)** Scientists cannot decide how to classify symbiotic relationships among species.
- **B)** The majority of interspecies interactions are parasitic because most species do not get along.
- **C)** If two species are involved in a parasitic relationship, one of the species will eventually become extinct.
- **D)** Symbiotic relationships evolve as the species that live in a community adapt to their environments and each other.

49. What is the meaning of the word *controversial* in the last paragraph?

- **A)** debatable
- **B)** objectionable
- **C)** confusing
- **D)** upsetting

Popcorn is often associated with fun and festivities, both in and out of the home. It's eaten in theaters, usually after being salted and smothered in butter, and in homes, fresh from the microwave. But popcorn isn't just for fun—it's also a multimillion-dollar-a-year industry with a long and fascinating history.

While popcorn might seem like a modern invention, its history actually dates back thousands of years, making it one of the oldest snack foods enjoyed around the world. Popcorn is believed by food historians to be one of the earliest uses of cultivated corn. In 1948, Herbert Dick and Earle Smith discovered old popcorn dating back 4000 years in the New Mexico Bat Cave. For the Aztec Indians who called the caves home, popcorn (or *momochitl*) played an important role in society, both as a food staple and in ceremonies. The Aztecs cooked popcorn by heating sand in a fire; when it was heated, kernels were added and would pop when exposed to the heat of the sand.

The American love affair with popcorn began in 1912, when popcorn was first sold in theaters. The popcorn industry flourished during the Great Depression when it was advertised as a wholesome and economical food. Selling for five to ten cents a bag, it was a luxury that the downtrodden could afford. With the introduction of mobile popcorn machines at the World's Columbian Exposition, popcorn moved from the theater into fairs and parks. Popcorn continued to rule the snack food kingdom until the rise in popularity of home televisions during the 1950s.

The popcorn industry reacted to the decline in sales quickly by introducing pre-popped and unpopped popcorn for home consumption. However, it wasn't until microwave popcorn became commercially available in 1981 that at-home popcorn consumption began to grow exponentially. With the wide availability of microwaves in the United States, popcorn also began popping up in offices and hotel rooms. However, the home still remains the most popular popcorn eating spot: today, 70 percent of the 16 billion quarts of popcorn consumed annually in the United States are eaten at home.

50. What can the reader conclude from the passage above?

    A)   People ate less popcorn in the 1950s than in previous decades because they went to the movies less.

    B)   Without mobile popcorn machines, people would not have been able to eat popcorn during the Great Depression.

    C)   People enjoyed popcorn during the Great Depression because it was a luxury food.

    D)   During the 1800s, people began abandoning theaters to go to fairs and festivals.

51. What is the meaning of the word *staple* in the second paragraph?

    A)   something produced only for special occasions

    B)   something produced regularly in large quantities

    C)   something produced by cooking

    D)   something fastened together securely

52. What is the author's primary purpose in writing this essay?

    A)   to explain how microwaves affected the popcorn industry

    B)   to show that popcorn is older than many people realize

    C)   to illustrate the history of popcorn from ancient cultures to modern times

    D)   to demonstrate the importance of popcorn in various cultures

53. Which factor does the author of the passage credit for the growth of the popcorn industry in the United States?

    A)   the use of popcorn in ancient Aztec ceremonies

    B)   the growth of the home television industry

    C)   the marketing of popcorn during the Great Depression

    D)   the nutritional value of popcorn

54. What is the best summary of this passage?

    A)   Popcorn is a popular snack food that dates back thousands of years. Its popularity in the United States has been tied to the growth of theaters and the availability of microwaves.

    B)   Popcorn has been a popular snack food for thousands of years. Archaeologists have found evidence that many ancient cultures used popcorn as a food staple and in ceremonies.

    C)   Popcorn was first introduced to America in 1912, and its popularity has grown exponentially since then. Today, over 16 billion quarts of popcorn are consumed in the United States annually.

    D)   Popcorn is a versatile snack food that can be eaten with butter or other toppings. It can also be cooked in a number of different ways, including in microwaves.

55. Which of the following is NOT a fact stated in the passage?

    A)   Archaeologists have found popcorn dating back 4000 years.

    B)   Popcorn was first sold in theaters in 1912.

    C)   Consumption of popcorn dropped in 1981 with the growing popularity of home televisions.

    D)   70 percent of the popcorn consumed in the United States is eaten in homes.

Vocabulary

1. Select the meaning of the underlined word in the sentence.

   The <u>adverse</u> outcome was expected but still upsetting.

   A) unlikely

   B) unfavorable

   C) different

   D) difficult

2. Select the word that means "based on observable and diagnosable symptoms."

   The new residence program allows medical practitioners to build on their clinical knowledge and to learn to assess patients more accurately.

   A) residence

   B) practitioners

   C) clinical

   D) accurately

3. Select the meaning of the underlined word in the sentence.

   Her <u>chronic</u> back pain led her to seek new treatments.

   A) continual

   B) recent

   C) severe

   D) dull

4. Select the meaning of the underlined word in the sentence.

   An <u>impartial</u> panel will decide on the appropriate punishment.

   A) overbearing

   B) incomplete

   C) objective

   D) heartless

5. *Distal* refers to a part of the body located _____.

   A) away from the point of origin

   B) toward the midline

   C) close to the surface

   D) at the back

6. Which is the best description of the word *pacify*?

   A) soothe

   B) transport

   C) motivate

   D) nurture

7. Select the meaning of the underlined word in the sentence.

   The doctor made the <u>judicious</u> decision to keep the patient in the hospital overnight.

   A) wise

   B) quick

   C) brave

   D) mistaken

8. Select the meaning of the underlined word in the sentence.

   Their relationship was <u>acrimonious</u> and prevented them from working well together.

   A) complex

   B) brief

   C) practical

   D) bitter

9. <u>Pragmatic</u> is best defined as being _____.

   A) accurate

   B) realistic

   C) imaginative

   D) spontaneous

10. What is the best description for the word *accountable*?

    A)   able to perform

    B)   responsible for

    C)   likely to forget

    D)   a part of

11. Select the word that means "regular or steady without variation."

The nurse kept copious notes to ensure the patient received consistent care while being transitioned to a palliative care center.

    A)   copious

    B)   ensure

    C)   consistent

    D)   palliative

12. A medication administered sublingually would be

    A)   held between the gums and cheek.

    B)   injected into the spine.

    C)   placed under the tongue.

    D)   sprayed into the nose.

13. Select the meaning of the underlined word in the sentence.

The <u>deleterious</u> effects of smoking should be explained to patients receiving respiratory therapy.

    A)   harmful

    B)   forgotten

    C)   undetectable

    D)   catastrophic

14. Select the meaning of the underlined word in the sentence.

The patient requires at-home care due to her <u>impaired</u> mobility.

    A)   dangerous

    B)   typical

    C)   uncertain

    D)   weakened

15. Select the meaning of the underlined word in the sentence.

Poor diet and lack of exercise have likely <u>exacerbated</u> her symptoms.

    A)   delayed

    B)   worsened

    C)   suppressed

    D)   generated

16. A person who is *lethargic* is _____.

    A)   tired

    B)   confused

    C)   angry

    D)   rushed

17. Select the meaning of the underlined word in the sentence.

The guidelines are <u>rudimentary</u> and will need to be improved before being implemented.

    A)   confusing

    B)   basic

    C)   available

    D)   innovative

18. A hematologist is a doctor who treats diseases of the _____.

    A)   heart

    B)   kidneys

    C)   blood

    D)   bones

19. Select the word that means "related to the treatment of disease or beneficial to the body."

    A)   symptomatic

    B)   endogenous

    C)   resilient

    D)   therapeutic

20. Which word means "wise or judicious"?

- **A)** prudent
- **B)** inquisitive
- **C)** terrified
- **D)** modest

21. Select the meaning of the underlined word.

The suspected toxin was sent for testing, but it was found to be <u>innocuous</u>.

- **A)** susceptible
- **B)** suspicious
- **C)** harmless
- **D)** beneficial

22. Select the meaning of the underlined word.

The lawsuit claimed the doctor's <u>negligence</u> resulted in serious injury to the patient.

- **A)** malice
- **B)** immorality
- **C)** inattention
- **D)** aggression

23. Select the meaning of the underlined word.

Her history of high blood pressure made her <u>predisposed</u> to heart disease.

- **A)** immune to
- **B)** likely to get
- **C)** in favor of
- **D)** an opponent of

24. Select the meaning of the underlined word.

The <u>dominant</u> theme of the speech was the importance of empathy toward patients.

- **A)** typical
- **B)** distinct
- **C)** convincing
- **D)** principal

25. To *interpret* something is to

- **A)** put an end to it.
- **B)** write it down.
- **C)** explain its meaning.
- **D)** make it stronger.

26. What is the best description for the word *resilience*?

- **A)** recovering easily
- **B)** a large quantity
- **C)** quick to anger
- **D)** creating excitement

27. Select the word that means "to occur again after an interval."

The patient's symptoms recur when she deviates from the regimen prescribed by her doctor.

- **A)** symptoms
- **B)** recur
- **C)** deviates
- **D)** prescribed

28. Select the meaning of the underlined word.

He was <u>anxious</u> about the test results.

- **A)** angry
- **B)** sad
- **C)** excited
- **D)** worried

29. Select the word that would best complete the sentence.

After updating to a new software program, the billing department had to make _____ changes to their procedures.

- **A)** unfortunate
- **B)** justified
- **C)** substantial
- **D)** unlikely

30. Select the meaning of the underlined word.

The employee made an <u>egregious</u> error, and his employer fired him immediately.

- **A)** extreme
- **B)** accidental
- **C)** malicious
- **D)** understandable

31. What is the best description for the word *illness*?

A) injury

B) ailment

C) irritation

D) symptom

32. What is the best description for the word *concurrent*?

A) up to date

B) rushing

C) sophisticated

D) simultaneous

33. Select the meaning of the underlined word.

Tardiness is not tolerated, and you will be counted absent.

A) illness

B) absence

C) lateness

D) attendance

34. Select the meaning of the underlined word.

They were uncertain whether the condition was contagious, so the patient was quarantined.

A) transmissible

B) poisonous

C) aseptic

D) common

35. Select the meaning of the underlined word.

The staff was concerned about the rash of flu cases at the hospital.

A) flood

B) severity

C) mixture

D) symptoms

36. Select the meaning of the underlined word.

The patient complained of bilateral weakness.

A) right side

B) both sides

C) lower body

D) upper body

37. What is the best description for the word *mediation*?

A) an argument

B) a negotiation

C) a civil lawsuit

D) a financial settlement

38. Select the meaning of the underlined word in the sentence.

Careful hand washing is an essential precaution in the workplace.

A) protocol

B) virtue

C) safeguard

D) rule

39. Select the word that best completes the sentence.

The change in the patient's condition was_____, so the doctors were unprepared.

A) reasonable

B) insignificant

C) abrupt

D) consistent

40. Select the meaning of the underlined word in the sentence.

Many medical tests should be scheduled annually.

A) every year

B) every month

C) every other year

D) every decade

41. Select the meaning of the underlined word in the sentence.

   The mixture will need to be <u>diluted</u> before it can be safely applied to the skin.

   A) solidified
   B) analyzed
   C) clarified
   D) weakened

42. Which word means "related to the stomach"?

   A) renal
   B) osteo
   C) nasal
   D) gastric

43. What is the best description of the term *efficient*?

   A) completed with little waste
   B) completed quickly
   C) completed without error
   D) completed on time

44. What is the best description for the term *complication*?

   A) an emergency
   B) a secondary condition
   C) an unlikely outcome
   D) a substantial change

45. Select the word that means "something that makes a treatment unadvisable."

   Arrhythmias are a contraindication for some therapies, but medication can still be prescribed.

   A) arrhythmias
   B) contraindication
   C) therapies
   D) prescribed

46. Select the meaning of the underlined word.

   A vitamin <u>deficiency</u> can cause many serious symptoms.

   A) lack
   B) dependence
   C) excess
   D) regimen

47. Select the meaning of the underlined word.

   The patient complains that the medications are <u>aggravating</u> her symptoms.

   A) dominating
   B) monitoring
   C) worsening
   D) stimulating

48. What is the best description of the term *audible*?

   A) able to be seen
   B) able to be heard
   C) able to move
   D) able to speak

49. Which of the following statements uses a euphemism?

   A) He passed away last week.
   B) The laceration will require stitches.
   C) The baby was born last month.
   D) The dog ran away but was found after two days.

50. Which word is NOT spelled correctly in the context of this sentence?

   It is the responsibility of the nurse to confirm the patient's identity before treatement begins.

   A) responsibility
   B) confirm
   C) identity
   D) treatement

51. Select the meaning of the underlined word.

The pupils should <u>dilate</u> in low light.

A) expand

B) move

C) brighten

D) shine

52. Which word is NOT spelled correctly in the context of this sentence?

Firing her without a replacement will crate more work for everyone else.

A) firing

B) replacement

C) crate

D) everyone

53. Select the meaning of the underlined word in the sentence.

The new weight loss drug will <u>suppress</u> production of hormones that cause hunger.

A) update

B) instigate

C) inhibit

D) continue

54. Select the meaning of the underlined word in the sentence.

The results of the study will be groundbreaking if they can be <u>reproduced</u>.

A) understood

B) forgotten

C) duplicated

D) integrated

55. Select the meaning of the underlined word in the sentence.

The patient's <u>prognosis</u> improved after a successful surgery.

A) mood

B) forecast

C) habits

D) insight

GRAMMAR

1. Which word from the following sentence is a conjunction?

   We went to the grocery store, stopped for coffee, and picked up our dry cleaning.

   A) our
   B) for
   C) and
   D) to

2. Select the best word for the blank in the following sentence.

   You need to get up now in order ___ make it to class on time.

   A) for
   B) to
   C) when
   D) of

3. Which of the following sentences is grammatically incorrect?

   A) Who goes to school on South Street.
   B) The boy goes to school on South Street.
   C) The girl attends the South Street School.
   D) Which of the children go to school on South Street?

4. Which of the following sentences is grammatically correct?

   A) The boy started school yesterday.
   B) The boy starts school yesterday.
   C) The boy started school tomorrow.
   D) The boy did start school tomorrow.

5. Select the best word for the blank in the following sentence.

   Please _____ your mom today.

   A) calling
   B) calls
   C) called
   D) call

6. Which word from the following sentence is a conjunction?

   Did you go to class, or did you stay home sick today?

   A) Did
   B) stay
   C) today
   D) or

7. Select the best word for the blank in the following sentence.

   The flight _____, so we will have to wait at the airport.

   A) delays
   B) delayed
   C) is delayed
   D) will delay

8. Which of the following sentences is grammatically incorrect?

   A) Monitors track the patient's heart rate and oxygen levels.
   B) Monitor track the patient's heart rate and oxygen levels.
   C) You should carefully monitor the patient's vital signs.
   D) Watch the monitors from the nurses' station.

9. Which of the following sentences is grammatically correct?

   A) I need to do my homework now, so I can go to the movie now.
   B) I need to do my homework now, so I cannot go to the movie now.
   C) I need to doing my homework now, so I cannot go to the movie now.
   D) I need to do my homework now, so I cannot going to the movie now.

10. Which word from the following sentence is a noun?

The puppy's favorite toy is pink and fuzzy.

A) pink

B) fuzzy

C) favorite

D) toy

11. Which word from the following sentence is the subject?

The bell will ring in five minutes.

A) bell

B) five

C) will

D) ring

12. Which of the following sentences is grammatically correct?

A) You can have either the cake nor the cookie.

B) You can't have neither the cake or the cookie.

C) You can have either the cake or the cookie.

D) You can having either the cake or the cookie.

13. Which word from the following sentence is a noun?

Put the groceries on the table, please.

A) table

B) Put

C) please

D) on

14. Which word from the following sentence is a preposition?

He checked into the hospital early that morning for his surgery.

A) checked

B) He

C) into

D) hospital

15. Which of the following sentences is grammatically correct?

A) Who is going to class on Saturday.

B) Who is goes to class on Saturday?

C) Whose going to class on Saturday?

D) Who is going to class on Saturday?

16. Which word from the following sentence is a subject?

After the children finished painting, they had to clean up their mess.

A) mess

B) painting

C) finished

D) they

17. Which word from the following sentence is a subject?

She popped popcorn, grabbed a drink, and sat down to watch her favorite show.

A) She

B) popcorn

C) drink

D) show

18. Select the best word for the blank in the following sentence.

_____ you want to work in home health care after graduation?

A) Does

B) Do

C) Was

D) Doing

19. Which word in the following sentence is incorrect?

The members of the team, all of whom played good in the game last night, are having a celebratory dinner.

A) team

B) whom

C) good

D) are

20. Select the best word or phrase for the blank in the following sentence.

    She _____ a doctor's appointment in the morning, so she was late to work that day.

    A) has
    B) had
    C) will have
    D) was

21. Which of the following sentences is grammatically correct?

    A) The baby is due in December.
    B) The baby dues in December.
    C) The babies is due in December.
    D) The baby are due in December.

22. Which word from the following sentence is a direct object?

    She finished decorating the kitchen for the party early that morning.

    A) morning
    B) She
    C) kitchen
    D) early

23. Which word from the following sentence is a direct object?

    He was scheduled to work a long shift.

    A) shift
    B) He
    C) long
    D) work

24. Which of the following sentences is grammatically correct?

    A) I learned to write good working at the paper.
    B) I learned to write well working at the paper.
    C) I teached to write well working at the paper.
    D) I learned to write well working to the paper.

25. Which of the following sentences is grammatically incorrect?

    A) The librarian at the reference desk is very helpful.
    B) The reference desk librarian is very helpful.
    C) Is the reference desk librarian helpful?
    D) Can the reference desk librarian helpful?

26. In the following sentence, which is the dependent clause?

    The librarian who works on Saturday had to leave early because she wanted to see a play.

    A) The librarian who works on Saturday
    B) had to leave early
    C) because she wanted to see a play
    D) The librarian who works on Saturday had to leave early

27. In the following sentence, which is the dependent clause?

    Although we left the baseball game early, we still got stuck in heavy traffic.

    A) Although we left the baseball game early
    B) we left
    C) we still got stuck in heavy traffic
    D) in heavy traffic

28. Which of the following sentences is grammatically correct?

    A) The baseball game was canceled because of rain.
    B) The baseball game will canceled because of rain.
    C) The baseball game was cancel because of rain.
    D) The baseball games was canceled because to rain.

29. Which word or phrase from the following sentence is the predicate?

The boy threw the ball across the field.

- **A)** The boy
- **B)** threw the ball across the field
- **C)** across the field
- **D)** The boy threw the ball

30. Which of the following sentences is grammatically incorrect?

- **A)** The dance was scheduled for next Saturday night.
- **B)** The dance is scheduled for next Saturday night.
- **C)** Schedule the dance for next Saturday night.
- **D)** Scheduling the dance for next Saturday night.

31. Which word or phrase from the following sentence is the predicate?

Michelle and her dog walk in the park every day.

- **A)** Michelle
- **B)** Michelle and her dog
- **C)** walk in the park every day
- **D)** in the park every day

32. Which of the following sentences is grammatically correct?

- **A)** I heard about the plane crash on the news.
- **B)** I read about the plane crash on the news.
- **C)** I heard on the plane crash on the news.
- **D)** I hear about the plane crash to the news.

33. Which of the following sentences contains a predicate adjective?

- **A)** Dinner smells amazing.
- **B)** We are going to dinner.
- **C)** He ate a sandwich.
- **D)** The car has a leak in the radiator.

34. Which of the following sentences contains a predicate adjective?

- **A)** The doctor is concerned about her symptoms.
- **B)** I scheduled an appointment.
- **C)** I have to work on Tuesday.
- **D)** He bought a new phone.

35. What word is best to substitute for the blank in the following sentence?

Although both girls enjoyed the movie, _____ decided not to see it again.

- **A)** she
- **B)** we
- **C)** they
- **D)** her

36. Which of the following sentences is grammatically incorrect?

- **A)** Nurses may work in the home, doctor's office, or hospital.
- **B)** Nurses works in the home, doctor's office, or hospital.
- **C)** Nurses can work in the home, doctor's office, or hospital.
- **D)** Nurses may work in either the home, doctor's office, or hospital.

37. What word is best to substitute for the underlined word in the following sentence?

The ambulance <u>took</u> the patient to the hospital after he called 911.

- **A)** brought
- **B)** accompanied
- **C)** assisted
- **D)** went

38. Select the word in the sentence that is not used correctly.

He swimmed across the lake last summer.

- **A)** across
- **B)** lake
- **C)** swimmed
- **D)** summer

39. Select the word in the sentence that is not used correctly.

Neither the dog or the cat like going to the vet.

A) Neither

B) like

C) going

D) or

40. Select the best word or phrase for the blank in the following sentence.

I _____ never going to work there.

A) am not

B) will

C) will not

D) am

41. Which of the following sentences is grammatically incorrect?

A) Take the patient into the examining room.

B) Takes the patient into the examining room.

C) You should take the patient into the examining room.

D) He takes the patient into the examining room.

42. The following sentence contains which part of speech or can be described in which way?

The butcher, who has his own shop, is known for the quality of his meat.

A) prepositional phrase

B) adverb

C) compound sentence

D) conjunction

43. Select the best word for the blank in the following sentence.

_____ you planning to attend the meeting?

A) Is

B) Are

C) Will

D) Was

44. Which of the following sentences is grammatically incorrect?

A) I checked the patient's vital signs and entered them into the computer.

B) I changed into scrubs at the beginning of my shift.

C) The patient, who had surgery that day, was nervous.

D) The patients was prepped for surgery that morning.

45. The following sentence contains which type of phrase or clause?

We are baking cookies to take to the school bake sale.

A) dependent clause

B) prepositional phrase

C) predicate adjective

D) adverbial phrase

46. Select the best word for the blank in the following sentence.

Can you _____ on the patient in room 302?

A) watch

B) check

C) talk

D) care

47. Select the best word for the blank in the following sentence.

She was scared ____ spiders, so she avoided the basement.

A) to

B) for

C) of

D) from

48. Select the best word for the blank in the following sentence.

They were _____ for a new car to purchase.

A) looks

B) looking

C) wanting

D) shops

49. Select the best word for the blank in the following sentence.

I am waiting _____ the bus.

A) for

B) to

C) catch

D) catching

50. Select the best word or phrase for the blank in the following sentence.

I _____ overtime later this week, so I cannot go out tonight.

A) will work

B) am work

C) working

D) works

51. Select the best word for the blank in the following sentence.

_____ to school and study hard to do well in life.

A) Go

B) Goes

C) Going

D) Gone

52. Which of the following sentences is grammatically correct?

A) Take the dog of the vet.

B) You need to take the dog to the vet.

C) The dog need to go to the vet.

D) The dogs need to going to the vet.

53. Which of the following is grammatically incorrect?

A) Take the garbage to the curb.

B) You should take the garbage to the curb.

C) The garbage needs to go to the curb.

D) You takes the garbage to the curb.

54. Select the best word for the blank in the following sentence.

The hospital cafeteria opens _____ 8:00 a.m.

A) for

B) at

C) when

D) to

55. Which of the following sentences is grammatically correct?

A) My best friend and I has tickets to a concert on Friday.

B) My best friend and I have tickets to a concert on Friday.

C) Me and my best friend has tickets to a concert on Friday.

D) Me and my best friend have tickets to a concert on Friday.

BIOLOGY

1. Which of the following choices would contain the code for making a protein?

   A) mRNA
   B) tRNA
   C) rRNA
   D) DNA polymerase

2. Which of the following is NOT present in an animal cell?

   A) nucleus
   B) mitochondria
   C) cytoplasm
   D) cell wall

3. Which of the following is the number of chromosomes found in a human gamete?

   A) 17
   B) 22
   C) 23
   D) 46

4. Which of the following biological macromolecules is non-soluble, composed of hydrocarbons, and acts as an important source of energy storage for the body?

   A) carbohydrates
   B) nucleic acids
   C) lipids
   D) proteins

5. Consider a prokaryotic organism that typically lives in a 10 percent saline concentration environment. Which of the following environments would cause the organism to lose mass at the greatest rate due to osmosis?

   A) a solution of pure water
   B) a solution of 3 percent saline concentration
   C) a solution of 10 percent saline concentration
   D) a solution of 20 percent saline concentration

6. Alleles for brown eyes (B)are dominant over alleles for blue eyes (b). If two parents are both heterozygous for this gene, what is the percent chance that their offspring will have brown eyes?

   A) 25
   B) 50
   C) 75
   D) 100

7. Which of the following cell organelles are the site of lipid synthesis?

   A) smooth endoplasmic reticulum
   B) ribosome
   C) rough endoplasmic reticulum
   D) Golgi apparatus

8. Mature red blood cells are adapted to not contain a nucleus. This allows them to carry more hemoglobin. As a result of this adaptation, red blood cells

   A) cannot undergo mitosis.
   B) have large energy reserves.
   C) never die.
   C) reproduce very quickly.

9. Photosynthesis takes place in which organelle of a photosynthetic, eukaryotic organism?

   A) nucleus
   B) chloroplast
   C) ribosome
   D) endoplasmic reticulum

10. Which of the following is the molecule found in red blood cells that binds to up to four oxygen molecules?

    A) hemoglobin
    B) erythrocyte
    C) globulin
    D) antigens

11. Which of the following is true of cellular respiration?

   A)   Two molecules of ATP are produced during electron transport.

   B)   Thirty-four molecules of ATP are produced during glycolysis.

   C)   Thirty-four molecules of ATP are produced during the Krebs cycle.

   D)   Thirty-eight molecules of ATP are produced during the entire process of cellular respiration.

12. The chromosomes of a eukaryotic organism would be found in the

   A)   chloroplast.

   B)   nucleus.

   C)   ribosome.

   D)   cytoplasm.

13. A distinct difference between a plant cell and an animal cell is the presence of

   A)   ribosomes.

   B)   mitochondria.

   C)   a cell wall.

   D)   a nucleus.

14. The result of meiosis is

   A)   two haploid (1n) cells.

   B)   four haploid (1n) cells.

   C)   two diploid (2n) cells.

   D)   four diploid (2n) cells.

15. The monomer of a nucleic acid is

   A)   DNA.

   B)   RNA.

   C)   a nucleotide.

   D)   an amino acid.

16. Which nitrogenous base is not found in a DNA molecule?

   A)   adenine

   B)   cytosine

   C)   guanine

   D)   uracil

17. The mitotic spindle forms during which phase of mitosis?

   A)   prophase

   B)   metaphase

   C)   anaphase

   D)   telophase

18. Sugars are built using which of the following monomers?

   A)   monosaccharides

   B)   nucleotides

   C)   amino acids

   D)   fatty acids

19. During which of the following phases of cellular respiration is the most ATP generated?

   A)   glycolysis

   B)   fermentation

   C)   the Krebs cycle

   D)   electron transport

20. Which of the following pairs of organelles perform similar functions?

   A)   the nucleus and ribosomes

   B)   vacuoles and mitochondria

   C)   chloroplasts and mitochondria

   D)   ribosomes and chloroplasts

21. Centrioles replicate in which of the following stages of cell division?

   A)   interphase

   B)   mitosis

   C)   cytokinesis

   D)   meiosis

22. The information stored in DNA is used to make which of the following molecules?

   A)   amino acids

   B)   proteins

   C)   fatty acids

   D)   monosaccharides

23. If a plant that is homozygous dominant (*T*) for a trait is crossed with a plant that is homozygous recessive (*t*) for the same trait, what will be the phenotype of the offspring if the trait follows Mendelian patterns of inheritance?

   A)   All offspring will show the dominant phenotype.

   B)   All offspring will show the recessive phenotype.

   C)   Half the offspring will show the dominant trait, and the other half will show the recessive phenotype.

   D)   All the offspring will show a mix of the dominant and recessive phenotypes.

24. Which of the following molecules can be found in abundance in a fatigued muscle?

   A)   glucose

   B)   lactic acid

   C)   ATP

   D)   myoglobin

25. Which of the following processes uses the information stored in RNA to produce a protein?

   A)   replication

   B)   translation

   C)   transcription

   D)   mutation

26. Which of the following does NOT correctly match the part of the cell and its primary function?

   A)   mitochondria: production of ATP through oxidative phosphorylation

   B)   nucleus: DNA replication and transcription

   C)   smooth endoplasmic reticulum: translation of mRNA into proteins

   D)   Golgi apparatus: packaging and transportation of proteins within and in/out of cells

27. Which of the following units is most appropriate for measuring the mass of an ant?

   A)   meters

   B)   grams

   C)   liters

   D)   kilograms

28. Muscle tissues will often require quick bursts of energy. As a result, which of the following organelles would be most likely to be found in higher than normal amounts in muscle cells?

   A)   ribosomes

   B)   lysosomes

   C)   vacuoles

   D)   mitochondria

29. The result of mitosis is

   A)   two haploid (1n) cells.

   B)   four haploid (1n) cells.

   C)   two diploid (2n) cells.

   D)   four diploid (2n) cells.

30. In a eukaryotic cell, DNA is transcribed in the

   A)   cytoplasm.

   B)   ribosome.

   C)   Golgi body.

   D)   nucleus.

CHEMISTRY

1. Which ion has the greatest number of electrons?

    A) Ca^{+2}

    B) Cl^-

    C) Ca^+

    D) P^{-3}

2. Which of the following correctly describes a strong acid?

    A) A strong acid completely ionizes in water.

    B) A strong acid donates more than one proton.

    C) A strong acid contains at least one metal atom.

    D) A strong acid will not decompose.

3. Which of the following is a decomposition reaction?

    A) $2Na + Cl_2 \rightarrow 2NaCl$

    B) $Zn + 2HCl \rightarrow ZnCl_2 + H_2$

    C) $CH_4 + 2O_2 \rightarrow CO_2 + 2H_2O$

    D) $H_2CO_3 \rightarrow H_2O + CO_2$

4. Which of the following is NOT a homogeneous mixture?

    A) air

    B) sandy water

    C) brass

    D) salt dissolved in water

5. How many electrons are included in the double bond between the two oxygen atoms in O_2?

    A) 2

    B) 4

    C) 6

    D) 8

6. Which of the following types of reactions is shown below?

    $CaCl_2 + 2NaOH \rightarrow Ca(OH)_2 + 2NaCl$

    A) single-replacement

    B) double-replacement

    C) synthesis

    D) acid-base

7. Which of the following processes produces a gas from a solid?

    A) melting

    B) evaporation

    C) condensation

    D) sublimation

8. What will happen to the pH of a nitric acid solution that is diluted by a factor of ten?

    A. The pH will go up ten units.

    B. The pH will go down ten units.

    C. The pH will go up one unit.

    D. The pH will go down one unit.

9. Which of the following correctly describes atomic number?

    A) the number of atoms in a mole of a given substance

    B) the number of neutrons in an atom

    C) the number of protons and neutrons in an atom

    D) the number of protons in an atom

10. Which of the following groups on the periodic table will typically adopt a charge of +1 when forming ionic compounds?

    A) alkaline earth metals

    B) lanthanides

    C) actinides

    D) alkali metals

11. How many neutrons are in an atom of the element $^{88}_{38}Sr$?

    A) 38
    B) 88
    C) 50
    D) 126

12. In a molecule of methane (CH_4), carbon shares four electrons with four atoms of hydrogen. What are the bonds called that form between the carbon and four hydrogen atoms?

    A) metallic
    B) ionic
    C) covalent
    D) hydrogen

13. Which of the following properties of water causes water droplets to form beads on surfaces, such as on a leaf?

    A) adhesion
    B) specific heat
    C) surface tension
    D) ability to dissolve substances

14. Which of the following terms describes an atom that has donated an electron to become a positively charged particle?

    A) anion
    B) cation
    C) compound
    D) molecule

15. The mass number of an atom is 23, and its atomic number is 11. How many protons, electrons, and neutrons does this atom have?

    A) 11 protons, 11 electrons, and 12 neutrons
    B) 11 protons, 11 electrons, and 1 neutron
    C) 11 protons, 1 electron, and 11 neutrons
    D) 6 protons, 5 electrons, and 12 neutrons

16. Which of the following is an anion?

    A) Br^-
    B) K^+
    C) Na
    D) CO_2

17. Hydrogen bonds influence all the interesting and incredibly important properties of water. These bonds form between the hydrogen atom of one water molecule and the oxygen atom of another water molecule because oxygen is

    A) a cation.
    B) an anion.
    C) electronegative.
    D) cohesive.

18. Using the following equation, how many moles of P_4O_6 would be produced from 6 moles of O_2, assuming excess P_4 is present?

    $$P_4 + 3O_2 \rightarrow P_4O_6$$

    A) 1
    B) 2
    C) 3
    D) 6

19. What happens to the atomic radius when moving left to right on the periodic table?

    A) It decreases.
    B) It increases.
    C) It stays constant.
    D) It does not follow a set pattern.

20. Which statement about radioactive particles is true?

    A) Alpha particles consist of two protons and two electrons.
    B) Alpha particles are NOT deflected by electric and magnetic fields.
    C) Beta particles are positively charged and are deflected by electric and magnetic fields.
    D) Gamma rays are not deflected by the electric and magnetic fields because they do not possess any charge.

21. How many O_2 molecules are required to balance the following reaction?

$CS_2 + O_2 \rightarrow CO_2 + SO_2$

A) 1

B) 2

C) 3

D) 4

22. Which is NOT a definition of an acid?

A) A substance that contains hydrogen and produces H^+ in water.

B) A substance that donates protons to a base.

C) A substance that reacts with a base to form a salt and water.

D) A substance that accepts protons.

23. Which element has chemical properties most similar to sulfur?

A) fluorine

B) argon

C) phosphorus

D) oxygen

24. Identify the reactant(s) and product(s) in the following equation:

$4Al\ (s) + 3O_2\ (g) \rightarrow 2Al_2O_3\ (s)$

A) reactant: Al_2O_3; products: Al and O_2

B) reactant: Al; products: O_2 and Al_2O_3

C) reactants: Al and O_2; product: Al_2O_3

D) reactants: O_2 and Al_2O_3; product: Al

25. If the following reaction is at equilibrium, what would happen if the pressure of the reaction was decreased?

$N_2(g) + 3H_2(g) \rightarrow 2NH_3(g)$

A) There would be no effect on the equilibrium.

B) The reaction will shift toward the products.

C) The reactions will shift toward the reactants.

D) It cannot be determined which way the reaction will shift.

26. Which of the following has the lowest first ionization energy?

A) Ca

B) K

C) Na

D) Mg

27. Which of the following is a double-replacement reaction?

A) $HNO_3\ (aq) + NaOH\ (aq) \rightarrow NaNO_3\ (aq) + H_2O\ (l)$

B) $CS_2\ (g) + CO_2\ (g) \rightarrow 2COS\ (g)$

C) $2N_2O\ (g) \rightarrow 2N_2\ (g) + O_2\ (g)$

D) $BaCl_2\ (aq) + H_2SO_4\ (aq) \rightarrow 2HCl\ (aq) + BaSO_4\ (s)$

28. Which of the following molecules experience London dispersion forces?

A) all atoms and molecules

B) atoms and molecules with full valence shells

C) atoms and molecules with a large dipole moment

D) atoms and molecules that contain at least one metal atom

29. Which of the following elements is the most electronegative?

A) chlorine

B) iron

C) magnesium

D) silicon

30. Which of the following is the best definition of an isotope?

A) atoms of the same element that have different ionic charges

B) atoms of elements within the same group on the periodic table

C) atoms of the same element that have different numbers of neutrons

D) atoms of the same element with different electron configurations

1. Which of the following is the cartilaginous flap that protects the larynx from water or food while still allowing the flow of air?

   A) epiglottis

   B) bronchioles

   C) epithelium

   D) tongue

2. Which of the following is a type of white blood cell that plays a key role in adaptive immunity by seeking out, attacking, and destroying targeted pathogens?

   A) B-cells

   B) goblet cells

   C) antibodies

   D) T-cells

3. Which of the following layers of skin acts as an energy reserve by storing adipocytes and releasing them into circulation when energy is needed?

   A) epidermis

   B) dermis

   C) hypodermis

   D) stratum basale

4. Which of the following is a dense, interconnected mass of nerve cells located outside of the central nervous system?

   A) ganglion

   B) dendrite

   C) cranial nerve

   D) pons

5. Which of the following is specialized tissue in the right atrium that acts as the heart's natural pacemaker by generating the electrical signal for the heartbeat?

   A) sinus venosus

   B) sinoatrial node

   C) atrioventricular node

   D) septa

6. The pineal gland is located in which of the following areas in the body?

   A) below the larynx

   B) above the kidney

   C) at the center of the brain hemispheres

   D) at the base of the brain

7. Which of the following sets of valves is primarily responsible for preventing blood flow from major blood vessels to the heart?

   A) atrioventricular valves

   B) semilunar valves

   C) tricuspid valves

   D) bicuspid valves

8. Which of the following is NOT a tissue layer found in skeletal bone?

   A) periosteum

   B) bone marrow

   C) enamel

   D) cancellous bone

9. Which of the following describes the primary function of the respiratory system?

   A) to create sound and speech

   B) to take oxygen into the body while removing carbon dioxide

   C) to transport nutrients to the cells and tissue of the body

   D) to act as a barrier between the body's organs and outside influences

10. Which of the following is NOT a hormone-producing gland of the endocrine system?

   A) prostate

   B) pituitary

   C) adrenal

   D) thyroid

11. Which of the following initiates the breakdown of carbohydrates?

   A) salivary amylase
   B) stomach acid
   C) bile salts
   D) peristalsis

12. Which of the following groups of bones are part of the axial skeleton?

   A) pectoral girdle
   B) rib cage
   C) arms and hands
   D) pelvic girdle

13. Which of the following is NOT a type of white blood cell?

   A) helper T-cell
   B) plasma cell
   C) antibody
   D) phagocyte

14. Which of the following is the final vessel through which semen must pass before being expelled from the body?

   A) ejaculatory duct
   B) penile urethra
   C) membranous urethra
   D) vas deferens

15. Which type of cell is responsible for the degradation of bone tissue?

   A) osteoclasts
   B) osteoblasts
   C) osteocytes
   D) lining cells

16. Which of the following supplies blood to the lower body?

   A) superior vena cava
   B) inferior vena cava
   C) iliac artery
   D) aortic arch

17. In which region of the small intestine are most of the nutrients absorbed?

   A) jejunum
   B) ileum
   C) duodenum
   D) colon

18. Which of the following parts of the brain is responsible for memory and language processing?

   A) pons
   B) cerebrum
   C) cerebellum
   D) medulla oblongata

19. Which of the following joints is formed by the humerus and the ulna?

   A) ball-and-socket joint
   B) hinge joint
   C) saddle joint
   D) gliding joint

20. Oxygen is exchanged between blood and tissues at which of the following areas?

   A) capillaries
   B) veins
   C) ventricles
   D) arteries

21. Which of the following is the anterior bone of the lower leg?

   A) ulna
   B) fibula
   C) tibia
   D) radius

22. After air is inhaled through the mouth, nose, and throat, which of the following structures does it travel through?

   A) alveoli
   B) bronchi
   C) bronchioles
   D) trachea

23. When exhaling, the diaphragm

   A) relaxes, reducing the space available for the lungs

   B) relaxes, increasing the space available for the lungs

   C) contracts, reducing the space available for the lungs

   D) contracts, increasing the space available for the lungs

24. Which of the following type of bone tissue gives bone its hardness and strength?

   A) osseous bone

   B) cancellous bone

   C) spongy bone

   D) cortical bone

25. Which of the following glands provides nourishment for sperm, as well as the majority of the fluid that combines with sperm to form semen?

   A) seminal vesicles

   B) prostate gland

   C) bulbourethral glands

   D) Cowper's glands

26. In the digestive system, the majority of nutrients are absorbed in which of the following organs?

   A) esophagus

   B) stomach

   C) small intestine

   D) large intestine

27. Which of the following is NOT part of the innate immune system?

   A) interferon

   B) neutrophils

   C) antibodies

   D) natural killer lymphocytes

28. Which of the following is an appendage of a neuron that sends electrical signals away from the neuron cell?

   A) axon

   B) dendrite

   C) neurite

   D) neuroglia

29. Which of the following is the primary muscle that drives ventilation?

   A) pectoralis major

   B) rectus abdominis

   C) trapezius

   D) diaphragm

30. Which of the following is the muscular action that moves a part of the body away from its median plane?

   A) abduction

   B) adduction

   C) pronation

   D) supination

PHYSICS

1. Which of the following quantities is a vector?

   A) 37 seconds
   B) 23 kilometers; east
   C) 178°F
   D) 1,500 calories

2. A box sliding down a ramp experiences all of the following forces EXCEPT

   A) tension.
   B) friction.
   C) gravity.
   D) normal.

3. A person starts from rest and increases his velocity to 5 m/s over a time period of 1 second. What is his acceleration?

   A) −5 m/s^2
   B) 0 m/s^2
   C) 5 m/s^2
   D) 10 m/s^2

4. A car has an initial velocity of 13.4 m/s. The car then takes 30 seconds to slow to a speed of 2.8 m/s. What was the car's acceleration while it slowed?

   A) 0.35 m/s^2
   B) 0.54 m/s^2
   C) 318 m/s^2
   D) 486 m/s^2

5. A person with a mass of 80 kg travels to the moon, where the acceleration due to gravity is 1.62 m/s^2. What will be her mass on the moon?

   A) greater than 80 kg
   B) 80 kg
   C) less than 80 kg
   D) The answer cannot be determined without more information.

6. What is the acceleration required to accelerate an object from rest to 10 m/s in 5 seconds?

   A) 0.5 m/s^2
   B) 2 m/s^2
   C) 50 m/s^2
   D) 500 m/s^2

7. At its maximum height, the velocity of a projectile shot straight up will be

   A) equal to its launch velocity.
   B) greater than zero.
   C) equal to zero.
   D) less than zero.

8. Which of the following objects would have the greatest momentum if they were all moving at the same velocity?

   A) a fly
   B) an elephant
   C) an airplane
   D) a car

9. An object is experiencing an upward force of 45 N and a downward force of 12 N. What is the net force on the object?

   A) 3.75 N
   B) 12 N
   C) 33 N
   D) 57 N

10. What is the momentum of an object with a mass of 15 kg moving with a velocity of magnitude 10 m/s in the −y direction?

    A) 15 kg · m/s
    B) 150 kg · m/s
    C) −15 kg · m/s
    D) −150 kg · m/s

11. If an object is launched from the roof of a building at an angle of 30°, which of the following statements is true? (Assume there is no air resistance.)

A) The horizontal acceleration of the object is positive.

B) The horizontal acceleration of the object is always negative.

C) The horizontal acceleration of the object is zero.

D) The horizontal acceleration of the object is positive while the object moves up and negative while the object moves down.

12. What is the kinetic energy of a bullet with a mass of 0.5 kg traveling with a velocity of 215 m/s?

A) 54 J

B) 108 J

C) 11,556 J

D) 23,112 J

13. What is the potential energy of a boulder with a mass of 50 kg resting on a cliff that is 250 m high?

A) 12,500 J

B) 61,250 J

C) 122,500 J

D) 30,625,000 J

14. What is the current flowing through a 15 Ω resistor when 120 V is applied to the circuit?

A) 80 mA

B) 125 mA

C) 8 A

D) 12.5 A

15. What is the momentum of a mass of 100 kg that is traveling at 2 m/s?

A) 50 kg · m/s

B) 100 kg · m/s

C) 200 kg · m/s

D) 400 kg · m/s

16. A single pulley is attached to the ceiling. If the pulley is holding a rope that is attached to the floor on one side and a person of weight 100 N on the other, what is the tension in the rope?

A) 0 N

B) 50 N

C) 100 N

D) 200 N

17. A ball is dropped from rest and falls due to gravity at 9.8 m/s² toward the center of the earth. What is its speed after 1 second?

A) 0 m/s

B) 4.9 m/s

C) 9.8 m/s

D) 14.7 m/s

18. Which of the following is an example of a longitudinal wave?

A) a wave on a string

B) a light wave

C) a sound wave

D) ripples in a pond

19. A 1 k Ω resistor is attached to a 1.5-volt battery. What will be the current through the resistor?

A) 0.0015 A

B) 0.15 A

C) 15 A

D) 150 A

20. Three resistors each with a resistance of 15 Ω are wired in series. What voltage is required to produce a current of 2.5 A in the wire?

A) 18.0 V

B) 37.5 V

C) 112.5 V

D) 8,437.5 V

21. If a ball is thrown in a horizontal direction from a height of 4.8 m, how long will it stay in the air?

   A)   1 second
   B)   2 seconds
   C)   5 seconds
   D)   10 seconds

22. A man is pushing against a heavy rock sitting on a flat plane, and the rock is not moving. The force that holds the rock in place is

   A)   friction.
   B)   gravity.
   C)   normal force.
   D)   buoyant force.

23. Two waves with amplitudes of 9.2 m and 2.1 m overlap and experience constructive interference. What will be the amplitude of the resulting wave?

   A)   4.4 m
   B)   7.1 m
   C)   11.3 m
   D)   19.3 m

24. How fast will an object with a mass of 10 kg accelerate when pushed with 50 N of force?

   A)   2.5 m/s^2
   B)   5.0 m/s^2
   C)   8.0 m/s^2
   D)   15.0 m/s^2

25. How far will a car moving at 40 m/s travel in 2 seconds?

   A)   10 m
   B)   20 m
   C)   40 m
   D)   80 m

26. If a baseball thrown straight up in the air takes 5 seconds to reach its peak, how long will it need to fall back to the player's hand?

   A)   2.5 seconds
   B)   9.8 seconds
   C)   5.0 seconds
   D)   10.0 seconds

27. Which unit of measurement is NOT used in the International System of Units?

   A)   newton
   B)   milliliter
   C)   gram
   D)   inch

28. What is the torque experienced by a wrench that is turned using 4 N of force at a distance of 0.5 m from the axis of rotation? (Assume the force is being applied perpendicular to the arm.)

   A)   2 N · m
   B)   8 N · m
   C)   20 N · m
   D)   80 N · m

29. A wave with a frequency of 44 Hz is traveling with a velocity of 10 m/s. What is the wave's wavelength?

   A)   0.23 m
   B)   4.4 m
   C)   54 m
   D)   440 m

30. A ball with a mass of 0.5 kg is moving at 10 m/s. How much kinetic energy does it have?

   A)   15 J
   B)   25 J
   C)   50 J
   D)   55.5 J

ANSWER KEY

MATHEMATICS

1.   C)
Evaluate to find greatest.

$-4(3)(-2) = 24$

$-16 - 17 + 31 = -2$

$18 - 15 + 27 = \mathbf{30}$

$-20 + 10 + 10 = 0$

2.   C)

total seats $= 4,500 + 2,000$

$\dfrac{\text{lower seats}}{\text{all seats}} = \dfrac{4,500}{6,500} = \mathbf{\dfrac{9}{13}}$

3.   B)
Plug the given values into the equation and solve for t.

$d = v \times t$

$4000 = 500 \times t$

$t = \mathbf{8\ hours}$

4.   D)
Write a proportion and then solve for x.

$\dfrac{40}{45} = \dfrac{265}{x}$

$40x\ 11,925$

$x = 298.125 \approx \mathbf{298}$

5.   C)
Use the formula for percentages.

$percent = \dfrac{part}{whole}$

$= \dfrac{42}{48} = 0.875 = \mathbf{87.5\%}$

6.   A)
His profit will be his income minus his expenses. He will earn \$40 for each lawn, or 40m. He pays \$35 is expenses each week, or 35w.

$profit = \mathbf{40m - 35x}$

7.   D)
Write each value in decimal form and compare.

$-0.95 < 0 < 0.4 < 0.35 < 0.75$ FALSE

$-1 < -0.1 < -0.11 < 0.8\overline{3} < 0.75$ FALSE

$-0.75 < -0.2 < 0 < 0.\overline{66} < 0.55$ FALSE

$-1.1 < -0.8 < -0.13 < 0.7 < 0.\overline{81}$ TRUE

8.   C)
If each student receives 2 notebooks, the teacher will need $16 \times 2 = 32$ notebooks. After handing out the notebooks, she will have $50 - 32 = \mathbf{18}$ notebooks left.

9. C)

Use the equation for percentages.

$whole = \frac{part}{percentage} = \frac{17}{0.4} = \textbf{42.5}$

10. A)

Add the fractions and subtract the result from the amount of flour Allison started with

$2\frac{1}{2} + \frac{3}{4} = \frac{5}{2} + \frac{3}{4} = \frac{10}{4} + \frac{3}{4} = \frac{13}{4}$

$4 - \frac{13}{4} = \frac{16}{4} - \frac{13}{4} = \frac{\textbf{3}}{\textbf{4}}$

11. A)

Add the number of cupcakes he will give to his friend and to his coworkers, then subtract that value from 48.

# of cupcakes for his friend: $\frac{1}{2} \times 48 = 24$

# of cupcakes for his coworkers: $\frac{1}{3} \times 48 = 16$

$48 - (24 + 16) = \textbf{8}$

12. C)

Round each value and add.

$129,113 \approx 129,000$

$34,602 \approx 35,000$

$129,000 + 35,000 = \textbf{164,000}$

13. B)

Plug 4 in for j and simplify.

$2(j - 4)^4 - j + \frac{1}{2}j$

$2(4 - 4)^4 - 4 + \frac{1}{2}(4) = \textbf{-2}$

14. B)

There are 15 minutes between 7:45 a.m. and 8:00 a.m. and 20 minutes between 8:00 a.m. and 8:20 a.m.

15 minutes + 20 minutes = **35 minutes**

15. B)

The cost per mile is represented by cost per gallon divided by miles per gallon.

$c = \frac{p}{m}$

16. C)

$23 \div 4 = 5.75$ pizzas

Round up to **6 pizzas**.

17. C)

One way to find the answer is to draw a picture.

Put 24 cans into groups of 4. One out of every 4 cans is diet (light gray) so there is 1 light gray can for every 3 dark gray cans. That leaves 18 dark gray cans (regular soda).

Alternatively, solve the problem using ratios.

$\frac{Regular}{Total} = \frac{3}{4} = \frac{x}{24}$

$4x = 72$

$x = \textbf{18}$

18. D)

$\frac{150 \text{ cm}}{1} \times \frac{10 \text{ mm}}{1 \text{ cm}} = \textbf{1500 mm}$

19. B)

Set up an equaton to find the number of orders of chicken strips they can afford:

$\$10 - 2(\$2.00 + \$1.00) = x$

$\$10 - 2(\$3.00) = x$

$\$10 - \$6.00 = \$4.00$

Four dollars is enough money to buy 1 order of chicken strips to share.

20. D)

$300 \div 12 = 25$

Test each answer choice to see if it equals 25.

A) $2(150 - 6)$

$= 2(144)$

$= 288 \neq 25$

B) $(300 \div 4) \div 6$

$= 75 \div 6$

$= 12.5 \neq 25$

C) $(120 \div 6) + (180 \div 6)$

$= 20 + 30$

$= 50 \neq 25$

D) $(120 \div 12) + (180 \div 12)$

$= (10) + (15) = \textbf{25}$

21. D)

Assign variables and write the ratios as fractions. Then, cross-multiply to solve for the number of apples and oranges sold.

x = apples

$\frac{\text{apples}}{\text{bananas}} = \frac{3}{2} = \frac{x}{20}$

$60 = 2x$

$x = 30$ apples

y = oranges

$\frac{\text{oranges}}{\text{bananas}} = \frac{1}{2} = \frac{y}{20}$

$2y = 20$

$y = 10$ oranges

To find the total, add the number of apples, oranges, and bananas together. $30 + 20 + 10 =$ **60 pieces of fruit**

22. C)

Use the formula for finding percentages. Express the percentage as a decimal.

part = whole × percentage = **1560 × 0.15**

23. D)

Find the time that Erica spends on break and subtract this from her total time at work.

$30 + 2(15) = 1$ hour

$8\frac{1}{2} - 1 = 7\frac{1}{2} =$ **7 hours, 30 minutes**

24. B)

Multiply the cost per pounds by the number of pounds purchased to find the cost of each fruit.

apples: $2(1.89) = 3.78$

oranges: $1.5(2.19) = 3.285$

$3.78 + 3.285 = 7.065 =$ **$7.07**

25. B)

Plug each value into the equation.

$4(3 + 4)^2 - 4(3)^2 + 20 = 180 \neq 276$

$4(6 + 4)^2 - 4(6)^2 + 20 =$ **276**

$4(12 + 4)^2 - 4(12)^2 + 20 = 468 \neq 276$

$4(24 + 4)^2 - 4(24)^2 + 20 = 852 \neq 276$

26. A)

Subtract the amount of the bills from the amount in the checking account.

$792.00 + 84.63 + 112.15 = 988.78$

$2,386.52 - 988.78 =$ **$1,397.74**

27. D)

Set up a proportion and solve.

$\frac{8}{650} = \frac{12}{x}$

$12(650) = 8x$

$x =$ **975 miles**

28. A)

The amount of money in Jane's bank account can be represented by the expression 275 + 15h ($275 plus $15 for every hour she works). Therefore, the equation 400 = 275+15h describes how many hours she needs to babysit to have $400.

29. C)

Multiply the car's speed by the time traveled to find the distance.

$1.5(65) = 97.5$ miles

$2.5(50) = 125$ miles

$97.5 + 125 =$ **222.5 miles**

30. C)

Divide 1.3208 by 5.2.

```
        .254
  52) 13.208
      104
      ---
      280
      260
      ---
      208
      208
      ---
        0
```

There is a **5** in the hundredths place.

31. B)

Set up an equation. If p is the original number of pears, the store has sold 0.30p pears. The original number minus the number sold will equal 455.

$p - 0.30p = 455$

$p = \frac{455}{0.7} =$ **650 pears**

32. C)

Round each number and multiply.

$16,000 \times 200 = 3,200,000 \rightarrow$ close to **3,300,000**

33. D)

Reduce the fraction; divide to change the reduced fraction to a decimal.

$$\frac{15}{25} = \frac{15 \div 5}{25 \div 5} = \frac{3}{5}$$

$$3 \div 5 = \mathbf{0.6}$$

$$= \frac{39}{48} - \frac{16}{48}$$

$$= \frac{\mathbf{23}}{\mathbf{48}}$$

34. D)

Create a proportion and solve.

$$\frac{\text{part}}{\text{whole}} = \frac{\%}{100}$$

$$\frac{15}{x} = \frac{8}{100}$$

$$15(100) = 8(x)$$

$$x = \mathbf{187.5}$$

35. C)

Multiply the total bill by 0.2 (20%) to find the amount of the tip. Then add the tip to the total.

$$\$48.30 \times 0.2 = \$9.66$$

$$\$48.30 + \$9.66 = \mathbf{\$57.96}$$

36. A)

If $\frac{2}{5}$ of the houses are painted yellow, then $\frac{3}{5}$ of the houses are NOT painted yellow. Since there are 24 houses that are not yellow, divide 24 by $\frac{3}{5}$ to find the total number of houses. Then subtract to find the number of yellow houses.

$$24 \div \frac{3}{5} = 24 \times \frac{5}{3} = 40$$

$$40 - 24 = \mathbf{16}$$

37. C)

To divide fractions, multiply by the reciprocal.

$$\frac{8}{15} \div \frac{1}{6} = \frac{8}{15} \times \frac{6}{1} = \frac{48}{15} = \frac{48 \div 3}{15 \div 3} = \frac{\mathbf{16}}{\mathbf{5}}$$

38. D)

Create a proportion and solve.

$$\frac{\text{part}}{\text{whole}} = \frac{\%}{100}$$

$$\frac{35}{14} = \frac{x}{100}$$

$$35(100) = x(14)$$

$$x = \mathbf{250}$$

39. B)

Find the least common denominator and subtract.

$$LCD = 48$$

$$\frac{13}{16} - \frac{1}{3}$$

40. C)

The ratio of hosts to the total number of employees is 2:12. Set up a proportion and solve.

$$\frac{2}{12} = \frac{x}{36}$$

$$2(36) = x(12)$$

$$72 = 12x$$

$$x = \mathbf{6}$$

41. D)

Find the least common denominator, and then add the whole numbers and fractions separately.

$$LCD = 8$$

$$1\frac{6}{8} + 2\frac{3}{8} = 3\frac{9}{8}$$

$$3\frac{9}{8} = 3 + 1\frac{1}{8} = \mathbf{4\frac{1}{8}}$$

42. A)

Isolate the variable x on one side of the equation.

$$5x - 4 = 3(8 + 3x)$$

$$5x - 4 = 24 + 9x$$

$$-4 - 24 = 9x - 5x$$

$$-28 = 4x$$

$$\frac{-28}{4} = \frac{4x}{4}$$

$$x = \mathbf{-7}$$

43. C)

Convert the fractions to decimals by dividing. The decimal equivalents do not terminate, but in order to compare to the other numbers in the list, only three decimal places are necessary.

$$\frac{1}{7} = 0.142 \ldots$$

$$\frac{6}{9} = 0.666 \ldots$$

$$0.125 < 0.142 \ldots < 0.600 < 0.666 \ldots$$

Therefore, the numbers from least to greatest are $\mathbf{0.125, \frac{1}{7}, 0.60, \frac{6}{9}}$.

44. B)

All of the decimal numbers are expressed in ten-thousandths. 55 is between 47 and 162, so **0.0055** is between 0.0047 and 0.0162.

45. B)

Find the least common denominator and subtract. This problem requires borrowing.

$LCD = 6$

$4\frac{3}{6} - 1\frac{4}{6}$

$= 3\frac{6}{6} + \frac{3}{6} - 1\frac{4}{6}$

$= 3\frac{9}{6} - 1\frac{4}{6}$

$= \mathbf{2\frac{5}{6}}$

46. D)

Create a proportion and solve.

$\frac{\text{part}}{\text{whole}} = \frac{\%}{100}$

$\frac{7}{60} = \frac{x}{100}$

$7(100) = x(60)$

$x \approx \mathbf{11.67}$

47. A)

Isolate the variable on one side of the equal sign.

$3a + 4 = 2a$

$4 = -1a$

$\mathbf{-4} = a$

48. D)

Convert the mixed number to an improper fraction. Multiply by the reciprocal of $\frac{1}{3}$.

$10\frac{3}{8} \div \frac{1}{3} = \frac{83}{8} \div \frac{1}{3} = \frac{83}{8} \times \frac{3}{1} = \frac{249}{8} = \mathbf{31\frac{1}{8}}$

49. D)

The ratio of sedans to the total number of vehicles is 6:10.

$\frac{6}{10} = \mathbf{\frac{3}{5}}$

50. C)

If 60% of the students are male, then 40% of the students are female. Create a proportion and solve.

$\frac{\text{part}}{\text{whole}} = \frac{\%}{100}$

$\frac{380}{x} = \frac{40}{100}$

$380(100) = 40(x)$

$x = \mathbf{950}$

51. D)

Write a proportion and solve.

$\frac{\frac{2}{1}}{\frac{1}{4}} = \frac{x}{\frac{2}{3}}$

$2\left(\frac{2}{3}\right) = x\left(\frac{1}{4}\right)$

$x = \frac{4}{3} \div \frac{1}{4} = \frac{4}{3} \times \frac{4}{1} = \frac{16}{3} = \mathbf{5\frac{1}{3}}$

52. D)

Add zeros as needed so that each number is expressed in thousandths; then add the numbers.

$951.400 + 98.908 + 1.053 =$

$1,051.361 \rightarrow \mathbf{7\ digits}$

53. A)

$\mathbf{1.068} < 1.086 < 1.608 < 1.680$

54. A)

Find the least common denominator to compare the fractions.

$LCD = 96$

$\frac{1}{24} = \frac{4}{96}$

$\frac{3}{32} = \frac{9}{96}$

$\frac{5}{48} = \frac{10}{96}$

$\frac{2}{16} = \frac{12}{96}$

$\frac{3}{16} = \frac{18}{96}$

$\frac{4}{96} < \frac{9}{96} < \frac{10}{96} < \frac{12}{96} < \frac{18}{96}$; therefore,

$\frac{1}{24} < \frac{3}{32} < \frac{5}{48} < \frac{2}{16} < \frac{3}{16}$.

55. C)

The ratio of solute to solution is 1:5. Write a proportion and solve.

$\frac{1}{5} = \frac{x}{90}$

$1(90) = x(5)$

$\mathbf{18} = x$

1. A)

The second paragraph of the passage states that "[u]sing the rectum also has the added benefit of providing a much more accurate reading than other locations can provide."

2. A)

This detail is not stated in the passage. The other choices can all be found in the passage.

3. B)

In the first paragraph, the author writes, "But what's the best way to get an accurate reading? The answer depends on the situation." She then goes on to describe various options and their applications.

4. A)

The final paragraph states that "agitated patients...won't be able to sit still long enough for an accurate reading." The reader can infer that an agitated patient is a patient who is visibly upset, annoyed, or uncomfortable.

5. B)

The author indicates that "[t]he most common way people measure body temperature is orally" but that "[t]here are many situations [...] when measuring temperature orally isn't an option." She then goes on to describe these situations in the second and third paragraphs.

6. C)

The passage states that babies' senses are much like those of their adult counterparts with the exception of their vision, which develops later.

7. B)

The passage states that "infants rely primarily on hearing."

8. A)

9. D)

The author writes that "hands 'cleaned' with hand sanitizer may still harbor pathogens"

because sanitizer "does nothing to remove organic matter" from the hands. The bacteria are not completely washed off, and therefore some are able to continue living on the surface of the hands.

10. B)

In the second paragraph, the author writes, "The [hand washing] process doesn't even require warm water—studies have shown that cold water is just as effective at reducing the number of microbes on the hands. Antibacterial soaps are also available, although several studies have shown that simple soap and cold water is just as effective."

11. B)

The author writes that because hand sanitizer "isn't rinsed from hands [as is water], it only kills pathogens and does nothing to remove organic matter."

12. C)

Together, these sentences provide an adequate summary of the passage overall. The other choices only provide specific details from the passage.

13. A)

Each paragraph examines hand washing from a different angle.

14. A)

In the first paragraph, the author writes, "Many illnesses are spread when people touch infected surfaces, such as door handles or other people's hands, and then touch their own eyes, mouths, or noses." The reader can infer from this sentence that hand washing prevents the spread of surface-borne illnesses.

15. D)

The passage describes human studies as the study of "the relationship between human activity and the environment," which would include farmers interacting with river systems.

16. A)

The passage explains what the study of geography involves and outlines its main sub-disciplines.

17. B)

Only this choice summarizes the two main points of the passage: the definition of geography and the breakdown of its sub-disciplines.

18. C)

The author opens the passage saying, "Because the needs of every patient will be different, it's the task of every health care facility to ensure that patients receive the proper nutrition." He then goes on to detail some of the factors that determine each patient's unique needs and describes some of the effects of proper and poor nutrition.

19. B)

The author writes, "However, many patients, bedridden or otherwise, have hidden energy needs. The process of healing can be extremely energy intensive—even an immobile patient can use up vast reserves of calories as her body fights infection, knits a fracture, or heals bed sores." While a bedridden patient's activity levels may be low, he or she is consuming energy at a high rate while healing.

20. B)

The author writes that "[g]enerally, energy needs are directly related to a person's weight and inversely related to age; it's also generally true that men require more calories than women." Additionally, he points out that "[t]he process of healing can be extremely energy intensive[.]"

21. A)

The author writes, "Thus, a thirty-five-year-old woman who weighs 135 pounds will require around 1800 calories a day[.]"

22. D)

The author writes, "Generally, energy needs are directly related to a person's weight and inversely related to age; it's also generally true

that men require more calories than women." However, he does not relate calorie needs to weight gain.

23. B)

The author writes, "All other explanations for the war are either a direct consequence of the South's desire for wealth at the expense of her fellow man or a fanciful invention to cover up this sad portion of our nation's history."

24. A)

The author writes, "But people who try to sell you this narrative are wrong. The Civil War was not a battle of cultural identities—it was a battle about slavery."

25. B)

The author writes, "The Civil War was not a battle of cultural identities—it was a battle about slavery. All other explanations for the war are either a direct consequence of the South's desire for wealth at the expense of her fellow man or a fanciful invention to cover up this sad portion of our nation's history."

26. A)

This choice addresses all of the main ideas of the passage: the flu is potentially deadly, highly infectious, and difficult to contain due to viral shedding.

27. D)

According to the passage, "the flu is...relatively difficult to contract[,]" and "[w]hile many people who contract the virus will recover, many others will not."

28. C)

The second paragraph states that the flu is "relatively difficult to contract" because it "can only be transmitted when individuals come into direct contact with bodily fluids of people infected with the flu or when they are exposed to expelled aerosol particles[.]"

29. A)

The author uses the term *measures* to describe the steps that people to take to prevent the spreading of the influenza virus.

30. C)

The final paragraph of the passage states that viral shedding is "the process by which the body releases viruses that have been successfully reproducing during the infection[.]"

31. A)

The second paragraph of the passage states that "the virus can be contained with fairly simple health measures like hand washing and face masks."

32. A)

The passage indicates that snakes' "intricate diamonds, stripes, and swirls help the animals hide from predators, but perhaps most importantly (for us humans, anyway), the markings can also indicate whether the snake is venomous."

33. A)

The passage states that "intricate diamonds, stripes, and swirls help the animals hide from predators[,]" implying that these markings are complex enough to allow the animals to blend in with their surroundings.

34. B)

The final paragraph of the passage states that the two species "frequently [share] a habitat" and that "[a] predatory hawk or eagle, usually hunting from high in the sky, can't tell the difference between the two species, and so the kingsnake gets passed over and lives another day."

35. C)

The first paragraph states that "[w]hile it might seem counterintuitive for a venomous snake to stand out in bright red or blue, that fancy costume tells any nearby predator that approaching him would be a bad idea." The coral snake's markings do not allow it to hide from predators but rather to "ward [them] off[.]"

36. D)

This summary captures the main ideas of each paragraph.

37. C)

The second paragraph states that "[t]he scarlet kingsnake, for example, has very similar markings to the venomous coral snake with whom it frequently shares a habitat. However, the kingsnake is actually nonvenomous[.]"

38. A)

The bulk of the passage is dedicated to showing that conventional wisdom about "fewer calories in than calories out" isn't true for many people and is more complicated than previously believed.

39. D)

People misreporting the amount of food they ate would introduce error into studies on weight loss and might make the studies the author cites unreliable.

40. B)

The author writes that "[j]azz music was played by and for a more expressive and freed populace than the United States had previously seen." In addition to "the emergence of the flapper[,]" the 1920s saw "the explosion of African American art and culture now known as the Harlem Renaissance."

41. A)

The author writes that "[j]azz music was played by and for a more expressive and freed populace than the United States had previously seen." In addition to "the emergence of the flapper[,]" the 1920s saw "the explosion of African American art and culture now known as the Harlem Renaissance."

42. C)

The author opens the passage saying, "In recent decades, jazz has been associated with New Orleans and festivals like Mardi Gras, but in the 1920s, jazz was a booming trend whose influence reached into many aspects of American culture." He then goes on to elaborate on what these movements were.

43. B)

At the end of the first paragraph, the author writes, "Ella Fitzgerald, for example, moved from

Virginia to New York City to begin her much-lauded singing career, and jazz pioneer Louis Armstrong got his big break in Chicago."

44. B)

The author writes that "[a]s these communities have evolved, the species in them have developed complex, long-term interspecies interactions known as symbiotic relationships." She then goes on to describe the different types of symbiotic relationships that exist.

45. D)

The author writes, "Often, relationships described as commensal include one species that feeds on another species' leftovers; remoras, for instance, will attach themselves to sharks and eat the food particles they leave behind. It might seem like the shark gets nothing from the relationship, but a closer look will show that sharks in fact benefit from remoras, which clean the sharks' skin and remove parasites."

46. C)

The author writes, "A relationship where one individual benefits and the other is harmed is known as parasitism."

47. A)

The author writes, "But is it possible for two species to interact and for one to remain completely unaffected?... In fact, many scientists claim that relationships currently described as commensal are just mutualistic or parasitic in ways that haven't been discovered yet."

48. D)

The author writes, "The bacteria, fungi, insects, plants, and animals that live together in a habitat have evolved to share a pool of limited resources...As these communities have evolved, the species in them have developed complex, long-term interspecies interactions known as symbiotic relationships."

49. A)

The author writes that "[t]here's another class of symbiosis that is controversial among scientists" and goes on to say that "many scientists claim the relationships currently described as commensal are just mutualistic or parasitic in ways that haven't been discovered yet." This implies that scientists debate about the topic of commensalism.

50. A)

The author states that "[p]opcorn continued to rule the snack food kingdom until the rise in popularity of home televisions during the 1950s" when the industry saw a "decline in sales" as a result of the changing pastimes of the American people.

51. B)

The author states, "For the Aztec Indians who called the caves home, popcorn (or *momochitl*) played an important role in society, both as a food staple and in ceremonies." This implies that the Aztec people popped popcorn both for special occasions ("in ceremonies") and for regular consumption ("as a food staple").

52. C)

In the opening paragraph the author writes, "But popcorn isn't just for fun—it's also a multimillion-dollar-a-year industry with a long and fascinating history." The author then goes on to illustrate the history of popcorn from the ancient Aztecs, to early twentieth century America, to the present day.

53. C)

The author writes, "The popcorn industry flourished during the Great Depression when it was advertised as a wholesome and economical food."

54. A)

This statement summarizes the entire passage, including the brief history of popcorn in ancient cultures and the growth in the popularity of popcorn in America.

55. C)

The author writes, "However, it wasn't until microwave popcorn became commercially available in 1981 that at-home popcorn consumption began to grow exponentially. With the wide availability of microwaves in the

United States, popcorn also began popping up in offices and hotel rooms."

Vocabulary

1. B)

Adverse means "acting against or causing harm," so an adverse outcome would be unfavorable.

2. C)

Clinical means "direct observation of a patient" or "based on observable and diagnosable symptoms."

3. A)

Chronic means "persistent or recurring over a long period of time," so her back pain has been continual.

4. C)

The prefix *im–* means "not," and the word root *partial* means "biased," so an impartial jury is one whose members are not biased and are therefore able to evaluate evidence in an objective, unprejudiced manner.

5. A)

Distal means "farther from the origin or point of attachment."

6. A)

The word root *pax* means "peace," and the suffix *–ify* means "to cause to become more," so to pacify someone means to cause that person to become more peaceful or to soothe them.

7. A)

The root word *judicium* means "judgment," and the suffix *–ous* means "possessing or full of," so the doctor made a decision based on good judgment or wisdom.

8. D)

Acrimonious means "angry or bitter."

9. B)

Pragmatic means "related to practical matters," so a pragmatic person is one who evaluates the facts and makes a realistic plan before acting.

10. B)

Accountable means "having to give an account," which makes the person answerable or responsible for something.

11. C)

Consistent means "regular or steady without variation."

12. C)

Sub– means "under," and *lingual* means "related to the tongue," so a medication administered sublingually would be placed under the tongue.

13. A)

Deleterious means "harmful or damaging."

14. D)

Impaired means "weakened or unable to fully function."

15. B)

Exacerbate means "to make more severe," so her symptoms have become worse.

16. A)

Lethargic means "tired."

17. B)

Rudimentary means "basic or elementary." Familiarity with the alphabet is a rudimentary reading skill that children learn at a young age.

18. C)

The root word *hema/hemo/hemato–* means "related to blood," so a hematologist studies diseases of the blood.

19. D)

Therapeutic means "related to the treatment of disease or beneficial to the body."

20. A)

Prudent means "wise or judicious." A prudent decision is a wise and practical one.

21. C)

Innocuous means "harmless or inoffensive."

22. C)

The root word *neglegere* means "to neglect," and the suffix *–ence* means "the act of," so negligence is the act of neglecting—not paying proper attention to—someone or something.

23. B)

The prefix *pre–* means "before," and the word *dispose* means "inclined to," so *predispose* means to be already inclined or more likely to.

24. D)

Dominant means "commanding or prevailing over others," so the dominant theme of a speech would be the principal, or most important, theme.

25. C)

Interpret means "to explain or tell the meaning of."

26. A)

Resilience is the ability to recover easily from change or damage.

27. B)

Recur means "to occur again after an interval."

28. D)

Anxious means "full of uneasiness or fear."

29. C)

Substantial means "an ample or considerable amount." For example, wealthy people have a substantial amount of money.

30. A)

Egregious means "obviously and extremely bad."

31. B)

An *illness* is an ailment or disease.

32. D)

The prefix *con–* means "with or together," the root word *concurrere* means "to run together," and the suffix *–ent* means "doing a certain action," so two or more concurrent events happen at the same time, or simultaneously.

33. C)

The root word *tard* means "slow," so someone who is tardy is slow or late.

34. A)

Contagious means "transmissible by direct or indirect contact."

35. A)

In addition to its common meaning of "a skin ailment," *rash* also means "a large number in a short period of time."

36. B)

The prefix *bi–* means "two," and *lateral* means "side," so *bilateral* means two (or both) sides.

37. B)

Mediation is the process of two conflicting parties negotiating a settlement or compromise.

38. C)

The prefix *pre–* means "before," so a precaution is a measure taken beforehand to prevent damage or as a safeguard.

39. C)

If the doctors were unprepared, the change was likely abrupt, which means "sudden and without warning."

40. A)

Annual means "every year."

41. D)

Dilute means "to diminish strength by addition or make thinner."

42. D)

Gastric means "related to the stomach," as in gastric ulcer (an ulcer in the stomach) or gastric bypass (surgery to reduce the size of the stomach).

43. A)

Efficient means "to be productive without waste."

44. B)

A *complication* is a secondary disease or condition that arises because of a primary disease or condition.

45. B)

A *contraindication* is "something that makes a treatment unadvisable."

46. A)

A *deficiency* is "an amount that is lacking or inadequate."

47. C)

Aggravating means "to cause to become worse."

48. B)

Audible means "able to be heard."

49. A)

Passed away is a euphemism (an indirect way to say something harsh) for "died."

50. D)

Treatement should be spelled *treatment*.

51. A)

Dilate means "to expand."

52. C)

Crate should be spelled *create*.

53. C)

Suppress means "to restrain or inhibit."

54. C)

The prefix *re–* means "again," so the word *reproduce* means "to produce again" or "to duplicate."

55. B)

Prognosis means "forecast or prospect of recovery."

GRAMMAR

1. C)

And is a conjunction, joining two things.

2. B)

To is the correct choice.

3. A)

Option A is a question but has no question mark.

4. A)

Yesterday implies past tense, so *started* is the correct verb choice.

5. D)

The implied subject is *you*, tense is present, so *call* is correct.

6. D)

Or, joining two parts of the sentence, is a conjunction.

7. C)

Present passive is the best choice here, so the correct choice is *delayed*.

8. B)

Subject and verb do not match.

9. B)

A is incorrect because you cannot attend a movie and do your homework at the same time. C and D both have verb errors.

10. D)

Toy, as a noun, is a person, place, or thing.

11. A)

The bell is carrying out the action *(ringing)*.

12. C)

Either has to go with *or*. Option D has a verb error.

13. A)

Table is a noun.

14. C)

Into is a preposition.

15. D)

Option A does not have a question mark; B has a verb error; and C uses the possessive *whose*.

16. D)

The first part of the sentence is a dependent clause; *they*, referring to the children, is the subject.

17. A)

She is the one who did everything and is therefore the subject.

18. B)

Do is correct because it's in the second person, present tense.

19. C)

Good, describing how the team played, must be replaced by an adverb, *well*.

20. B)

The appointment has already happened, so *had*, or the past tense, is correct. *Was* does not make sense in this context.

21. A)

Subject and verb agree.

22. C)

Kitchen is the direct object, or the thing being decorated.

23. A)

Shift is the direct object.

24. B)

I learned to write well working at the paper is the only correct option. A has an incorrect adjective, C has an incorrect verb, and D has an incorrect preposition.

25. D)

D is incorrect since *can* requires a verb, not *helpful*, an adjective.

26. C)

Because she wanted to see a play is the dependent clause: it starts with a subordinating conjunction (because) and cannot stand alone.

27. A)

Although we left the baseball game early is a dependent clause; therefore it can't stand on its own in a statement.

28. A)

B and C have verb errors, while D has a preposition error.

29. B)

The predicate is the verb, plus anything following.

30. D)

D is a sentence fragment because it's lacking a subject.

31. C)

The predicate is the verb, plus anything following.

32. A)

C and D use incorrect prepositions. B is technically correct; however, *on the news* implies something heard, rather than something read.

33. A)

A predicate adjective directly describes the subject of the sentence.

34. A)

A predicate adjective directly describes the subject of the sentence.

35. C)

The two girls are the subject of the clause; therefore, the pronoun must be third person plural.

36. B)

The subject and verb do not agree.

37. A)

Brought is the best substitute.

38. C)

Swam is the past tense of *swim*.

39. D)

Neither goes with *nor*, not *or*. The verb agrees with the subject or noun it's closest to.

40. D)

Am is correct. *Will* does not agree with the verb tense, and the others produce a double negative.

41. B)

The verb does not agree with the implied subject, *you*.

42. C)

Who has his own shop is a dependent clause.

43. B)

Are is the only verb that agrees with the subject *you*.

44. D)

Subject and verb disagree.

45. B)

To take to the school bake sale is a prepositional phrase.

46. B)

Only *check* can be paired with the word *on*.

47. C)

Of is the only correct response when paired with *scared*.

48. B)

Looking is the only choice that works with both *were* and *for*.

49. A)

For is correct. *Catch* would require the addition of *to*.

50. A)

Will work is correct, because it is in the future tense.

51. A)

Go agrees with the implied subject, *you*.

52. B)

A has a preposition error; C and D have verb errors.

53. D)

Subject and verb do not agree.

54. B)

At refers to time or place.

55. B)

The pronoun is the subject of the sentence, so it should be *I*, not *me*. Also, the subject is plural, so the verb should be *have*, not *has*.

BIOLOGY

1. A)

mRNA is a sequence of nucleotides in which each triplet codes for a particular amino acid. The sequence of triplets in the mRNA would translate into the sequence of amino acids that make up a protein.

2. D)

The cell wall is the structure that gives plant cells their rigidity.

3. C)

Human gametes have 23 unpaired chromosomes; human somatic (body) cells have 23 pairs, or 46, chromosomes.

4. C)

Lipids, which include but are not limited to fats, are an efficient source of energy storage due to their ability to store nearly twice as much energy as carbohydrates and proteins.

5. D)

Water will leave the cell through osmosis when the concentration of solute outside the cell is greater than that inside the cell. Water will leave the cell when it's placed in a 20 percent solute solution, decreasing the mass of the cell.

6. C)

The Punnett square shows that there is a 75 percent chance the child will have the dominant B gene, and thus have brown eyes.

	B	b
B	BB	Bb
b	Bb	bb

7. A)

The smooth endoplasmic reticulum is a series of membranes attached to the cell nucleus and plays an important role in the production and storage of lipids. It is called smooth because it lacks ribosomes on the membrane surface.

8. A)

Red blood cells are created in bone marrow instead of through mitosis. They are the only type of cell to be created in this way. Without a nucleus, red blood cells are unable to undergo mitosis.

9. B)

Photosynthesis takes place in the chloroplast.

10. A)

Hemoglobin in red blood cells binds to oxygen molecules and transports them from the lungs throughout the body.

11. D)

A total of thirty-eight molecules of ATP are produced: two molecules from glycolysis, two molecules from the Krebs cycle, and thirty-four molecules from electron transport.

12. B)

The nucleus is the organelle that carries the DNA of eukaryotic organisms.

13. C)

A plant cell is enveloped by a cell wall, but animal cells do not possess cell walls.

14. B)

Four haploid (1n) cells are produced during meiosis.

15. C)

Both DNA and RNA consist of chains of nucleotides.

16. D)

Uracil (U) is a base of RNA.

17. A)

In addition to the condensation of chromosomes, the mitotic spindle forms during prophase.

18. A)

Sugars are built from monosaccharides like glucose.

19. D)

Thirty-four molecules of ATP are usually produced during electron transport.

20. C)

These two organelles use an ATP synthase to generate ATP.

21. A)

In interphase, the cell prepares to divide, so centrioles, which are small organelles involved in cell division, will replicate if present.

22. B)

Proteins are the expressed products of a gene.

23. A)

Because each offspring will inherit the dominant allele, all the offspring will show the dominant phenotype. The offspring would only show a mix of the two phenotypes if they did not follow Mendelian inheritance patterns.

24. B)

Lactic acid, a byproduct of anaerobic respiration, builds up in muscles and causes fatigue. This occurs when the energy exerted by the muscle exceeds the amount of oxygen available for aerobic respiration.

25. B)

Translation is the process of matching codons in RNA to the correct anti-codon to manufacture a protein.

26. C)

Ribosomes are the organelles primarily responsible for translating mRNA into proteins; the primary function of the smooth endoplasmic reticulum is the synthesis of lipids.

27. B)

The gram is the appropriate unit to measure the mass of light objects, such as ants.

28. D)

The mitochondria found in cells are what power the cell and provide it with the energy it needs to carry out its life functions. Muscle cells need a lot of ATP in order to provide the energy needed for movement and exercise.

29. C)

The daughter cells produced during mitosis are genetically identical to their diploid (2n) parent.

30. D)

Transcription occurs in the nucleus while translation occurs in the cytoplasm.

CHEMISTRY

1. C)

Ca^+ has nineteen electrons. All the other ions have eighteen electrons.

2. A)

Strong acids break apart into their constituent ions immediately when placed in water.

3. D)

This is a decomposition reaction where one reactant breaks apart into two products.

4. B)

Sandy water is not a homogeneous mixture. Sand and water can be easily separated, making it a heterogeneous mixture.

5. B)

The two oxygen atoms in a covalent double bond share two pairs of electrons, or four total.

6. B)

A double-replacement reaction occurs when one part of each of the two reactants are exchanged with the other, resulting in two new compounds. In this equation, Ca and Na switch places.

7. D)

Sublimation is the phase change in which a material moves directly from the solid phase to the gas phase, bypassing the liquid phase.

8. C)

The pH will go up one unit because the proton concentration will go down by a factor of 10 (pH = $-\log[H^+]$).

9. D)

The atomic number is the number of protons in an atom and defines the type of atom. Elements are arranged on the periodic table in order of increasing atomic number.

10. D)

The noble gas electron configuration consists of a complete valence electron shell. This is the lowest energy electron configuration, and elements will typically form bonds in order to achieve this electron configuration. By losing one electron and thereby adopting a +1 charge, alkali metals achieve a noble gas electron configuration. By losing two electrons, adopting a +2 charge, alkaline earth metals achieve a noble gas electron configuration.

11. C)

Subtracting the atomic number from the mass number gives the number of protons: $A - Z = 88 - 38 = 50$.

12. C)

In a covalent bond, two atoms share a pair of electrons.

13. C)

Surface tension pulls together the molecules on the surface of water, forcing them to form a sphere, or bead.

14. B)

An atom that loses an electron becomes a positively charged ion called a cation.

15. A)

The number of protons in the nucleus of an atom equals the atomic number (in this case, 11). The number of protons and neutrons in the nucleus of an atom equals the mass number (23 − 11 protons = 12 neutrons). And the number of protons and electrons in an atom are equal, because atoms are electrically neutral.

16. A)

An anion is a negatively charged atom.

17. C)

The hydrogen atoms and the oxygen atom in a molecule of water do not share electrons equally. Oxygen tends to draw electrons toward itself more strongly than hydrogen, which makes oxygen an electronegative atom.

18.   B)

Use dimensional analysis.

$$\frac{6 \text{ mol O}_2}{} \quad \left| \quad \frac{1 \text{ mol P}_4\text{O}_5}{3 \text{ mol O}_2} \quad \right| \quad = \mathbf{2} \text{ mol P}_4\text{O}_5$$

19.   A)

Atomic radius decreases from left to right on the periodic table because, as the number of protons in the nucleus increases, the attraction between the nucleus and the electrons increases.

20.   D)

Gamma rays are neutral in charge and are not deflected by electric and magnetic fields.

21.   C)

The balanced equation has the coefficients 1:3:1:2.

$$\_CS_2 + \_O_2 \rightarrow \_CO_2 + \_SO_2$$

Carbon is already balanced (one atom on each side). There are two S atoms on the left, so add 2 to SO_2 on the right.

$$\_CS_2 + \_O_2 \rightarrow \_CO_2 + 2SO_2$$

There are six O atoms on the right, so add 3 to O_2 on the left.

$$CS_2 + 3O_2 \rightarrow CO_2 + 2SO_2$$

22.   D)

Acids increase the concentration of hydrogen ions in solution and do not accept protons.

23.   D)

Oxygen is in the same group as sulfur and is also a non-metal.

24.   C)

The reactants are always on the left side of a chemical equation, and the products are on the right.

25.   C)

An equilibrium always responds to a change by trying to reverse it. The equilibrium will shift to the reactants to increase the number of moles of gases and thus increase the pressure.

26.   B)

Elements in Group 1 have the lowest first ionization energy because they will form a noble gas when one electron is removed. Elements toward the bottom of a group will have a lower first ionization energy because the valence electrons are farther from the nucleus. Thus, potassium (K) will have the lowest first ionization energy of all the choices.

27.   D)

This reaction is a double-replacement reaction in which the two reactants change partners. Ba^{+2} combines with SO_4^{-2} and H^{+1} combines with Cl^{-1}.

28.   A)

London dispersion forces arise due to the random movement of electrons and may be found in all atoms and molecules.

29.   A)

Electronegativity increases from left to right and bottom to top along the periodic table. Chlorine is higher and more to the right on the table than the other answer choices, so it is the most electronegative.

30.   C)

Isotopes are atoms that differ in their number of neutrons but are otherwise identical.

ANATOMY AND PHYSIOLOGY

1. A)
The epiglottis is the protective flap at the entrance of the larynx.

2. D)
T-cells are a type of white blood cell that originates in the thymus. There are four different varieties of mature T-cells, each of which serves a different function in the immune system.

3. C)
The hypodermis is the thickest layer of skin and is the site of much of the stored fat in the human body.

4. A)
Ganglions are dense clusters of nerve cells responsible for processing sensory information and coordinating motor activity.

5. B)
The sinoatrial (SA) node is an area of specialized muscle tissue in the right atrium that generates an electrical signal which spreads from cell to cell to generate the heartbeat.

6. C)
The pineal gland is located in the epithalamus and is a gland involved in the production of melatonin.

7. B)
Semilunar valves are present in the pulmonary trunk and the aortic trunk; they allow blood to enter the vessels and prevent its return back to the heart.

8. C)
Enamel is a tissue found in teeth, but not skeletal bones.

9. B)
Oxygen intake and carbon dioxide disposal are the primary functions of the respiratory system.

10. A)
The prostate is an exocrine gland that secretes the alkaline fluid found in semen. It does not produce hormones.

11. A)
Salivary amylase in the mouth begins the breakdown of carbohydrates.

12. B)
The rib cage, which consists of the ribs and the sternum, is part of the axial skeleton.

13. C)
Antibodies are proteins produced by plasma cells, a type of lymphocyte, which is a type of white blood cell.

14. B)
Both urine and semen travel through the penile urethra, the longest portion of the male urethra, to be expelled through the urethral opening.

15. A)
Osteoclasts break down and absorb bone tissue.

16. C)
The iliac artery receives blood from the aorta to supply blood to the lower body.

17. A)
The jejunum, the middle section of the small intestine, is the site of most of the food absorption in the body after it is broken down in the duodenum.

18. B)
The cerebral cortex is the most developed part of the human brain and is responsible for memory, language processing, and other higher brain functions.

19. B)
The humerus and ulna connect at the elbow to form a hinge joint.

20. A)

Capillaries are very small blood vessels found where veins and arteries meet. They are the site of material exchange.

21. C)

The tibia, or shin bone, is the larger of the lower leg bones and is located slightly to the front of the smaller fibula.

22. D)

The trachea, or windpipe, is a passageway for air as it moves from the mouth, nose, and throat to the bronchi.

23. A)

During exhalation, the diaphragm relaxes causing the tissue to move up into the chest cavity. This movement reduces the space available for the lungs and forces air out of the lungs.

24. D)

Cortical bone, also known as compact bone, is dense and solid and provides critical strength to the bone.

25. A)

The seminal vesicles provide nourishment for sperm and up to 70 percent of the total volume of semen.

26. C)

Much of the nutrient absorption in the body occurs in the jejunum, which is the middle section of the small intestine.

27. C)

Antibodies are part of the body's adaptive immune system and only respond to specific pathogens.

28. A)

Neurons typically have one long, thick axon that transmits signals away from the neuron.

29. D)

The diaphragm is a muscle that increases the thoracic cavity when contracted, allowing more space for the lungs during respiration.

30. A)

Abduction occurs when muscles contract and move a body part away from the midline; the muscle completing this movement is called an abductor muscle.

PHYSICS

1. B)

Vectors always have a magnitude (23 kilometers) and direction (east).

2. A)

Tension is the force that results from objects being pulled or hung. The box experiences friction as it slides against the ramp. Gravity is the force pulling the box down the ramp, and the normal force is the upward force of the ramp on the box.

3. C)

Use the formula for acceleration:

$$a = \frac{\Delta v}{t} = \frac{5\ m/s - 0\ m/s}{1\ s} = \textbf{5 m/s}^2$$

4. A)

Identify the variables and plug into the appropriate formula to solve for acceleration:

$v_i = 13.4\ m/s$

$v_f = 2.8\ m/s$

$t = 30\ s$

$v_f = v_i + at$

$$a = \frac{v_f - v_i}{t} = \frac{(2.8\ m/s) - (13.4\ m/s)}{30\ s} = \textbf{0.35 m/s}^2$$

5. B)

The mass of an object is constant, so the mass would still be 80 kg. (However, the person's weight would be lower on the moon than on the earth.)

6. B)

Identify the variables and plug into the appropriate formula to solve for acceleration:

$v = 10\ m/s$

$t = 5\ s$

$$a = \frac{\Delta v}{t} = \frac{10\ m/s}{5\ s} = \textbf{2 m/s}^2$$

7. C)

The velocity of a projectile is zero at its maximum height.

8. C)

Momentum is directly proportional to mass ($p = mv$), so the heaviest object will have the greatest momentum.

9. C)

Add the two forces to find the net force:

$45\ N + (-12\ N) = \textbf{33 N}$

10. D)

Use the formula for momentum:

$p = mv = (15\ kg)(-10\ m/s) = \textbf{-150 kg} \cdot \textbf{m/s}$

11. C)

The only force acting on the object is gravity. Because no force is acting in the horizontal direction, the object's horizontal acceleration is zero.

12. C)

Use the formula for kinetic energy:

$KE = \frac{1}{2}(mv^2) = \frac{1}{2}(0.5\ kg)(215\ m/s)^2 = \textbf{11,556 J}$

13. C)

Use the formula for potential gravitational energy:

$PE = mgh = (50\ m)(9.8\ m/s)(250\ m) = \textbf{122,500 J}$

14. C)

Use Ohm's law:

$$I = \frac{V}{R} = \frac{120\ V}{15\ \Omega} = \textbf{8 A}$$

15. C)

Use the formula for momentum:

$p = mv = (100\ kg)(2\ m/s) = \textbf{200 kg} \cdot \textbf{m/s}$

16. C)

The tension will be equal to the weight it supports, **100 N**.

17. C)

Use the formula for acceleration:

$$a = \frac{v_2 - v_1}{t}$$

$$a = \frac{v_2 - 0}{t}$$

$$v_2 = at = (9.8 \text{ m/s}^2)(1 \text{ s}) = \textbf{9.8 m/s}$$

18. C)

Sound is a longitudinal wave; the other three answer choices are transverse waves.

19. A)

Use Ohm's law to solve for the current:

$$V = IR$$

$$I = V/R = \frac{1.5 \text{ V}}{1000 \text{ }\Omega} = \textbf{0.0015 A}$$

20. C)

Find the total equivalent resistance of the three series resistors:

$$R_{eq} = R_1 + R_2 + R_3 = 15 \text{ }\Omega + 15 \text{ }\Omega + 15 \text{ }\Omega = 45 \text{ }\Omega$$

Use Ohm's law to find the voltage:

$$V = IR = (2.5 \text{ A})(45 \text{ }\Omega) = \textbf{112.5 V}$$

21. A)

Identify the variables and plug into the appropriate formula to solve for time:

$$d = 4.8 \text{ m}$$

$$a = 9.8 \text{ m/s}^2$$

$$v_i = 0 \text{ m/s}$$

$$d = v_i + \frac{1}{2}at^2$$

$$t = \sqrt{\frac{2d}{a}} = \sqrt{\frac{2(4.8 \text{ m})}{9.8 \text{ m/s}^2}} = \textbf{1 s}$$

22. A)

When the man pushes on the rock, static friction points opposite the direction of the applied force with the same magnitude.

23. C)

Constructive interference means the waves' amplitudes are in sync, so the amplitude will be the sum of the two waves' individual amplitudes:

$$9.2 \text{ m} + 2.1 \text{ m} = \textbf{11.3 m}$$

24. B)

Use Newton's second law:

$$F = ma$$

$$a = \frac{F}{m} = \frac{50 \text{ N}}{10 \text{ kg}} = \textbf{5.0 m/s}^2$$

25. D)

Use the formula for displacement:

$$d = vt = (40 \text{ m/s})(2 \text{ s}) = \textbf{80 m}$$

26. C)

The time to the peak and the time to fall back to the original height are equal.

27. D)

Newtons, millimeters, and grams are SI units for force, distance, and mass, respectively.

28. A)

Use the formula for torque:

$$\tau = rF = (0.5 \text{ m})(4 \text{ N}) = \textbf{2 N} \cdot \textbf{m}$$

29. A)

Use the formula for the velocity of a wave to solve for the wavelength:

$$v = \lambda f$$

$$\lambda = \frac{v}{f} = \frac{10 \text{ m/s}}{44 \text{ Hz}} \approx \textbf{0.23 m}$$

30. B)

$$KE = \frac{1}{2}mv^2 = \frac{1}{2}(0.5 \text{ kg})(10 \text{ m/s})^2 = \textbf{25 J}$$

CPSIA information can be obtained
at www.ICGtesting.com
Printed in the USA
LVHW10s1448071018
592736LV00005B/215/P

9 781635 302592